sharing the
delirium

sharing the delirium

second generation AIDS plays and performances

THE BADDEST OF BOYS by Doug Holsclaw
MYRON, A FAIRY TALE IN BLACK AND WHITE
by Michael Kearns
QUEEN OF ANGELS by James Carroll Pickett
SATAN AND SIMON DESOTO by Ted Sod
AIDS! THE MUSICAL! by Wendell Jones and David Stanley,
music by Robert Berg
WHAT ARE TUESDAYS LIKE? by Victor Bumbalo
MY QUEER BODY by Tim Miller

Selected and introduced by Therese Jones

HEINEMANN  *Portsmouth, NH*

Heinemann
A division of Reed Elsevier Inc.
361 Hanover Street
Portsmouth, NH 03801-3912
Offices and agents throughout the world

Editor: Lisa A. Barnett
Production: Vicki Kasabian
Cover design: Diana Coe
Cover illustration: Reginald Marsh, *Lifeguards*, 1933, tempera on
  masonite panel, 35½ × 23⅜": sight. Reprinted with permission by
  Georgia Museum of Art, University of Georgia, University Purchase
  GMOA 48.205

Library of Congress Cataloging-in-Publication Data

Sharing the delirium: second generation AIDS plays and
  performances/selected and introduced by Therese Jones.
    p.   cm.
   Includes bibliographical references.
   Contents: The baddest of boys/Doug Holsclaw—Myron, a fairy
tale in black and white/Michael Kearns—Queen of angels/James
Carroll Pickett—Satan and Simon Desoto/Ted Sod—AIDS! the
musical!/Wendell Jones and David Stanley—What are Tuesdays
like?/Victor Bumbalo—My queer body/Tim Miller.
   ISBN 0-435-08633-2
   1. AIDS (Disease)—Patients—United States—Drama.   2. Gay
men—United States—Drama.   3. American drama—20th
century.   4. Gay men's writings, American.   I. Jones, Therese.
PS627.A53S53 1994
812'.54080356—dc20   93-44972
                                            CIP

Performance rights information will be found at the end of this book.

Printed in the United States of America on acid-free paper
98 97 96 95 94   EB   1 2 3 4 5 6

For Keith,
"The feeling of my loss will n'er be old;/
This, which I know, I speak with mind serene."

contents

acknowledgments   viii

introduction   ix
therese jones

the baddest of boys   1
doug holsclaw

myron, a fairy tale in black and white   55
michael kearns

queen of angels   87
james carroll pickett

satan and simon desoto   141
ted sod

AIDS! the musical!   207
*wendell jones and david stanley,
music by robert berg*

what are tuesdays like?   265
victor bumbalo

my queer body   309
tim miller

about the authors   337

acknowledgments

My greatest acknowledgment goes to the artists who have contributed to this collection. Their commitment to AIDS art and activism inspires all who are touched by their creativity and concern. I have been especially grateful for the opportunity to share the delirious humor and know the great courage of Jim Pickett. I would also like to thank Lisa Barnett of Heinemann who believed in this project from the beginning and worked to make it a reality.

I am indebted to the Boulder Queer Collective who provided me with a timely fellowship early on and to my students in The AIDS Crisis and the Humanities, who taught me as much as I taught them.

Finally, I would like to express my sincere gratitude for the support of friends and family: Max Tibbits, Greg Smith, Susan McMorris, Gary Green, Michele Tarter, Sara Jones, and Chris Jones.

A portion of the income from the sale of this book will benefit Artists Confronting AIDS.

introduction

The theatre like the plague invites the mind to share a delirium which exalts its energies . . . causes the mask to fall, reveals the lie, the slackness, baseness, and hypocrisy of our world; it shakes off the asphyxiating inertia of matter which invades even the clearest testimony of the senses.

—Antonin Artaud
The Theatre and Its Double

I.

In May of 1992, I made one final, frenzied trip to San Antonio to be with my friend in the last week of his life. From all over the country we came to San Antonio—best woman friend, best bar buddy, best colleague, best ex-lover—to join his caregivers at the AIDS Foundation Hospice, just a few minutes away from the Alamo (a site equally renowned for dramatic last stands).

Like a chorus, we gathered round his bed that first night, formal and solemn. The silence between attempts at conversation was punctuated by a man coughing in the adjacent room. This was no simple, dry hacking; this was not even a more complicated, bronchial wheezing. This was coughing that was bigger than all of Texas, coughing that one might hear if the planet were to spasm and expectorate, coughing with sufficient force, volume and regularity that it was like the Old Faithful of coughing.

We began to smirk, then to giggle, finally, to collapse with laughter—festive laughter, universal laughter, ambivalent laughter, laughter that expressed denial and affirmation, that transformed terror into comedy. Carnival laughter.

II.

The theatre of AIDS begins in 1985 with Larry Kramer's *The Normal Heart,* written because the artist/activist said he felt an obligation to become a message queen, to inform the gay community about AIDS and the straight community about the gay community. Educational messages, behavioral models, and social practices designed to ensure and enhance the physical, emotional, spiritual, and political survival of the gay community shape and color first generation plays of the eighties such as *The Normal Heart,* William Hoffman's *As Is,* and Harvey Fierstein's *Safe Sex.*

However practical, the chronological marker of a decade proves to be an insufficient division for first and second generation AIDS theatre. Dramatic mode becomes as important a distinction as dramatic matter in attempting to categorize plays about AIDS as either one or the other. Generally, first generation works are traditional in form, sentimental in tone and assimilationist in aim. Similar to first generation AIDS novels whose characteristics Emmanuel Nelson elucidates, such plays are serious portrayals in which the characters reject sex as the core cultural characteristic of urban gay life, affirm monogamy and reinvent the traditional family;[1] they are conservative constructions of disrupted gay male identity and nostalgic reconstructions of familiar social structures and practices, what Miranda Joseph describes as "unifying community origin stor[ies]" with embedded maturation narratives;[2] and they are, above all, poignant expressions of loss.

Director Anne Bogart offers her own critical checklist for distinguishing between first and second generation plays:

> First generation, the disease has just happened.
> The playwright's obligation is to present the
> material, to present the facts, and mourn them,
> and mourn the situation. So they [are] very
> serious and very, very responsible . . . a second
> generation AIDS play . . . it's angry and it's funny
> and kind of abstract.[3]

Second generation works represent a radical shift in theatrical representations of AIDS, no longer an event to be comprehended but a reality to be accommodated. Described in articles and reviews as "defiant celebrations of gay life," the "pushy pairing of AIDS and entertainment" that "mourns the passing of Gay nakedness and sexual freedom with rage and laughter," "activism and art fused into a Mobius strip," "blithely satiric," "eerily realistic," and "going where no teary-eyed AIDS plays have gone before," the multiplicitous comedies, multimedia performances, and revisioned folk dramas defiantly postulate an alternative discourse which opposes hierarchical structures, asserts subjectivity, and challenges cultural suppression of sexuality without, as one critic puts it, "the whiff of the pathos or bathos that's dominated most AIDS drama."[4] Unlike first generation plays, humor is not incidental but essential in second generation theatre, an entire spectrum of comedic drama: satire, farce, romance, slapstick, and burlesque.

In form, second generation AIDS plays and performances answer the call, which David Roman has articulated, for a theatre that extends beyond the "tragic classical realist dramas that characterize the majority of plays about AIDS produced by gay men."[5] In tone, these plays and performances fit the bill, which Douglas Crimp has stipulated, for a "critical, theoretical, activist alternative to the personal, elegiac expressions that appeared to dominate the art-world response to AIDS."[6] The seven pieces I have chosen for this collection reflect the creative genius and political commitment of the artists/activists who produced them and who share with us the exhilarating and empowering fusion of carnival—a festive perception of the world that succeeds moments of natural and social crisis, consecrates inventive freedom, and liberates from established truths—and the politics of representation[7]—the assertion of subjectivity and foregrounding of individual experience. I will discuss the works in the order in which they appear.

III.

Critics have called Doug Holsclaw's *The Baddest of Boys* the first second generation AIDS play,[8] making it an appropriate choice to begin this anthology. The farcical black comedy coalesces many of the elements that characterize second generation AIDS theatre. First, there is a variety of charac-

ters reflecting the multiple roles of the gay community and
their myriad responses to AIDS. The youngest and baddest
of these characters, a Queer Nation activist/waiter, literally
incorporates the postmodern concept of identity as dynamic
and performative, as he is a multiple personality who spontaneously dissociates throughout the play. Second, the tone
is fearless and festive. One employee of the cafe in which
the action is set has called in dead four times in one month.
Finally, the material body of the person with AIDS is represented in grotesque images, simultaneously provoking horror and hilarity. Perry, created onstage as a kind of Mr.
Potato Head, is being treated by an African American lesbian physician who resorts to microwaves, bungee cords, and
blowtorches to fight his rare opportunistic infections. Doug
Holsclaw has evoked the frantic scramble for survival and
defensive callousness to suffering of these, our plague years.

Michael Kearns has been at the center of AIDS theatre
and AIDS activism since 1984. *Myron, A Fairy Tale in Black
and White,* his first full-length, multiple-character play, is an
updated version of Rostand's *Cyrano de Bergerac* in which the
obtrusive and offensive body part is not a nose but the
diseased arm of an African American gay man with AIDS, a
character who by virtue of everything that makes him who
he is—race, sexual identity, diseased body—makes him other
in either dominant culture or minority subculture. His grotesque arm localizes difference and festers with self-hatred.
Myron regards it as an appropriate, ironic punishment from
God (he is a writer, and it is his "write arm") and brandishes
it as a weapon to strike out at others and as a shield to
protect himself: "Well, get ready for reality, honey: I look
like Miss Jane Pittman on a bad day." The playwright wittily
and touchingly reminds us that those boundaries we set up
and those rituals we create to separate ourselves from all
others—those blacks and whites—are not only grossly inhuman but also patently absurd.

As the Showman informs us, *Queen of Angels* is a postmodern tale without an ending ("4 the playg . . . [iz] stil desen-
dun") but with plenty of laughs ("Thatz y weer heer. 2
provyde sum komikul releef 2 thayr dizpayr"). James Carroll

Pickett captures the ritual spectacles, the playful forms, and the ambivalent laughter of carnival in this revision of the myth of Gilgamesh, the precursor to Orpheus who descended into the underworld to rescue his beloved. Max is the poet/hero, sentenced to live when all he loved have died. He is surrounded by a company of Clowns, the funny but frightening representatives of the carnival spirit, entertained by the violent antics of Punch and Judy, guided by one El Coyote who warns of the twin dangers of silence and infighting among oppressed groups, and confronted by the evil Queen of Angels who cruelly mocks all attempts to construct gay identity and to validate people with AIDS.

How far would you go to change an HIV positive to an HIV negative? Would you undergo experimental treatments? Take illegal drugs? Make a pact with the devil? In Ted Sod's *Satan and Simon DeSoto,* the title character opts for "Satanism . . . an alternative approach to holistic healing." In order to alter his antibody status, Simon must consciously and completely transform himself by denying his sexual identity, repudiating his community, and betraying his loved ones. The playwright raises many complex and controversial issues in his own darkly comic version of the Faust legend.

The promotion reads as follows: "You've had the disease! You've been to the demonstration! Now see the musical!" *AIDS! The Musical!* is described by its creators, Wendell Jones, David Stanley, and Robert Berg, as "an all-singing, all dancing, all queer voyage into a world of AIDS activism, new age gatherings, sleazy sex clubs, radical faeries, lesbian love, and fags bashing back!" Their dramatic intention is to reflect queer lives in America at the present time and to celebrate the distinctiveness and diversity of queer identity. Their intended audience is a gay one because, they say, they have grown tired of heterosexuals reacting to AIDS. Thus, in the convoluted logic of retroviruses, *AIDS! The Musical!* represents a Brechtian staging of reverse transcriptase: reclaiming AIDS from the heterosexual community, rescripting AIDS for the gay and lesbian community, and re-visioning that community's response: "The whole epidemic is so tragic, it's ridiculous." After the Scene One passing of Bob whose last wish is that death be like a big musical with angels and songs (the ensuing show honors that request), the audience accompanies the protagonist, Thomas, on a journey through contemporary gay culture and arrives with him at the final destination—a collective and activist response to AIDS.

Victor Bumbalo's *What Are Tuesdays Like?* removes the fourth wall of an outpatient waiting room so that the audience can observe the weekly comings and goings of people living with AIDS. From the outset of the pandemic, the construction of AIDS has relied on the establishment of boundaries between sick and healthy, black and white, gay and straight, poor and rich, guilty and innocent, risk groups and general population. Thus, a "fourth wall play" is itself a metaphor for such polarization: those who are actively involved in the ongoing struggle of AIDS are watched by others who are comfortably ensconced at a safe, however sympathetic, distance. Within the play, Bumbalo embeds other metaphors which suggest the unstable and relative positions of observer/observed, so that onlookers are aware of the paradoxical position of being an objective yet implicated viewer, of being separate from but not immune to a drama of the drama of AIDS. For example, the play opens with a character attempting to project himself imaginatively into a landscape of the Grand Canyon—a scene that seems a simultaneous performance of the willed suspension of disbelief taking place on the other side of the proscenium. In a later scene, two characters—Howard and Denise—fantasize about the public execution of a particularly callous social worker. As they envision his hanging, Howard fills in the details: "He'd hear us. Talking about a new restaurant we'd be going to as soon as the show is over." Such a line hits far too close for comfort, leaving an audience feeling a little less sure, a little less smug about their or anyone's distance from AIDS.

Shifting from the body of the community which incorporates individuals to the individual body of the artist which incorporates the community, Tim Miller merges autobiography—the search for personal identity—and cultural history—the concomitant search for community identity—in

My Queer Body. We begin with the comic reenactment of the conception and birth of the performance artist ("ECCE HOMO!!!"), move to the sweet story of his sexual coming of age ("born once again"), then witness his exorcism of the ghosts of those he once knew and loved. *My Queer Body* is an American epic in the tradition of Walt Whitman's *Song of Myself.* Tim Miller constructs a queer self in a world that has either denied or destroyed queer existence and superimposes the contours of his own body on the landscape of America. Like Whitman, the artist momentarily stops and waits for us on his journey to a future that includes "a symphonic homoerotic performance art cantata that will exorcise homophobia and bigotry from our land."

I hope that you enjoy this extraordinary collection of plays and performances.

Therese Jones
University of Colorado, Boulder

notes

[1]Emmanuel S. Nelson, "AIDS and the American Novel," in *Journal of American Culture* (Spring 1990): 48–49.

[2]Miranda Joseph, "Constructing Gay Identity and Community: The AIDS Plays of Theatre Rhinoceros," in *Theatre Insight* (Spring 1991): 10.

[3]Michael King, "Don't Call Me Avant-Garde: An Interview With Anne Bogart," *Houston Press*, 2 April 1992.

[4]The order of the following sources correspond to the order of descriptions in the text: Sylvie Drake, "Rock," *Los Angeles Times*, 18 January 1992. Karen Ocamb, "Send In the Clowns!," *Update*, 7 October 1992. David Roman, "'It's My Party and I'll Die If I Want To!': Gay Men, AIDS, and the Circulation of Camp in U.S. Theatre," in *Theatre Journal* (October 1992): 319. Sylvie Drake, "'Sex/Love/Stories': Miller's Explosive Ode to Gay Life," *Los Angeles Times*, 20 March 1991. Steven Winn, "Fierce Humor in Holsclaw's AIDS Farce," *San Francisco Chronicle*, 19 May 1992. Carol Tice, "The Plague's The Thing in New Musical," *In These Times*, 4 September 1991. Winn, "Fierce Humor," and Tice, "The Plague's The Thing."

[5]David Roman, "'It's My Party and I'll Die If I Want To!': Gay Men, AIDS, and the Circulation of Camp in U.S. Theatre," in *Theatre Journal* (October 1992): 305.

[6]Douglas Crimp, "AIDS: Cultural Analysis/Cultural Activism," in *AIDS: Cultural Analysis/Cultural Activism*, ed. Douglas Crimp (Cambridge: The MIT Press, 1988): 15.

[7]The inherent features of carnival as the symbolic destruction of authority and assertion of popular renewal are from the literary theories of Mikhail Bakhtin set forth in *Rabelais and His World*, trans. Helene Iswolsky (Bloomington: Indiana University Press, 1984): 7–11.

[8]Noreen C. Barnes, "AIDS in the Twilight Zone," *Bay Area Reporter*, 21 May 1992, and Steven Winn, "Fierce Humor in Holsclaw's AIDS Farce," *San Francisco Chronicle*, 19 May 1992.

doug holsclaw

the baddest
of boys

author's note

Welcome to Cafe Carl . . .

Death is a powerful thing; frightening, intoxicating, illuminating. It can draw people together or send them into orbit. When the unthinkable becomes incorporated into the fiber of one's day-to-day life, when daily stress alone has been known to cause people to open fire in fast-food restaurants, what you get is a unique blend of compassion, tolerance, generosity of spirit, and fear. When fear becomes a common nuisance, like looking for parking on a crowded street, we enter a new, distinct, uncharted reality . . . causing one to ponder, to seriously imagine . . . as strange as things are now what must Rod Serling's childhood have been like?

The Baddest of Boys stems from an idea of how the gay community might appear to someone who had pulled a Rip Van Winkle for ten or so years. It is this perspective that is responsible for the off-kilter and at times nightmarish quality of the play. It is ultimately a play about trying to maintain one's sanity in an insane world, and my own view of how so many imperfect human beings have inadvertently risen to a level of nobility in response to the circumstances thrust upon them. Special thanks to the bravery of Theatre Rhinoceros, Adele Prandini, David Clayton, and Sabin Epstein for bringing *The Baddest of Boys* to the stage.

performances and productions

The Baddest of Boys was originally produced by Theatre Rhinoceros, Adele Prandini Artistic Director, at the Cowell Theatre in San Francisco, premiering May 16, 1992, with the following cast:

CHARLES: Ken Steinmetz
ERIC: Phil Vo
ANGELA: Melissa Baer
LAZLO: B.G. Lacquemont
IRIS: Melanie Moore

DIRECTED BY: Sabin Epstein
SET DESIGN: Chris Grant
LIGHTING DESIGN: Wendy Gilmore
COSTUME DESIGN: Dana Peter Porras
SOUND DESIGN: Bob Davis
STAGE MANAGER: Deborah Philips

characters

CHARLES: mid-thirties. Mild mannered, long-suffering manager of Cafe Carl

ERIC: twenty-one. Very attractive Asian waiter. Queer Nation type

ANGELA: thirties. Eccentric Buddhist chef

LAZLO: forty. Performance artist, co-owner of the cafe

IRIS: mid-thirties. Black, pregnant physician

PERRY: a head. Terminally ill co-owner of the cafe

setting

A two-level set. Downstairs is the dining room of Cafe Carl, a trendy South of Market restaurant in San Francisco. Upstairs is Perry's room.

act one

Ethereal music and lights suggest that we are in a dream.
Perhaps fog drifts across the stage. Charles is sitting stage center
with his head, face down, on a table. A bus tray filled with
dishes is on the table next to him, the dishes are stacked at an
angle that defies gravity. Everything in the cafe is subtly out of
whack. Tables may have only three legs, the bar may be slant at
an angle. The cafe should look slightly surreal in a way that
could also just be trendy decorating run amuck. A large
Picassoesque head or mask is suspended upstage and begins to
glow. We hear a booming male voice, perhaps speaking in a New
York Jewish accent.

VOICE. He that toucheth the dead body of any man shall be
unclean. *(Charles' head pops up)*
CHARLES. But I had to touch him. No one else was there.
VOICE. He that toucheth the dead body of any man shall be
unclean.
CHARLES. He held out his hand to me . . . *(He looks at his hand)*
Oh God, How do I get it off me? Please, tell me how do I
become clean again?
VOICE. And the Lord spake unto Moses saying, bring thee a red
heifer without spot. And ye shall give her unto a priest, that
he may slay her before his face. *(Eric enters dressed as a hip-hop
looking version of Jack and the Beanstalk)*
ERIC. That is so gross!
CHARLES. Where am I going to find a red heifer?
ERIC. I had one, but I sold it.
CHARLES. You sold it!
ERIC. For a handful of pine nuts. Magic pine nuts.
CHARLES. But baby, baby, I need a red cow.
ERIC. And then I met this man.
CHARLES. You met a man?
ERIC. A *big* man.
CHARLES. But you promised me!
ERIC. He was sooo big!

CHARLES. You didn't do anything bad, did you?

ERIC. I was very bad. *(Eric exits)*

VOICE. And the priest shall take of her blood with his finger, and sprinkle it before the congregation seven times. *(Angela enters dressed as a funky high priestess)*

ANGELA. Why seven?

CHARLES. Just do it!

ANGELA. Do you know how much cholesterol is in this stuff? Never mind the steroids and antibiotics.

VOICE. And one shall burn the heifer in his sight. Her skin, and her flesh, and her blood, with her dung, shall he burn.

ANGELA. Does anybody have a light?

VOICE. And the priest shall take cedar wood, and hyssop, and scarlet, and cast it into the midst of the burning heifer.

ANGELA. *(Singing)* Scarlet ribbons for his hair.

VOICE. Then the priest shall bathe his clothes in water, and bathe his flesh in water.

ANGELA. *(Singing)* I'm gonna wash that cow right out of my hair.

VOICE. And a man that is clean. *(Lazlo enters, perhaps dressed in a metallic jumpsuit like a spaceman)*

LAZLO. That's me. My hygiene has always been above reproach.

VOICE. Shall gather up the ashes of the heifer, and wash his clothes in water, and bathe his flesh in water.

LAZLO. Where is the red cow, Charles? Don't tell me we've run out of red cow again? That's the third time this week!

CHARLES. What are you talking about? We don't have red cow on the menu.

LAZLO. I've never seen a red cow, I never hope to see one, but if there was a red cow, I'd rather see than be one. *(He laughs at his own joke)* That's good, that's really quite good. *(As he exits)* I've never seen a red cow, I never hope to see one . . .

VOICE. He that has touched the dead body of a man shall be unclean.

CHARLES. Out damn spot! I didn't want to touch him, but he reached out to me.

VOICE. This is the law, when a man dieth in a tent: all that is in the tent, and every open vessel, which hath no covering is unclean.

CHARLES. Gather up all the creamers!

VOICE. And whosoever toucheth one that is slain with a sword, or a bone of a man, or a grave, shall be unclean.

CHARLES. You just can't win, can you.

VOICE. And a clean person shall take the ashes of the burnt heifer and running water shall be put thereto in a vessel. *(Iris enters. She is extremely pregnant—beyond reality—and dressed as an exaggeration of a doctor with a huge light reflector on her forehead)*

IRIS. Somebody boil some water. A big pot of water.

CHARLES. I need a red heifer, a red cow, have you seen one?

IRIS. And what are the properties of this cow? Has this been documented? Has it been published? *(We hear a loud screeching sound which scares Charles)*

CHARLES. AAAhhh! What was that?

IRIS. I've been beeped. They must need me down at the slaughter house. *(Iris exits)*

VOICE. And the unclean person shall take hyssop, and dip it in the water and sprinkle it upon him that touched a bone, or one slain, or one dead.

CHARLES. Didn't we do that already?

VOICE. *(Booming)* Do it again!

CHARLES. Jesus!

VOICE. Who?

CHARLES. Never mind. *(He sits and rests his head on the table)*

VOICE. And whatsoever the unclean person toucheth shall be unclean; and the soul that toucheth it shall be unclean. And his soul shall be unclean! *(The last line is echoed as Charles wakes up screaming. Lights come up to full)*

CHARLES. AAAHHHH! *(Eric enters from the street)*

ERIC. Charles, what's the matter?

CHARLES. You!

ERIC. You're pissed, right?

CHARLES. Start talking, Mister.

ERIC. I'm not going to tell you anything if you use that tone with me.

CHARLES. I'm your boss, I'll use any tone with you that I please.

ERIC. Well, if you don't want to know, that's fine.

CHARLES. Don't do this to me.

ERIC. I may have had a very good excuse for missing the lunch shift but now you'll never know.

CHARLES. I demand to know.

ERIC. Keep it up.

CHARLES. You can't just miss a shift, it makes me look ridiculous.

ERIC. I guess you'll have to fire me then.

CHARLES. Don't treat me this way. I'm the manager.

ERIC. We have a naughty waiter here, I guess the big bad boss will have to fire him.

CHARLES. I don't want to fire you.

ERIC. What choice do you have?

CHARLES. Well, maybe you have an excuse, maybe you were trapped underground in a Muni car or your hair dried funny or one of your other personalities took over.

ERIC. My other personalities would never miss a shift.

CHARLES. What about Phil?

ERIC. How dare you throw Phil in my face. You're so insensitive. Maybe I'd be better off if you did fire me.

CHARLES. I don't want to fire you.

ERIC. Then you know what to do.

CHARLES. I don't. I don't know what to do.

ERIC. Ask nice and I'll tell you.

CHARLES. Please, what should I do?

ERIC. I mean ask me nice where I was and I might tell you.

CHARLES. Please, my precious, I've been sick with worry. Where were you?

ERIC. You're going to feel like such an ass when you find out.

CHARLES. Good. I don't want to fire you, honey, but how do I explain to Perry that my boyfriend skips shifts and doesn't get fired?

ERIC. Perry's in the hospital, he need never know.

CHARLES. He's coming home today, and I know he'll find out. Lazlo will tell him.

ERIC. Don't you dare throw Lazlo in my face.

CHARLES. Why do you hurt me like this?

ERIC. Because I love you.

CHARLES. Do you?

ERIC. You're the only man I've ever loved.

CHARLES. I love you too, you know I do.

ERIC. I've loved you ever since that first day when you stood on that table and changed a light bulb and your T-shirt rose up and I saw your stomach and I lost all track of time and let that party of four wait two hours before I took their order.

CHARLES. I've forgiven you for that.

ERIC. I was arrested.

CHARLES. Arrested?

ERIC. It was so cool. I went to a kiss-in at a Macy's fashion show.

CHARLES. That's your excuse? You were kissing someone?

ERIC. I was making a statement to all those uptight, over-rich Junior Leaguers who will spend thousands of dollars on a queer-designed gown and then vote Republican. Our message is accept us now or wear Norma Kamali for the rest of your life.

CHARLES. Who were you kissing?

ERIC. That's not the point. I was making a statement.

CHARLES. It was a good statement. Statements are good. But couldn't you just throw water balloons or tear gas or something? Did you have to kiss someone?

ERIC. It was no one you know.

CHARLES. Really?

ERIC. It was no one I know. In fact, I think it may have been an employee. Things got very confusing, everyone was trying on clothes and after awhile you couldn't tell the enemy from the radicals, everyone was wearing catsuits and color blocks and French kissing.

CHARLES. Why can't you meet some *nice* radicals?

ERIC. And I picked up the most adorable little Madonna shorts. I can't wait to try them on for you. Now don't you feel foolish making such a scene?

CHARLES. Well, I was worried. I didn't know, and I've been so busy trying to get everything ready upstairs for Perry's return. Then when Dexter didn't show, I was down to two waiters. At least he called.

ERIC. Dexter called?

CHARLES. Well, his roommate called.

ERIC. And what was his big excuse?

CHARLES. Dexter died.

ERIC. He didn't die.

CHARLES. His roommate said he died last night, you know he hasn't been well.

ERIC. That queen's used that excuse four times this month. Are you sure it was his roommate and it just wasn't Dexter disguising his voice?

CHARLES. I know it's a shock, honey, and I know how close you were. I'm really sorry.

ERIC. Dexter was with me. He was last seen on a podium at Macy's fighting over a Day-Glo burnoose with Jennifer Montana.

CHARLES. Well, thank God he's alive. I guess I'll have to fire him.

ERIC. Don't you dare. He had a good excuse. He was dead. Just leave it at that.

CHARLES. This place is falling apart and Perry's coming home and I'm afraid Lazlo will find out about the lunch shift and fire me. You know Lazlo hates me.

ERIC. Don't you dare throw Lazlo in my face. I told you it was only once and it wasn't that great, so just get over it.

CHARLES. I can't get over it, you slept with one of my bosses.

ERIC. And you have to stop leaving the room every time he comes in. It's rude. You can't avoid him forever.

CHARLES. I'll try. I'll have to for Perry's sake. I mean, Lazlo and I are his two closest friends, but whenever I hear Lazlo's voice my heart starts pounding and my veins start bulging and I . . .

ERIC. You're so uptight! *(Lazlo enters from street)*

LAZLO. Who wrote these specials on here? There's chalk dust all over the floor.

CHARLES. I have to go put fresh sheets on Perry's bed.

ERIC. Charles . . .

CHARLES. I have to go. I love you. *(Charles exits upstairs)*

LAZLO. Where is everybody?

ERIC. I don't know. I'm just cleaning up from the noon rush.

LAZLO. Was it busy?

ERIC. Swamped. I am totally exhausted. I had to work a double station.

LAZLO. Why? Didn't Charles schedule enough help?

ERIC. Dexter cancelled.

LAZLO. What was his excuse?

ERIC. He called in dead.

LAZLO. Again? Well, he has been looking thin lately. I guess we should give him one more chance. What about Jean-Luc?

ERIC. Dead.

LAZLO. He can't be dead. He called in dead on Wednesday. Does he take us for complete fools?

ERIC. Still dead. Wednesday was the real thing.

LAZLO. That's terrible.

ERIC. I know.

LAZLO. It's getting impossible to keep a waiter in this town. Never mind what it's done to our insurance rates.

ERIC. Lucky thing I was here. It got really crazy. Charles became completely unglued.

LAZLO. Charles needs to get a grip. He's been behaving abominably.

ERIC. He knows about us.

LAZLO. He knows?

ERIC. Everything.

LAZLO. You told him?

ERIC. I didn't mean to—I dissociated and Phil took over. He told him. I can't be held responsible.

LAZLO. Phil is such a squealer.

ERIC. It just came out.

LAZLO. Well, that explains the way he acted in the hospital this morning. He was visiting Perry when I came in and he was totally rude. He acted like I wasn't there.

ERIC. He can be so childish.

LAZLO. Perry was very upset. As sick as he is he still worries about this place. He wants everybody to get along after he's gone. Well, Charles better change his tune if he wants to manage this place after Perry dies.

ERIC. You couldn't fire Charles.

LAZLO. There are going to be some big changes around here. I'm tired of the way Perry let Charles push him around.

ERIC. Charles is a wonderful manager.

LAZLO. When Perry and I bought this place, I wanted to just be a silent partner so I could concentrate on my performance work.

ERIC. I loved your last piece.

LAZLO. Thank you, thank you very much. But soon I will be in a position where I can't keep silent. I don't know about the restaurant business. I'm a performance artist. I've been a performance artist since . . .

ERIC. Since when?

LAZLO. Since my trust fund matured. I've kept my mouth shut for Perry's sake but if this place is going to be mine, I'm going to run it my way. No more of his bourgeois bent. The discreet music, the carefully concealed lighting, the constant emphasis on service. I've had it.

ERIC. You're so bold, Lazlo. What are you planning?

LAZLO. A more visceral experience, visual contradictions, enveloping sound. So what if they can't hear each other. If they want to talk they should stay home. And enough of this service shit. Fuck good service, make them wait. They'll appreciate it more when it comes. Let people wait for tables. I want to see yuppies pressed up against the glass by the bar. Let people on the street know they're missing something.

ERIC. Oh, Lazlo.

LAZLO. This place will be just like my performance pieces. Vibrant, assaulting, insulting. I want them to leave with an empty feeling in the pits of their stomachs.

ERIC. That's exactly how I felt after I saw your last piece.

LAZLO. Really?

ERIC. In fact, that's how I felt after I slept with you.

LAZLO. And you still prefer Charles over me?

ERIC. He's hung like a race horse, Lazlo. Sometimes I don't want an empty feeling. And besides, he lets me make my own schedule.

LAZLO. That could all change when Perry dies.

ERIC. But then Charles will be half owner.

LAZLO. Half owner? Of this?

ERIC. Perry is leaving him his share in his will.

LAZLO. That's ridiculous. When Perry dies, everything goes to me. Then we'll see if he's too good to speak to me.

ERIC. He needs the job, Lazlo.

LAZLO. And I need him. At least until I learn how things run around here. Where is he, anyway?

ERIC. He's getting Perry's room ready.

LAZLO. I wish I could stay to greet him.

ERIC. Where are you going?

LAZLO. I'm premiering a new piece tonight.

ERIC. Oh no, I'll miss it. I promised Charles I'd work tonight.

LAZLO. But you worked today.

ERIC. I don't want thanks, I know things are tough with Perry's condition. My needs can go on hold.

LAZLO. But it's really a stunning piece. I think you'd like it.

ERIC. I'm sure I would.

LAZLO. You wouldn't understand it, but you'd like it.

ERIC. So much the better. What's it about?

LAZLO. It's about our preoccupation with death. It started as a collaboration with Itzak Ubatande.

ERIC. Itzak Ubatande!

LAZLO. But he died, so I'm going solo.

ERIC. Use it.

LAZLO. It's an AIDS benefit. I'm sorry you can't make it. Here's a ticket in case you change your mind.

ERIC. Well, if it's for a good cause . . . *(Angela enters from outside carrying grocery bags)*

ANGELA. Coming through.

LAZLO. Angela, let me help you. Eric, help her.

ERIC. What is all this stuff?

ANGELA. Groceries, girlfriend. We're almost out of chili. I've got to make a new batch. *(Eric exits into kitchen with groceries)*

LAZLO. What happened to the delivery man?

ANGELA. Brandon?

LAZLO. The cute one.

ANGELA. He's dead.

LAZLO. Oh my God.

ANGELA. I stopped by the mortuary to pay my respects on the way to Safeway. Now I have chili to make.

LAZLO. Without Perry?

ANGELA. We're famous for our chili. I can't take it off the menu.

LAZLO. Has he?

ANGELA. No, he still hasn't told me the secret ingredient.

LAZLO. Have you asked?

ANGELA. It's kind of touchy. I don't want him to think I think he's going to die soon.

LAZLO. But he is going to die soon.

ANGELA. And seasonings and spices seem insignificant in light of his suffering.

LAZLO. When he was healthy it was cute for him to be so guarded about his favorite recipe. Now it's some strange form of denial.

ANGELA. I've tried everything I can think of in the chili, but I just can't match it.

LAZLO. You've got to ask him.

ANGELA. Why do I have to ask him?

LAZLO. You're the chef, this is your domain.

ANGELA. You're the co-owner, you ask him.

LAZLO. I don't want to own this. It's your future at stake.

ANGELA. And what about yours?

LAZLO. I have my career.

ANGELA. Honey, you can't be getting too rich doing benefits, and that trust fund must be pretty tied up paying the mortgage on this place.

LAZLO. How did you know I had a trust fund?

ANGELA. I've seen your work.

LAZLO. I just don't want to say anything that will upset him.

ANGELA. You've known him since prep school, you're the logical one to ask him.

LAZLO. You've known him for years, too, ever since the Buddhist commune.

ANGELA. And even back then he wouldn't tell what he put in that chili. We served it in our cafe, of course it was veggie chili, but it still had that special twist. That's why they kicked him out. They said all recipes were communally owned even if he did discover it. So he left and took his recipe with him, and I followed a few weeks later.

LAZLO. Were you bumped too?

ANGELA. There were aesthetic differences in the kitchen.

LAZLO. I can't believe anyone wouldn't like your food.

ANGELA. I made hush puppies in the wok. They still pray for me. Look, I'm visiting him tomorrow morning. I'll see if it comes up then.

LAZLO. But he's coming home today.

ANGELA. How can they let him come home?

LAZLO. He wants to come home, Angela.

ANGELA. How's his condition?

LAZLO. It's grave. They wanted to try a new procedure on his lungs, but he refused.

ANGELA. Oh, Lord.

LAZLO. It's state of the art. Dr. Ainsworth takes a high voltage vacuum pump and sucks the lungs out through the nostrils, they turn inside out so they can treat them with topical antibiotics.

ANGELA. And he refused?

LAZLO. They can't use anesthesia.

ANGELA. Oy, girleen!

LAZLO. They tried it once but the anesthetic made the capillaries in the nasal passages dilate and they couldn't get the lungs back in. Perry said no. And they say the procedure can increase your life span for up to four days.

ANGELA. Well, we've got to stand by his decision.

LAZLO. Yes, we've all got to stand by him. And hope that Charles starts behaving himself.

ANGELA. What's wrong with Charles?

LAZLO. He found out I slept with Eric.

ANGELA. You slept with Eric?

LAZLO. Only once.

ANGELA. How did he find out?

LAZLO. One of Eric's multiple personalities told him.

ANGELA. Which one?

LAZLO. He suspects Phil.

ANGELA. Phil is such a bitch.

LAZLO. Charles made a scene at the hospital and it was very upsetting for Perry.

ANGELA. I'll talk to him. He's got to hold himself together for a few more days. Perry needs him.

LAZLO. Perry needs us all.

ANGELA. I've got to get started on this chili and then get to work on the burritos for the AIDS cook-a-thon.

LAZLO. It's tonight?

ANGELA. Yes, all the best chefs in town are donating the food and the diners have pledges for a certain dollar amount based on their calorie intake. It could be very Roman.

LAZLO. Well, it's for a good cause. But what about Perry? The hospital is sending him home in an ambulance. I told them someone would be here.

ANGELA. I have to make and deliver four hundred Middle Eastern lemon chicken burritos! Why can't you be here?

LAZLO. I have a performance tonight. It's a fifty-dollar a seat gala. I can't cancel.

ANGELA. But he needs someone.

LAZLO. Eric! *(Eric enters from kitchen)*

ERIC. Tell Charles I had to book. Dexter just called. The Vice President is in town, and they've found out his itinerary. We're going to storm Benihana. Tell Charles I love him.

LAZLO. But someone has to care for Perry.

ERIC. This is important to me, Lazlo. The media coverage will be awesome. I have to go! *(Eric exits to street)*

LAZLO. Wait, give me that ticket back. It cost fifty bucks. *(Lazlo exits after him. Charles enters from upstairs)*

CHARLES. What's going on down here?

ANGELA. Charles, I'm so glad you're here. The ambulance is on its way.

CHARLES. I was upstairs cleaning Perry's room.

ANGELA. What happened to Anatol? I thought he was paid to clean?

CHARLES. He died two weeks ago. The place is a pig sty.

ANGELA. Anatol dead?

CHARLES. And most of Perry's plants. Anataol had such a green thumb. Of course, I always suspected it was simply gangrene.

ANGELA. We really need to talk before Perry arrives.

CHARLES. I wish I could but I . . .

ANGELA. The sicker he gets, the more he shuts me out. And when I told him the community was creating a tanka for him, he did this—hmph—nostril thing.

CHARLES. I think right now he needs our practical support.

ANGELA. Charles, you don't have a spiritual bone in your body. And he hasn't even told me about the chili.

CHARLES. How can you think about chili at a time like this?

ANGELA. But he'll be gone soon. Dying is a process, death is the event.

CHARLES. I can't think about Perry dying. I just have to think about today when he comes home.

ANGELA. Dying is a catalyst for death.

CHARLES. Well, I wouldn't dream of arguing with that, but, Angela, he'll need help going to the bathroom . . .

ANGELA. Dying is a ray of light that illuminates a single thread but does not break it.

CHARLES. This could be a very messy business.

ANGELA. I'll do everything I can. I'll leave him some Middle Eastern lemon chicken burritos for dinner.

CHARLES. He can't eat burritos. Not after they botched that new laser tongue biopsy. It's still very tender.

ANGELA. I'll be there when the time comes. It's very important for me to be there when he passes over.

CHARLES. But will you be there when he passes burritos?

ANGELA. Don't get sanctimonious with me, Missy. I heard you were a big fat royal bitch at the hospital today.

CHARLES. I had just heard about Anatol. I was out of sorts.

ANGELA. You had just heard that Eric slept with Lazlo.

CHARLES. You know?

ANGELA. Everything.

CHARLES. Everything?

ANGELA. That's what I said.

CHARLES. You know about the pot holders?

ANGELA. Say pot holders?

CHARLES. I can't talk about it.

ANGELA. Lazlo wants me to speak with you.

CHARLES. Lazlo told you, of course.

ANGELA. Yes he did, but I already knew. I pretended I didn't because after all, he is my boss and a semiprofessional drama queen. I'm not a total kiss-up, but Mama didn't raise no fool.

CHARLES. How did you know?

ANGELA. Chantal.

CHARLES. Chantal? How did Chantal know?

ANGELA. Phil told her.

CHARLES. I hate Phil. And I hate Lazlo; this is all his fault.

ANGELA. You can't blame it all on Lazlo. Eric's so young, Charles. Do you really think he's not going to sleep around?

CHARLES. Kidney punch.

ANGELA. Why don't you date someone your own age? What was wrong with Marlon?

CHARLES. Kidney failure.

ANGELA. Fatal?

CHARLES. Girl, where have you been?

ANGELA. I'm sorry, Charles. Now, Eric's not a bad boy, but he's just a boy, and he doesn't understand yet.

CHARLES. Lazlo should. He just did this to hurt me. He wants me to quit. He's jealous of my friendship with Perry. He wants him all to himself. I've known ever since that skin graft incident.

ANGELA. He wasn't trying to exclude you.

CHARLES. Perry and I built this place. Side by side, we did everything together while Lazlo was out doing his unitard, rear-projection thing. And now that Perry's terminal, I'm just trash.

ANGELA. Can you put this on hold? For Perry?

CHARLES. For Perry. Of course I can. Perry is my first concern.

ANGELA. And he'll be so happy to find you waiting for him when they bring him home.

CHARLES. But I have to leave. I have to make my Open Hand deliveries.

ANGELA. But I've got the cook-a-thon and Lazlo and Eric just left.

CHARLES. Together? They left together? Oh my God.

ANGELA. Relax. Lazlo has another benefit and Eric's picketing the Feds.

CHARLES. But Eric said he'd work tonight.

ANGELA. You know how he is about politics.

CHARLES. Where am I going to find another waiter on such short notice?

ANGELA. Try the morgue. *(Eric enters from the street)*

CHARLES. Eric, you're back. Thank God.

ERIC. I can't stay. I forgot my new Madonna shorts. I'm storming Benihana. *(Eric exits to kitchen)*

ANGELA. I've got to run, too, honey. I can't back out now.

CHARLES. Please, Angela, don't go!

ANGELA. The Board of Supervisors will be there and I hear one of them is single. And, besides, it's for a very good cause. *(Angela exits into kitchen as Eric enters)*

CHARLES. Eric, you can't leave me. I need you. Perry's coming home and everything is falling apart.

ERIC. You need me? How can you be so selfish with so much at stake?

CHARLES. I know there's a lot of steak at Benihana, I mean at stake at Benihana, no I don't . . . what's at stake? I'm lost.

ERIC. An incredible opportunity to attract press attention to the lack of AIDS funding.

CHARLES. But what about Perry?

ERIC. It's too late to help Perry.

CHARLES. Someone's got to care for him.

ERIC. This is turning into a city full of caregivers. Where's your anger?

CHARLES. My anger's in my fingernails, okay? If I let my anger take over I wouldn't be any good to anyone. I'm trying to deal with my grief and care for Perry and I need your help.

ERIC. And if I let you drag me down with your grief and your caring, then I wouldn't be any good to anyone either. Can't you see I'm fighting for you?

CHARLES. In Madonna shorts?

ERIC. They're way cool, aren't they?

CHARLES. They're way short. Don't they have a dress code at Benihana?

ERIC. Fuck Benihana, this is war. *(Lazlo enters from the street)*

LAZLO. Give me back that ticket. It's worth fifty bucks.

ERIC. Well, it's for a good cause.

LAZLO. Cute shorts. *(Eric exits to street)*

CHARLES. Enough Lazlo, I know everything.

LAZLO. That Phil is such a Chatty Cathy.

CHARLES. But I'm putting Perry's needs first, we're in this together. I want you to stay.

LAZLO. But my benefit.

CHARLES. Please don't leave me alone with him.

LAZLO. Well, isn't this a rare turn of events. This morning you couldn't stand to be in the same room with me.

CHARLES. It's still not easy for me.

LAZLO. I suppose you want me to apologize.

CHARLES. It wouldn't help.

LAZLO. How about a hug?

CHARLES. I'm willing to put my feelings aside for Perry's sake.

LAZLO. And after that?

CHARLES. Don't say after, I'm still hopeful.

LAZLO. Hopeful about what? Some miracle will cure Perry?

CHARLES. Anything is possible.

LAZLO. Some miracle will make your boy-toy be faithful?

CHARLES. Okay, okay, I'm not counting on miracles. Let's just deal with Perry right now. The rest all depends . . .

LAZLO. On what? The will? The controlling interest in the cafe? Whether you still have a job after the way you've snubbed me?

CHARLES. A snubbing isn't good enough for you.

LAZLO. Whether you still have your boyfriend?

CHARLES. Eric loves me. I know he does.

LAZLO. Relax, I don't want your boyfriend.

CHARLES. He only slept with you because you're a performance artist.

LAZLO. But why do you think I became a performance artist?

CHARLES. And you have a trust fund.

LAZLO. How does everyone know about my trust fund?

CHARLES. But I have something money can't buy.

LAZLO. I know, he told me.

CHARLES. Honor, integrity . . .

LAZLO. And a schlong like a thoroughbred.

CHARLES. A triple crown winner and don't you forget it! *(Iris enters from upstairs)*

IRIS. There you are boys, I need to speak with you.

CHARLES. Dr. Ainsworth, how did you get in?

IRIS. We brought Perry up the side stairs.

LAZLO. Thank God you're here doctor, I've got to run. *(Lazlo exits to street)*

CHARLES. Lazlo! I'm sorry I didn't hear you, Dr Ainsworth, I would have helped. You shouldn't be lifting things in your condition.

IRIS. Dante and Tyrone, from the ambulance company, carried him up. It took three trips with all the equipment.

CHARLES. Where are they? I'd like to thank them.

IRIS. I'm afraid the strain was too much for Dante. Tyrone's taking him to the morgue.

CHARLES. How's Perry?

IRIS. It's not good. He's contracted another rare virus. It causes a rapid and painful growth of cartilage, you'll especially notice it around the ears, but he's a fighter.

CHARLES. Oh my God, can't anything be done?

IRIS. There is a new experimental procedure involving iodine and a blowtorch. Do you by any chance have a small propane stove in the kitchen?

CHARLES. No! No, we don't.

IRIS. Well, before I go I have some instructions.

CHARLES. You have to go?

IRIS. I have a Lamaze class

CHARLES. Can you come back later? I'll serve you dinner. We have the best chili in town.

IRIS. I'm speaking at a medical convention. They've got AIDS specialists from all over the world quarantined at the Civic Center. They're expecting me.

CHARLES. But I need you here.

IRIS. They're being deported at dawn, I can't put it off.

CHARLES. But what about Perry?

IRIS. I've given him something to calm him down. He's very disoriented. He thinks I'm from the FBI and I'm trying to kill him.

CHARLES. Are you sure it was a good idea to bring him home?
(A beeper goes off on Iris' belt)

IRIS. Is that me or something in the kitchen?

CHARLES. I think it's you.

IRIS. *(She takes out beeper and looks to see who is calling)* I have to run, I'm late for Lamaze. *(Iris exits. Charles looks towards the stairs and crosses slowly. He climbs the stairs to Perry's room. When he reaches the top he sees Perry's head illuminated, it is the same huge, grotesque head as in his dream, and he screams)*

Blackout.

act two

Lights up on Perry's room. We hear a loud beep which later will be identified as Perry's morphine pump. When visitors enter the room they press a button on his morphine pump, we hear the wail of the pump giving him a shot of morphine and then the lights and sounds change taking the room to another dimension of reality, perhaps what we are seeing is Perry's view of events through a haze of morphine. Tubes and hoses run everywhere. IV bags and bottles hold different colors of liquids. Some may glow, some may bubble like a lava lamp or smoke. Sounds of screams, bats, chains, etc., can be heard faintly in the background. As the play progresses, Perry's room becomes more and more like a house of horrors. We are in morphine-land as Lazlo begins his performance piece.

LAZLO. It used to be people would die in just about anything, but today's dying are younger, hipper, and more willing to take a fashion risk. They want to face the grim reaper with a "look." Those terminal cases on the cutting edge want to die in something new. That's who we cater to at Worn Once-Once Worn. Many find the angularity of emaciation frees them to try a slinky look they once only dreamed about. If you're still this side of decomposure, why wait? You'll find fabric drapes on you with stunning lines without the obstructions of fatty tissue and muscle mass. Perry Ellis, Halston, Willi Smith—we only carry dead designers. If they're alive, it's not their time.

But what if your blood pressure is stable and civil war hasn't yet erupted on your chem panel? Don't let the dead and dying have all the fun. We have a full line of previously worn clothing by people who no longer need threads where they've gone. And they call it paradise? Not my idea of heaven. All clothes in our Mortswear boutique are previously disowned. Love your dress, who died in that?

And for those who can afford it, in our Cafe Muerta Boutique—this year's coup—overalls! They're in, they're out—hello, they're back! In Farm Accident Overalls, everyone is an original. No two alike! We'll have more in stock soon after the fall harvest . . . I mean fall collection arrives. Hemorrhage stains for fall, crimsony earth tones to wear while the days are getting shorter.

And for those who want more than cloth, more than leather, more than memories. You can have a little piece of eternity with our new line of jewelry simply called "Truman." Pendants, brooches, earrings, and more. Enclosed in outré blends of pewter, chrome, and semiprecious metals you can keep the semiprecious ashes of a once precious friend. And just in time for the holidays—paperweights with snow scenes. The off-white look of the swirling snow suggests either a sooty urban setting or the remains of a cherished friend. Only you and your decorator will know for sure.

Once Worn-Worn Once and Morstwear for the Dying, and the dying to please.

Blackout. In the dark we hear the morphine pump screech. Lights up downstairs as Angela is looking for something behind the counter. Iris enters from the street.

ANGELA. I'm sorry, we're not open yet.

IRIS. Dr. Ainsworth, Iris Ainsworth, Perry's physician.

ANGELA. I'm sorry, Dr. Ainsworth.

IRIS. Did Brutus arrive?

ANGELA. Brutus?

IRIS. From the medical supply company. He was supposed to deliver a morphine pump this morning.

ANGELA. Yes, he did. He installed it about an hour ago. He went very peacefully.

IRIS. Perry's dead? Oh my God! I shouldn't have gone to the convention last night. I should have stayed here.

ANGELA. No, Brutus. It was all very sudden. We've placed him in the cooler until the Neptune Society arrives.

IRIS. Give me strength. How's Perry?

ANGELA. Lazlo is with him. He hasn't let me go up yet. He said his ears are huge.

IRIS. Well, that's to be expected, but he's a fighter. I've brought my blowtorch. Is Charles here?

ANGELA. No, he went to bail his boyfriend out of jail.

IRIS. Oh dear. I might have to enlist your assistance Ms. . . .

ANGELA. Dupree. Angela Dupree.

IRIS. You're the chef?

ANGELA. Yes.

IRIS. The Buddhist?

ANGELA. Yes.

IRIS. Perry's friend from the commune?

ANGELA. He mentioned me?

IRIS. I really couldn't say, that would violate doctor patient confidentiality. Are you squeamish, Ms. Dupree?

ANGELA. Angela. Tough as nails. Unless it involves harming any sentient beings.

IRIS. Isn't that difficult for a chef?

ANGELA. It's a conflict. But that's all going to change. Perry has promised me his share of the restaurant. I'm planning on going Buddhist veggie. I want it to be a very spiritual place. Have you tried the chili?

IRIS. Perhaps I'll just wait for Charles.

ANGELA. I haven't much faith in Western medicine, anyway.

IRIS. I see.

ANGELA. It just seems there must be something they could do.

IRIS. I am they, Ms. Dupree.

ANGELA. I'm not criticizing you.

IRIS. Then who are you criticizing?

ANGELA. I just wonder what Eastern medicine could teach us from this.

IRIS. Well, if they have a cure, I wish they'd tell us.

ANGELA. Perhaps we haven't asked the right questions. *(Lazlo enters from street)*

LAZLO. Hello, Dr. Ainsworth. *(To Angela)* Hasn't anyone showed up yet?

ANGELA. Chantal is in the back chopping vegetables. How was your benefit last night?

LAZLO. It was cancelled.

IRIS. No one showed up?

LAZLO. No, the emcee died. How was your speech?

IRIS. Fine, but I could barely be heard above all the hacking.

LAZLO. I trust everyone has been safely deported?

IRIS. Fog has closed the airport down. They've all been moved to a secret location.

ANGELA. Lazlo, honey, how is Perry? Did he ask to see me?

LAZLO. I'm sorry, no.

ANGELA. But the secret ingredient!

IRIS. How is Perry this morning?

LAZLO. I just performed my latest piece for him.

ANGELA. And he's still alive?

LAZLO. He's a bit confused. He thought I was Vincent Price but I think he enjoyed it.

IRIS. And his ears?

LAZLO. Enormous. And his eyebrows are doing something strange, too. They've sprouted these kind of green golf tee kind of things.

IRIS. It's a rare fungus, very painful, but he's a fighter. I'd better get up there. *(Iris exits upstairs)*

ANGELA. I'll be in the kitchen if anyone asks for me. *(Angela exits into kitchen. Charles enters from the street)*

LAZLO. It's about time, Charles. This place can't open itself, you know.

CHARLES. It couldn't be helped. How's Perry?

LAZLO. Not good. I think we better start looking for pallbearers.

CHARLES. Pallbearers? I can't even find a bus boy.

LAZLO. I'm going out for a paper. I want to see if the columns mention my canceled performance.

CHARLES. They'll probably be the best reviews you've ever gotten. *(Eric enters)*

ERIC. Excuse me.

LAZLO. Eric, how nice of you to drop in.

ERIC. Why are you calling me Eric?

CHARLES. He dissociated in the car. His night in jail must have been very traumatic.

LAZLO. Who is he now?

CHARLES. I think he's Prince Noir.

LAZLO. Well, whoever you are, you can start wiping off these tables. *(He throws Eric a dishrag)*

ERIC. Ahhh—cooties! Cooties!

CHARLES. Lazlo, please, the Prince has a phobia about germs, he can't get his hands dirty.

LAZLO. Don't you ever think he's just faking to get out of work?

CHARLES. Back off, Lazlo. I'll handle this.

LAZLO. What's he prince of?

CHARLES. Some island . . . Mesquite . . . Martinet . . . it's an *m* word.

ERIC. Everything must be spotless!

CHARLES. Prince Noir, look at me.

ERIC. Everything must be in its proper place.

CHARLES. Focus.

LAZLO. He's not royalty.

CHARLES. He's Crown Prince and neat as a fucking pin.

LAZLO. Oh, please. *(Lazlo exits)*

CHARLES. Eric, your hair looks like shit. It looks like you slept on it funny!

ERIC. Where am I? Who am I? Does my hair look okay?

CHARLES. Thank God, you're back. Now let's get to work. You start with the silver. I'll get the cream from the cooler. *(Charles exits into kitchen as Lazlo enters from the street)*

LAZLO. I have never been so insulted in my life.

ERIC. Bad reviews again, Lazlo?

LAZLO. Not a mention. And look at the front page.

ERIC. Total coolness—I made the front page! I've got to call Dexter.

LAZLO. 'Activists Storm Benihana. Three people were injured by flying shrimp when twenty-one-year-old Eric Huang dropped through a vent and engaged the Vice President in a lip-lock that took five secret service agents to disengage.'

ERIC. My shorts look cute, don't they? Oh no, I left the price tag on.

LAZLO. It's a look.

ERIC. Of course it is. Keep reading.

CHARLES. *(Offstage)* AAAAHHHHH!

LAZLO. What was that?

CHARLES. *(Offstage)* AAAAHHHHH!

ANGELA. *(Offstage)* Whoa Nelly!

ERIC. It's Charles! *(Angela and Charles enter from kitchen)*

ANGELA. I'm sorry, gal-pal, I forgot he was in there.

CHARLES. There's a dead man in the cooler!

ERIC. Is he cute?

LAZLO. Sit down, Charles. What a horrible shock. Why don't you try to relax and take a look at the morning paper.

ERIC. Give me that! *(Eric exits to kitchen, Iris enters from upstairs)*

IRIS. Is everything all right? I heard a scream.

ANGELA. Charles found the body in the cooler.

IRIS. Hasn't the Neptune Society arrived yet? They must have a full load this morning.

LAZLO. Those drivers can be such prima donnas. Especially if you don't make a reservation.

ERIC. *(Offstage)* Brutus!

CHARLES. How's Perry?

IRIS. Not good. He's very confused. He keeps asking what kind of a childhood Rod Serling had.

LAZLO. That's a scary thought.

ANGELA. Maybe I should go see him.

IRIS. Perhaps not. It could be quite a shock. The lesions on his face are beginning to form a sort of Laura Ashley print. I've only seen this twice before. But he's a fighter.

ANGELA. How long can this go on? How much worse can he get?

IRIS. It would be quite lovely on a pressed linen but with his features it's appalling.

ANGELA. Can't something be done?

IRIS. Mega-radiation might help. Do you have a microwave oven in the kitchen?

ANGELA. Miss Thing! Get a grip! How you die is as important as how you live. Isn't it about time we . . .

IRIS. And how do you know it's time?

ANGELA. Because I'm ready to know.

IRIS. I'm just doing my job. What time is it, anyway? I have an appointment for an amniocentesis at noon. *(Eric enters, he puts the newspaper on the bar)*

ERIC. It's only ten-thirty. *(To Charles)* How you doing, baby?

CHARLES. Don't serve the coleslaw today.

ANGELA. I had to prop him up in something.

IRIS. Angela, please show me to the kitchen.

ANGELA. I cannot be a party to this.

IRIS. I'm not asking you to be. I'm asking you to show me to the kitchen.

ANGELA. This way, Dr. Ainsworth.

IRIS. Lazlo, could you look in on Perry? I don't want to leave him alone.

ANGELA. Let me go up.

Everyone shouts no!

IRIS. Please, Angela, the kitchen. *(Angela and Iris exit into kitchen)*

LAZLO. Get a grip, Charles, we open in half an hour. Has anybody seen my newspaper?

ERIC. You're wanted upstairs, Lazlo. *(Lazlo exits upstairs)*

CHARLES. Why didn't you call me last night? I would have come down.

ERIC. I didn't want to disturb you. Let's go out on the patio.

CHARLES. You could never disturb me.

ERIC. It was one night in jail, what's the big deal? I missed you so much. *(Eric tries to kiss him)*

CHARLES. You could have been hurt. There are some pretty rough characters in there.

ERIC. Actually, I met the sweetest guy, who wouldn't let anyone else touch me. Let's get that tie off.

CHARLES. Anyone *else?*

ERIC. I've had it with your irrational jealousy, Charles.

CHARLES. You mean a grandfatherly guard looked out for your well-being?

ERIC. I've been through enough trauma, I don't need any dis from you. You should have seen what they made me wear. Come on, just let me see it. *(Trying to undo Charles' pants)*

CHARLES. Who? The guys in the cell block? They dressed you up in a little costume?

ERIC. No, Charles, the guards. I had to wear this horrible un-tailored jumpsuit—thing with no pockets . . . you're doing it again.

CHARLES. What am I doing?

ERIC. Casting doubts on my character.

CHARLES. Tell me it wasn't you in there. Tell me it was another personality. Tell me it was Phil.

ERIC. How dare you drag Phil into this. It's starting to grow.

CHARLES. I'm so ashamed.

ERIC. Proximity to death makes some people horny. Don't beat yourself up about it.

CHARLES. You're so good to me.

ERIC. Let's go outside. *(Eric and Charles exit to patio. Iris enters from kitchen carrying a microwave oven followed by Angela)*

ANGELA. I'm sorry, but I just can't allow you to go up there with that thing.

IRIS. I understand your reservations, Angela, but I am sworn to an oath and I must act in what I feel is the best interest of the patient.

ANGELA. I think death would be in Perry's best interest. Something should be done.

IRIS. Do you want to do it?

ANGELA. Me?

IRIS. I was trained to prolong life, not end it.

ANGELA. Perhaps if you allowed yourself to explore the spiritual side of your nature.

IRIS. I've lost twelve patients this month already and I . . . *(She becomes dizzy and has to sit)*

ANGELA. Are you all right?

IRIS. I just need to catch my breath. I'm a little tired from the convention last night. *(She starts to get up)*

ANGELA. You're having a baby, Iris. I simply will not allow you to expose yourself to that sort of radiation.

IRIS. Of course, what was I thinking.

ANGELA. You don't look well, maybe I should call your husband to come get you.

IRIS. I'm a dyke!

ANGELA. Well, I thought you were.

IRIS. Well, I knew you were.

ANGELA. I didn't want to ask because . . .

IRIS. So you make some crack about a husband?

ANGELA. I was concerned. *(Iris opens her medical bag)*

IRIS. This is the baby's father. *(She pulls a vial of sperm from her medical bag)*

ANGELA. I'm so relieved. Is it someone you know?

IRIS. Thurgood Marshall. I got it on the black market.

ANGELA. Well, it looks like nice sperm . . . not that I'm an expert on sperm. But it seems a nice consistency. Not too thick, not too thin. I'm sure it will be a lovely child.

IRIS. That means a lot coming from you.

ANGELA. From me?

IRIS. Being a chef you must . . . oh, I don't know why, it just does.

ANGELA. That's sweet, but why do you still carry that vial around with you?

IRIS. I just never seem to get around to cleaning that bag out. I save everything. I suppose you're like that with recipes.

ANGELA. I never use recipes. It's a Zen kind of thing. With one exception. *(Angela eyes Iris' bag. Lazlo appears at the top of the stairs)*

LAZLO. Angela, could you bring me some water? His tongue seems to be puffing up.

IRIS. That can only mean one thing. Have you a bungee cord?

ANGELA. Just let me get some water. *(Angela exits to kitchen)*

LAZLO. Iris, it's monstrous what's happening up there. I hate to be the one to bring it up, but isn't there something that can be done?

IRIS. I'm doing everything medical science has to offer. *(She pulls a blowtorch from her bag)*

LAZLO. I'm afraid Perry is beyond science. Right now he's up there carrying on a conversation with Sharon Tate!

IRIS. I'll go hit the morphine button, that should calm him down.

LAZLO. I just gave him a dose five minutes ago. *(Angela enters with a bowl of chili and a glass of water which she hands to Iris who drinks it)*

ANGELA. Here's some water.

IRIS. You're an angel, Angela.

ANGELA. Try this chili, Lazlo. What do you think?

LAZLO. It's missing a little . . .

ANGELA. Yes? Missing a little what?

LAZLO. I don't know. I can't quite put my finger on it.

ANGELA. I can't either, and I've tried almost everything.

LAZLO. Cumin?

ANGELA. No.

LAZLO. It wouldn't be dill?

ANGELA. No.

LAZLO. Well, be creative. How about this stuff? *(He picks up the vial of sperm)*

IRIS. No!

ANGELA. NO! *(The baby kicks and Iris spills the glass of water)*

IRIS. Oh, I'm sorry.

LAZLO. Here, let me. *(He finds the newspaper on the bar and places it over the spilled water. Eric enters from patio followed by Charles)*

CHARLES. Eric, come back. What about me?

ERIC. I thought you were in a hurry to set this place up. Do I have to do everything myself?

CHARLES. He's so conscientious, really he is. *(Eric exits into kitchen)*

IRIS. I'm sorry about the spill.

ANGELA. Just sit, I'll clean it up. *(Angela picks up newspaper and Charles sees photo of Eric with the Vice President)*

CHARLES. Oh my God! The front page! And he said he was in jail last night.

LAZLO. Of course he was, this is a photo of the crime. You're so dense, Charles. No wonder you don't understand my work. *(Eric enters carrying napkins)*

ERIC. All right, Chantal, I'll be right back.

LAZLO. Get the lead out, Eric. We open in thirty minutes

ERIC. You're mobile, Lazlo, go help Chantal. She lost an earring in the ratatouille and she's having a total shit fit. *(Lazlo exits into kitchen)*

CHARLES. *(Holding up newspaper)* Eric, my pumpkin, how could you humiliate me like this?

ERIC. Enough with the jealousy, Charles. Can't you see I'm working?

CHARLES. But look at the photos splashed all over the morning paper. You're kissing the Vice President and you seem to be enjoying it.

ERIC. It was for the cause. Besides, what makes you think I started it? Do you think the Vice President wouldn't find me attractive?

CHARLES. Of course not, Eric. I can certainly understand the attraction. I'm sorry, I . . .

ERIC. It was no big deal. He tasted like Tic Tacs.

CHARLES. How awful for you. I'm so sorry!

ERIC. Jesus Christ! *(Eric exits into kitchen)*

ANGELA. Charles, when are you going to stop making a fool of yourself over that boy?

CHARLES. We're just going through a rough period, things will get better.

ANGELA. You know what they say about mixed marriages.

CHARLES. Angela!

ANGELA. You're gay, he's queer. It will never work.

CHARLES. I really can't think about it right now. Perry is my only concern. Everything will get back to normal once he stabilizes. We've just got to open for lunch and carry on as usual. I've got to check on Perry. *(Charles exits upstairs, Lazlo follows him off)*

ANGELA. Do me a favor Iris. Try this chili. It's our specialty.

IRIS. Um, that's tasty.

ANGELA. It doesn't taste like it's missing something?

IRIS. Did you leave something out?

ANGELA. This is Perry's favorite recipe. But he never told anyone the secret ingredient.

IRIS. Who is that man?

ANGELA. Where?

IRIS. In the dark suit. He's been walking back and forth in front of the cafe ever since I arrived.

ANGELA. Charles! Charles, could you come down here for a minute? *(Charles enters from upstairs)*

CHARLES. Oh, I just can't bear to see him like this, Dr. Ainsworth, isn't there something that can be done?

IRIS. Well, there is a new radical procedure with ammonia and a curling iron. *(Iris exits upstairs)*

ANGELA. Charles. There is a strange man outside. He seems to be spying on us.

CHARLES. Him in the suit?

ANGELA. Yes.

CHARLES. Oh no. *(Eric enters with dishes)* Eric, I think the Secret Service is following you.

ERIC. Again?

ANGELA. There's a man out front walking back and forth.

ERIC. Where?

IRIS. There, by the Vespa.

ERIC. *(Goes to the front door)* Yo! Vinnie! Get a grip, you have a wife and children. Go home! *(To Charles)* I'm sorry you had to see that, Charles. *(Eric exits into kitchen)*

CHARLES. Eric, how could you? *(Charles exits into kitchen. Angela, left alone, sneaks over to Iris' medical bag and begins to look for something. She takes out a large syringe and sneaks up to Perry's room. She approaches the bed and hits the morphine button, the lights and sound take us into morphine-land)*

ANGELA. Perry? Are you awake? It's me, Angela . . . I know you

haven't wanted to see me, but I mean no harm, I only come
to learn from you. What's it like? Are you scared? Do you
see a white light? Do you see the black night? Do you see a
red sunset? Or perhaps red wine? Red vinegar? Red pepper,
red onion, red currents, red cow, red dates? Ready as I am
to accept your passing, for birth is not a beginning and
death is not an end, I come to you as the disciples of Master
Etsugen gathered one last time to be taught of Buddha's
enlightenment, and at dawn he bathed, put on his ceremonial robes and sitting erect in the lotus position composed
his death poem under a pepper tree. Was it a pepper tree?
I believe it was, of course, I don't know what kind of pepper
tree exactly. It could have been serrano peppers or tepin or
cascabel or chiptole, guajilo, guerro? Please, Perry, I've tried
Thai peppers, Texas peppers, Colorado, New Mexico—hell,
I've even tried Anaheim and Fresno peppers. Om. Om. Take
refuge in the Dharma and pray that you may with all beings
enter deeply into this treasure and your wisdom may grow
as vast as the ocean. For anointed with precious oil . . . olive
oil? Peanut oil? Safflower oil? Sesame oil? Oil of Olay? Oh
lay ye down and take refuge in the wisdom and warmth of
the Sangha . . . Sangria? Yes! No. Perry, this isn't funny. I've
tried mole, pepitos, epazole, elote, achriote—for Goddess
sake—I even spit in it once! Om. Om. Perhaps as Master
Etsugen said in his death poem—the inquisitiveness of man
is pure folly. Say it Perry! Say it! You must, you simply must,
you must . . . mustard! Dijon? Dusseldorf? Bordeaux, Ger-
man, English, French, French's, Grey Poupon? I'd hoped it
wouldn't come to this. *(She raises the syringe. Iris enters from
kitchen and crosses to stairs)*

IRIS. Everything will be fine. I just need some steel wool and
rubber tubing. *(Iris enters bedroom)*

ANGELA. Om . . . Om . . . eeanie meanie chili beanie.

IRIS. Angela! What are you doing? *(The lights and sound change,
returning the room to reality)*

ANGELA. Iris, don't jump to conclusions.

IRIS. Give me that syringe. *(Iris crosses downstairs, Angela follows
her)*

IRIS. Sodium Pentathol? Truth serum? What were you going to do with this?

ANGELA. It's not for me, Iris, it's for the chili.

IRIS. You were going to put the truth serum in the chili?

ANGELA. No, I was going to give it to Perry. What would Cafe Carl be without Perry's famous chili? I want him to live on, I want him to leave something behind for us to remember him by. I don't even like chili.

IRIS. I see.

ANGELA. I just don't want him to be forgotten.

IRIS. I think I misjudged you.

ANGELA. It was crazy, I know, but I'm desperate.

IRIS. Perry is very lucky to have a friend who cares so much. *(Iris goes to her and hugs her)* There, there.

ANGELA. *(The baby kicks her)* Ow.

IRIS. I'm sorry, it's the baby.

ANGELA. And Perry is lucky to have such a dedicated physician.

IRIS. Even a Western physician?

ANGELA. I'm sorry, I know you're doing your best, but . . .

IRIS. The stress is beginning to take its toll on all of us. *(They kiss)*

ANGELA. *(The baby kicks her again)* Ow!

IRIS. Damn.

ANGELA. You need to rest. There is a cot in Perry's office.

IRIS. But my tubing . . .

ANGELA. Your tubing won't help Perry now. Come with me. *(Angela leads Iris off to kitchen as Charles and Lazlo enter)*

LAZLO. Charles, you've got to face facts.

CHARLES. He's been bad before.

LAZLO. Get real, Charles.

CHARLES. Didn't Iris say something about a curling iron?

LAZLO. I think we better start being realistic about this. He asked me to call his lawyer shortly before the Laura Ashley thing started.

CHARLES. I thought all of his affairs were in order?

LAZLO. Have you actually seen the will?

CHARLES. Well . . . no.

LAZLO. Maybe it's time we started looking.

CHARLES. I will not have you going through this man's drawers while he's lying there helpless.

LAZLO. I think we should begin a dialogue about the future. The memorial, the cremation, changes here at my cafe . . .

CHARLES. Your cafe? After Perry's gone, you won't make a move without my consent.

LAZLO. And what makes you think that?

CHARLES. Perry's leaving his share to me. He said he wanted to thank me for my years of hard work and give me some security.

LAZLO. He told me he wanted to thank me for investing the money to make it all possible.

CHARLES. How quaint.

LAZLO. Let's not forget this is Cafe Carl and Carl was my grand-father . . .

CHARLES. I'm sick of hearing about your trust fund.

LAZLO. I've never even mentioned it.

CHARLES. Like it's a secret.

LAZLO. It might be time for you to make a change anyway. It might be good for you to have a life outside this place.

CHARLES. Always thinking of my well-being.

LAZLO. Believe it or not . . . I might be.

CHARLES. Well, you certainly weren't thinking about it when you shtupped my boyfriend.

LAZLO. That's just one more reason for a change. You shouldn't get involved with the help. It just creates problems.

CHARLES. What about you?

LAZLO. I wasn't involved. Eric loves my work, it was my way of thanking him for his support.

CHARLES. Do you hear drums pounding?

LAZLO. Now, about the memorial.

CHARLES. Please, Lazlo.

LAZLO. I've been preparing a new piece for the occasion.

CHARLES. I can't breathe.

LAZLO. It will be a celebration of his essence, in Sanskrit of course, but I think it will be accessible. I was hoping you could handle the food.

CHARLES. Handle this, Lazlo.

LAZLO. I was hoping we could be civilized about this. *(Charles exits upstairs, Eric enters from kitchen)*

ERIC. Have you seen Charles?

LAZLO. He's with Perry.

ERIC. Hud called in.

LAZLO. Dead I presume?

ERIC. He had a night sweat with his electric blanket on high.

LAZLO. And we just hired him last week. *(Eric exits upstairs and enters Perry's room)*

ERIC. Charles? Can I talk to you?

CHARLES. Yeah, come on in.

ERIC. Oh my God.

CHARLES. Don't look. Eric. I don't want you to upset yourself.

ERIC. I've never seen anything like this before in my life.

CHARLES. Don't overreact. Perry never did look very good before noon.

ERIC. It's about Hud.

CHARLES. Dead?

ERIC. So he claims.

CHARLES. Shucks. Chantal will have to help serve.

ERIC. I'm not going to tell her.

CHARLES. Please, baby, I don't want to leave Perry alone.

ERIC. What could you possible do for him at his point? I think the best thing you could do for him would be to unplug him, or at least get him a veil.

CHARLES. He's bounced back before.

ERIC. Charles, you've got to let go.

CHARLES. Please just go tell Chantal to put on an apron.

ERIC. What happened to his face?

CHARLES. It's a rare viral-fungal-bacterial sort of thing, but he's a fighter. The little flowers are kind of nice. Very summery.

ERIC. You're losing it, Charles. *(Eric exits downstairs)*

LAZLO. Where's Iris? She has a phone call.

ERIC. She's in Perry's office with Angela. I think she's practicing her breathing exercises.

LAZLO. Has the Neptune truck come for Brutus yet?

ERIC. No, he's still stirring the coleslaw.

LAZLO. Oh great, they'll probably arrive right during the noon rush. Just what we need for the customers to see . . . another dead body being hauled out of here.

ERIC. We are getting quite a reputation.

LAZLO. Perhaps I could do a short performance piece to distract them while they're carting him out.

ERIC. That would be so intense, Laz. I love your art.

LAZLO. Thank you. Thank you very much.

ERIC. If I could find a man with your talent and Charles' tool, I think I'd give up dating. I've got to talk to Chantal. *(Eric exits into kitchen)*

LAZLO. Sweet boy. *(Iris enters, passing Eric)*

ERIC. Lazlo has a message for you.

IRIS. Yes?

LAZLO. It seems the airport is still shut down and several of the conventioneers are near death. They need you there right away.

IRIS. Where are they?

LAZLO. He wouldn't say. He says it's top secret. You're to call this number.

IRIS. Damn Immigration.

LAZLO. But before you go we really need to talk about Perry.

IRIS. Can't it wait?

LAZLO. No, Iris, I think we should gather Charles and Angela and make a decision. *(He takes the phone out of her hand and places it on receiver. They both look up towards Perry's room)*

If the play is performed in two acts this is the place for the break. Action resumes where it was left off.

IRIS. Lazlo, don't ask me to do something that is contrary to my professional ethics. *(Angela enters from kitchen reading a letter)*

ANGELA. God damn, who would have believed it?

IRIS. I'm sorry but I have to leave. It's something of an emergency.

ANGELA. Where is Charles? I'm afraid I have some news he's not going to like.

LAZLO. *(From stairs)* Charles, could you come down here please? Don't anybody leave just yet.

ANGELA. I admire your dedication, but you're so busy taking care of others, who is taking care of you?

IRIS. Someone has to look out for those boys.

CHARLES. What is it?

LAZLO. We need to talk.

IRIS. I have to make a call.

LAZLO. This won't take long.

ANGELA. Charles, read this. It's from Eric.

CHARLES. Eric?

LAZLO. Dr. Ainsworth, we appreciate that you are on the cutting edge of technology but I fear that you've lost perspective on . . .

CHARLES. Oh no! Oh no! No! NO!

IRIS. Charles?

LAZLO. What is it?

CHARLES. Eric has eloped with Chantal.

IRIS. Chantal.

LAZLO. Right before the noon rush?

ANGELA. I'm sorry, Charles.

LAZLO. Whose idea was it to hire bisexuals around here, anyway?

CHARLES. This is too much for me to bear.

IRIS. Eric is bisexual?

CHARLES. No, Phil is.

ANGELA. I hate Phil.

LAZLO. I can't believe Chantal would leave with no notice.

ANGELA. She won't be licking my spoon anymore.

CHARLES. I can't go on.

LAZLO. Charles, you must. We open in ten minutes. Do something!

CHARLES. We'll all have to pitch in. I can wait tables.

ANGELA. I can cook.

IRIS. I can carve. Let me call Immigration and tell them there has been a delay.

ANGELA. I'll heat up the grill. Lazlo, you'll have to do dishes.

LAZLO. Dishes? If I'm going to perform I need to do my warm-ups.

CHARLES. Do it for Perry.

LAZLO. I hate it when you say that. *(Charles, Lazlo, Angela, and Iris exit to kitchen. Eric enters from patio. He looks to make sure no one is around. He takes the* specials *blackboard from the easel, then climbs the stairs and enters Perry's room. He approaches Perry, presses the morphine button, we hear it shriek and the lights and sound take us into morphine-land)*

ERIC. Hi, Perry? Can you hear me? It's me, Eric. Eric, I'm your waiter. I think it's time to make a decision. Take a look at your choices before you decide. *(He either hands Perry a menu or holds up a small chalkboard marked* specials*)* Can I answer any questions or make any recommendations? Well, of course, we have carbon monoxide. We have that in a garage or in the car itself. Of course you can park on the street and run a hose from the exhaust pipe through a window, but then there's the chance of someone seeing you and intervening. If you go with a garage I recommend starting with a specific amount of gas. That way you can knock yourself off and then the car will run out of gas before there is danger to others. If you'd like that, it comes with towels and tape for sealing windows and doors. The foreigns tend to get a little better mileage so you compensate with a little less gas, but the domestics, surprisingly, have a somewhat more subtle bouquet. If you're into red meats, look at the back. We have a wide selection of gauges and calibers for those with hearty stomachs. It really depends on your personal taste. I recommend a twenty-two in the roof of the mouth which will take out a good chunk of the brain but leave the face pretty much intact. That's especially good if you have a more traditional family and they plan on a buffet after and would like to have you there as a point of focus for the guests. The orals are also very popular. We have a long list of choices with the recommended dosages. Again, in foreign and domestic, depending on your pocketbook. That comes with a nice Kahlua and cream to coat your stomach and a Compazine suppository to ward off nausea. We don't want to end up with our head in the toilet like that movie star now do we? We're fresh out of razor blades, the specials go quickly, so that's just about it. Why don't I give you a few minutes to think about it? *(Lazlo enters from kitchen followed by Charles)*

CHARLES. Lazlo, come back here. I need you to chill the asparagus plates. *(Eric hears them downstairs and hides behind the door)*

LAZLO. Get Brutus to do it.

CHARLES. Is he still here?

LAZLO. Yes, he's the large blue man next to the cilantro.

CHARLES. It's getting so hard to get rid of a body these days.

LAZLO. Write your congressman, Charles. I need a few minutes to myself.

CHARLES. We don't have a few minutes.

LAZLO. Get off my back, Charles, I am still your superior around here.

CHARLES. We'll see about that. *(Iris enters)*

IRIS. Where is the blackboard? Angela wants me to write up the specials.

LAZLO. What are we serving?

IRIS. A Mediterranean American shrimp with orange pistachio couscous and chunky minted yogurt.

LAZLO. Again? Charles, that's the third time this week.

CHARLES. Back off, Lazlo, you know nothing about running a restaurant. *(Angela enters)*

ANGELA. Iris, there's been a change in the special.

LAZLO. Thank God.

ANGELA. Brutus fell in the chunky minted yogurt. We'll be serving a lemony hummus with tortillas instead.

LAZLO. That is so tired, Angela. When I take over we have to do some serious updating of the menu.

ANGELA. When you take over? Excuse me, but Perry promised me a full partnership.

LAZLO. Why would he do that?

ANGELA. Because he loves me, Lazlo, and he know it's my food they've been coming to eat.

CHARLES. I think we have a problem here.

ANGELA. There will be some changes in the menu, Lazlo—we're going Buddhist veggie or bust!

IRIS. Excuse me, I think I'll check on Perry. *(Iris exits upstairs. Eric hides under the bed when he hears her ascending the stairs)*

CHARLES. Angela, this probably isn't the time to tell you this, but Perry promised his to me, too.

ANGELA. To you? Why would he do that?

CHARLES. I'm his best friend.

ANGELA. I'm his spiritual counterpart.

CHARLES. And he knows that my hard work and common sense have kept this place from turning into a madhouse.

ANGELA. Why would he promise us both?

CHARLES. Maybe he forgot. He started getting a little fuzzy after his last bout with toxo.

LAZLO. Toxo my ass, Charles. You're just trying to get back at me for sleeping with Eric.

ANGELA. Lazlo, Charles wouldn't lie. Maybe Perry just got confused, what with the dementia and all.

LAZLO. He wasn't demented when he promised his share to me.

CHARLES. Maybe it was that cranial lymphoma thing.

ANGELA. Or the medication for his vascular edema.

CHARLES. Or that CPA thing when he started seeing spots.

ANGELA. Never mind the hairy leukplakia.

CHARLES. I forgot about that.

ANGELA. Maybe he was afraid we would desert him.

CHARLES. You mean he was trying to bribe us into sticking around?

LAZLO. I'd never desert Perry.

CHARLES. None of us would.

ANGELA. That's so sad. Poor Perry. *(Iris appears at top of the stairs)*

IRIS. Excuse me, but Perry's condition is worsening. He has developed a very obscure form of brainial elephantitus. I think you should all come up.

CHARLES. Oh my God. *(They all rush upstairs into the bedroom)*

IRIS. Be prepared, his head has begun to grow.

LAZLO. What about lunch?

IRIS. His brain has started leaking from his ears. But he's a fighter.

LAZLO. I just lost my appetite. *(In bedroom they gather around Perry)*

CHARLES. Perry, can you hear me?

ANGELA. It's me, Angela.

CHARLES. We're all here, Perry.

LAZLO. We just can't watch him suffer any longer.

IRIS. I'm beginning to think you're right.

ANGELA. Om. Do Re Mi Fa.

LAZLO. Please don't chant, Angela. You know that's why he hasn't wanted to see you.

ANGELA. I didn't know.

CHARLES. I guess he didn't want to tell you.

LAZLO. I think he started questioning his spirituality when his balls fell off.

ANGELA. Oh, Perry.

CHARLES. Can you hear me, Perry? We're all here for you.

LAZLO. I think it's time to act.

IRIS. I'm afraid I've exhausted reasonable medical responses.

CHARLES. I can't watch.

ANGELA. I would have understood, Perry.

IRIS. I guess it's time. *(Iris moves to turn off machines)*

LAZLO. So long, my friend. *(Angela lunges to his bedside)*

ANGELA. Anise? Cinnamon oil? Guava paste?

CHARLES. Angela, please!

ANGELA. I'm sorry . . . I . . . oh Goddess!

LAZLO. What?

ANGELA. Look at his chest.

LAZLO. What is it?

ANGELA. This can't be happening.

IRIS. I've never seen anything like it.

CHARLES. What? What's happening?

IRIS. The lesions. They look like . . .

ANGELA. They're changing.

LAZLO. It looks like . . .

ANGELA. A face.

LAZLO. Is that who I think it is?

IRIS. It can't be.

ANGELA. But it looks just like him.

LAZLO. Are you sure it's not Elton John?

ANGELA. Elton John is bald. *(Eric appears from under the bed and moves toward them)*

CHARLES. I can't believe my eyes.

IRIS. It's unprecedented.

ANGELA. It's a miracle.

CHARLES. It's . . . it's . . . *(Eric has moved into the circle and looks down at Perry)*

ERIC. Jesus Christ! *(Charles falls to his knees. Angela begins to chant. The others stare in disbelief as the lights fade to black)*

act three

During the blackout, we hear Eric addressing a crowd with a bullhorn.

ERIC. We are your sons and daughters and brothers and sisters

and we are dying and we are angry and we will fight! And
I challenge the fucking President to come down here and
see what I have seen. Gay men still get AIDS, you can say it.
And here today, a martyr in death just as the likeness he
now bears is . . . he is . . . one man, who has lost his voice
but is reaching out from death's door to say . . . is making
a statement to the media and the world that . . . well, it is
an incredible likeness and I'm sure it means something,
never mind it is the photo-op of the decade! If you'll just
be patient. And I challenge the President, and not the Vice
President who is a horrible, minty-mouthed kiss-and-tell who
I am definitely not speaking to, to come here today and bear
witness to the miracle that is happening amongst our belea-
guered ranks. And you, Vinnie, go home! *(Eric enters from the
street holding a bullhorn. Charles is lighting candles. He wears a
large cross around his neck)*

CHARLES. Eric, please shut the door! The draft is going to blow
out all the candles.

ERIC. I'm sorry you had to hear that last part.

CHARLES. I am not allowing the press corps in here and that is
final.

ERIC. We're sitting on a story of monumental proportions. How
can you be so selfish?

CHARLES. What about Perry? How can he have any peace with
that mob out front? And I hold you personally responsible
for calling the press.

ERIC. I didn't tell anyone.

CHARLES. I suppose it was Phil?

ERIC. You blame Phil for everything.

CHARLES. I still haven't forgiven you for eloping with Chantal.

ERIC. I came back.

CHARLES. And turned this place into a media circus.

ERIC. I only told Dexter.

CHARLES. Dexter is media mad and you know it.

ERIC. This is bigger than Perry now. Channel Five is going to
cancel their marine mammal report tonight if they get foot-
age.

CHARLES. My friend is dying, honey. This is just too personal to
share.

ERIC. You can't keep the cafe closed forever.

CHARLES. The waiters couldn't get through that mob even if they were alive. *(Angela and Iris enter from the kitchen. Angela is struggling with a huge vat of chili. Iris is trying to assist her)*

IRIS. Angela, let me give you a hand.

ANGELA. Iris, you are too far along to be lifting, now just sit and rest, my sweet.

ERIC. My sweet?

CHARLES. What are you doing?

ANGELA. Some of those pilgrims haven't eaten in hours. If we can't open the restaurant, at least I can give them this chili.

CHARLES. But it's not right. It's not Perry's chili.

ANGELA. They're hungry, Charles. They have been holding vigil all night. Three Jews for Jesus have already fainted.

ERIC. Charles, we've got to open.

CHARLES. We can't handle a crowd like that.

ERIC. Sure we can. Where's Chantal?

ANGELA. She's not here, she called in earlier this morning.

CHARLES. Oh my God! Chantal is dead?

ANGELA. No, PMS.

ERIC. Thank God.

IRIS. That's what you think.

ANGELA. Eric, open the door. I'm going out.

IRIS. I'll come with you.

ANGELA. Iris, sit. It's crazy out there, you've got to think of the baby.

IRIS. Be careful! *(Angela exits to street)* Aaaahhhh!

CHARLES. Iris!

IRIS. Aaaahhhh!

CHARLES. Holy shit!

IRIS. Everyone stay calm. It's just a little labor pain, that's all.

CHARLES. We've got to get you to a doctor.

IRIS. I am a doctor and I have plenty of time. I can't leave Perry now.

CHARLES. We've got to get you out of here before the crowd gets any bigger.

IRIS. I will not leave my patient in this condition.

CHARLES. I'll stay with Perry.

IRIS. But my oath.

ERIC. Forget about your oath, you're having a baby.

IRIS. Let me check in on Perry, then I'll call Erno, my obstetrician, if that will make you feel any better. I've also got to call the Ferry Building and check on the conventioneers.

ERIC. The Ferry Building?

IRIS. I shouldn't have said that. Their location is a closely guarded secret.

CHARLES. We won't tell anyone, will we, Eric? *(Eric bolts toward the front door)*

CHARLES. Eric!

ERIC. Dexter! *(Eric exits)*

CHARLES. Please, Eric! Eric! Phil! Come back here! *(Charles exits after him)*

IRIS. Ooowww! I hear you, baby. I hear you. *(She moves to stairs)* It won't be long now. *(She enters bedroom)* Perry? Can you hear me, Perry? *(She hits morphine button)* I know I said I'd stay with you until the end but little Thurgood is getting impatient. I was hoping you'd still be around to see him but . . . *(She checks vital signs. She speaks into dictaphone)* Day two: Condition remains unchanged. Patient slept fitfully last night experiencing bouts of confusion, kept calling me Damien . . . Damien. *(Turns off dictaphone)* When my brother died I swore I would fight this thing, but after all my years of training I feel utterly helpless. These eyes on your chest staring out at me . . . what does it mean? They just didn't prepare me for this in medical school. *(Turns on dictaphone)* Having exhausted any logical cause, can find no scientific explanation. No data detailing treatment exists. Therefore, having crossed into uncharted territory one must not rule out any means of treatment available be that medical . . . or mystical. In layman's terms, what the hell . . . I've tried everything else. Having been failed by science I turn to my ancestral traditions. *(She turns off dictaphone, digs into her bag and removes a feathered headdress and ceremonial cape and book of Swahili verse. We hear drums with a tribal rhythm as she puts on headdress and cape and moves around the bed performing an African ritual of dying)* With the ashes of a red cow I bless you.

O God, possessor of power,	Ya Allahu Mwenyi kuwa,
Receive me in Thy Heaven;	mikubali kwakowe mbinguno,
Now I am dying,	sasa mafa,
Give my soul peace	roho'pe amani, amani.

(Ritual builds to a conclusion. She stares down at Perry looking for a sign. Checks vital signs again. Turns on dictaphone) Patient's condition remains unchanged. Would like to suggest new medical theory—Murphy's Law of medicine—anything that can go wrong with the human body will. *(She turns off dictaphone)* And you have borne it bravely. Aaaaahhhh! *(She clutches her stomach. Angela enters from the street with empty vat of chili. Upstairs, Iris is removing her ceremonial costume)*

ANGELA. I'm sorry, there's no more. Thank you, thank you, no I'm sorry, the recipe is a secret.

IRIS. Ooooh boy! *(Angela hears a cry from upstairs and rushes to stairway)*

ANGELA. Iris? Iris, is that you? *(Iris opens the door and meets her at the top of the stairs)*

IRIS. No, that was Perry. He's mumbling about Rod Serling again.

ANGELA. I can't believe he's still alive.

IRIS. Has the crowd thinned out any?

ANGELA. It's gotten worse. An envoy from the Pope just arrived. He wants to verify the face and declare Perry a miracle. Unless his nipples in any way contribute to the outline, then he will be deemed obscene art.

IRIS. What's all that noise?

ANGELA. We're being picketed by WAGAMF.

IRIS. WAGAMF?

ANGELA. Women Against Giving All that Money to Faggots.

IRIS. Uuuaahh!

ANGELA. Was that what I think it was?

IRIS. Just a little gas from that chili yesterday.

ANGELA. Are you sure? Iris maybe you should go.

IRIS. I'll leave when I have to.

ANGELA. Perry would understand. How is he? Is the face still there?

IRIS. There's no getting around it. It's a very white male inter-pretation of his likeness, but it's him all right. I see they ate your chili.

ANGELA. They attacked it like wolves. Nina Totenberg said it was the best chili she's ever eaten. *(She starts to cry)*

IRIS. Why does that make you sad?

ANGELA. It was my chili, it wasn't Perry's, and nobody noticed. They like it just as well. Nobody cared.

IRIS. I'm sure Perry would be proud of you! *(She hugs Angela and the baby kicks her)*

ANGELA. Ow! Iris, honey, I'm calling the doctor.

IRIS. I'll call.

ANGELA. You're pushing yourself too hard.

IRIS. You go sit with Perry, I'll call Erno and then I'll lie down and rest. *(They kiss, Angela jumps back before the baby has a chance to kick her. Iris exits into kitchen. Angela exits to bedroom as Charles and Lazlo enter from the street)*

CHARLES. I tried to catch him, but I lost him in the crowd.

LAZLO. You worry about him too much.

CHARLES. Then I saw you performing.

LAZLO. They loved me, didn't they?

CHARLES. It was very powerful, Lazlo.

LAZLO. Really? You liked it?

CHARLES. I don't know that I liked it but it made me feel like . . . well, like I already feel but . . . you put it in a way that . . .

LAZLO. You could relate to? Well, imagine that.

CHARLES. I never thought we'd agree on anything.

LAZLO. Charles, we have more in common than you think.

CHARLES. You mean Perry?

LAZLO. Well, yes, we both love Perry.

CHARLES. And you slept with my boyfriend.

LAZLO. Well, that wasn't what I was getting at but . . .

CHARLES. You're hung like a bull, too?

LAZLO. No, I'm afraid that's not it. Charles, I know your pain. You may think I'm arrogant and pretentious.

CHARLES. I do.

LAZLO. But I understand you more than Eric ever could.

CHARLES. Do you?

LAZLO. We're men of a certain age who have had our worlds turned upside down, and we shouldn't be fighting.

CHARLES. Lazlo . . .

LAZLO. I feel your fear, I feel your grief, I feel your amazing unit stiffening against my leg.

CHARLES. I'm so ashamed.

LAZLO. Do it for Perry.

CHARLES. Jesus! *(In a mad embrace they disappear behind the counter. The lights shift to Angela upstairs)*

ANGELA. Remember the story of the master who asked for a pear on his deathbed? And he ate it and all of his disciples gathered around him and he said, "What a juicy pear." And then died? I didn't mean to make you feel pressured, I guess I felt I could learn something from you. I didn't mean to give you performance anxiety about dying. You have been a lesson to us all. But Perry, in the end, you've really outdone yourself. I mean, a Buddha on your chest would have been something too, but since the weight loss it would never fit. But this face, this final mystery, this last unanswered question . . . Perry, you have really outdone yourself. *(Charles and Lazlo pop up from behind counter)*

CHARLES. I'm sorry Lazlo, I just don't feel good about this.

LAZLO. You're purging your grief, it's not supposed to feel good.

CHARLES. But Eric . . .

LAZLO. Screw Eric!

CHARLES. You already did.

LAZLO. Let me make it up to you.

CHARLES. First, let's talk about the will.

LAZLO. Let me just see it.

CHARLES. Oh God.

LAZLO. For Perry. *(They disappear behind counter. Iris staggers in from kitchen as Angela enters from bedroom)*

IRIS. Ooh ooh child, things are gonna get easier . . . uh!

ANGELA. Iris, look at you.

IRIS. I'm fine, really I am.

ANGELA. . . . Did you call Erno?

IRIS. Yes.

ANGELA. What did he say?

IRIS. He's dead.

ANGELA. That is too profound. I've got to get you out of here. It's turning into a mob out there. The streets are filled with nuns doing line dances.

IRIS. Don't worry about me.

ANGELA. I do worry about you. I see you so caught up in trying to save Perry and the others when you have a new life inside you.

IRIS. After years of watching my patients wither away, no matter what I tried, I thought maybe a new life would revive me and give me new strength to carry on my work. I even thought maybe she would grow up and be the one to find a cure.

ANGELA. You can't do it alone, Iris. Let me take care of you. Let me help you raise the child.

IRIS. There's something you should know.

ANGELA. It would revive my faith in renewal. I've cared for Perry until the end, now I could nurture a new life. You could continue your practice and . . .

IRIS. I got the results back from my amniocentesis.

ANGELA. Yes?

IRIS. It's a boy.

ANGELA. Oh. How far along did you say you were?

IRIS. Ooooohhh!

ANGELA. Just kidding. Iris, we could start a whole new life together.

IRIS. But what about Perry?

ANGELA. We've done all we can. Let the nuns come in and take care of him.

IRIS. But Perry's Jewish.

ANGELA. Perry is a Buddhist. *(Charles pops up from behind counter)*

CHARLES. Perry is a shrine!

ANGELA. A shrine to what?

CHARLES. I don't know, I don't know what any of this means, but I was raised as a Christian and I must believe . . . *(Lazlo also appears)*

LAZLO. Did I hear something about nuns in a line dance?

ANGELA. Afraid you'll be upstaged?

LAZLO. I lost track of time. I'm going back out.

CHARLES. Lazlo, maybe we should just sit with Perry.

LAZLO. I won't be sitting for some time, Charles. *(Lazlo exits outside)*

CHARLES. Lazlo!

ANGELA. Where's Eric?

CHARLES. I don't know, I lost him in the crowd.

ANGELA. Uh oh.

IRIS. Oooohhh!

ANGELA. Charles, I'm taking Iris out through the back.

IRIS. I've got to tell Perry goodbye.

ANGELA. There's no time for that.

CHARLES. Will you be coming back later?

ANGELA. Charles. I'm not coming back at all. I'm going to help Iris raise her . . . son.

CHARLES. But what about your share in the restaurant?

ANGELA. You can have it. I've finished my work here—I'm moving on.

CHARLES. What about the chili recipe?

ANGELA. Maybe we weren't meant to know.

CHARLES. You're going to leave Perry like this?

ANGELA. Perry left us a long time ago. Goodbye, Charles.

CHARLES. Angela.

IRIS. Charles. *(Iris hugs him)*

CHARLES. Iris. *(The baby kicks)* Ow! *(Angela and Iris exit through kitchen. Lazlo enters from outside)*

LAZLO. Where's everybody going?

CHARLES. They're in labor. I'm so glad you came back.

LAZLO. I'm afraid I'm leaving, too.

CHARLES. Was it me?

LAZLO. No, I just met an old lover of mine in the crowd. He's a filmmaker now and he wants to document my work. He's going to follow me cross-country as I provoke and confuse the public.

CHARLES. Can't this wait until Perry is gone?

LAZLO. Are you kidding? Look at the crowd, we can get some fabulous reaction shots.

CHARLES. I think this is very selfish, Lazlo. Perry's up there with the face of Jesus-fucking-Christ on his chest and you're thinking about your career.

LAZLO. Charles, this isn't for me, you must believe that. Someday I want the world to know what this was like for people like you and me and Perry.

CHARLES. Who would believe any of this?

LAZLO. It will be on film. I want to leave a document behind, in case no one is around who remembers.

CHARLES. But the face, Lazlo, what does it mean?

LAZLO. It means that contrary to popular belief about the hearing, I think it's the sense of humor that's the last to go. Ciao, baby.

CHARLES. And the cafe?

LAZLO. It's yours, I don't need it. I have . . .

CHARLES. A trust fund.

LAZLO. No hard feelings?

CHARLES. Eehh. *(Lazlo hugs him then exits out front door. Charles turns and slowly walks toward stairs as Eric bursts in from the patio. He is covered in soot, his clothing is torn, he acts like he is being chased)*

CHARLES. Oh my God, Eric, what happened?

ERIC. Have the cops been here?

CHARLES. What did you do?

ERIC. It was so cool, Dexter and I blew up the Ferry Building!

CHARLES. Eric, this isn't funny.

ERIC. Okay, not the whole building. We blew the entrance off.

CHARLES. Where did you get the explosives?

ERIC. Dexter made a bomb out of hair care products. You should have seen it, we freed all the quarantined conventioneers. There was a sea of morphine pumps flowing up Market Street like wind surfers.

ERIC. This is very serious.

ERIC. I know it is, I have to leave.

CHARLES. Oh God.

ERIC. You can come with me.

CHARLES. I couldn't leave Perry.

ERIC. Enough with Perry, come with me.

CHARLES. Where? Where are you going?

ERIC. I'm going on the run . . . I don't know where.

CHARLES. I can't leave Perry and the cafe. And what about your condition? What if you dissociate in a strange city?

ERIC. When the bomb went off I integrated. I am Eric and I remember. Please come with me.

CHARLES. And what if I got sick? Where would I go? Who would take care of me?

ERIC. You don't know that you'll get sick, you haven't even been tested.

CHARLES. And I can't. I've got to have some hope to hang on to.

ERIC. I'm your hope now, Charles.

CHARLES. And Perry with his face. I know it means something.

ERIC. It's time to stop trying to figure out what things mean and start knocking some skulls together.

CHARLES. I won't resort to violence and I won't leave Perry!

ERIC. Charles, you're just too good.

CHARLES. Am I? I love you, Eric, please don't leave me.

ERIC. I'm not leaving you. I'm leaving you behind. I'm a fugitive now.

CHARLES. You can't leave me in the middle of this nightmare! I could hide you, Eric.

ERIC. I know you would, but you hide somebody who's blown up a building and you're in trouble too.

CHARLES. But where will you go?

ERIC. I'll be all around in the dark. I'll be everywhere. Wherever there's a fight so dying men can get the care they need. Wherever there's a bully beating up a queer on the playground, I'll be there. I'll be in the sound dykes make when they rev up their bikes. I'll be in the way queens laugh at an old movie. And when this is all over and gays and lesbians aren't afraid to love each other and they're living in their homes without fear, I'll be there too.

CHARLES. Later, when this all blows over, you'll come back to me?

ERIC. Sure, Charles. I love you.

CHARLES. Goodbye, Eric. *(Eric exits through patio)*

CHARLES. Eric! *(Charles collects himself and walks up the stairs to Perry's room. Charles enters Perry's room)*

CHARLES. Well, Perry, I guess it's just you and me . . . and the face. Now, in answer to your question about Rod Serling's childhood *(He hits morphine button)*—I've been giving it some thought. And it seems pretty clear that something must have happened when he was just a wee small lad. When the little boy down the block collected worms in a cigarillo box and the girl next door put her eye out when she was running with a popsicle in her hand—way back then he must have had dreams . . . bad dreams. Dreams about ticking clocks that skipped a beat, and puppies drowning in vats of mud, and eyes that watched him through the petals of flowers and a man who hid under the bed and untied his shoes while his mother was boiling cabbage. But why would a little tot have such peculiar thoughts while sleeping? Well, I've thought about that too—in fact, I haven't slept in three days, thinking of nothing else, for there seems but one logical conclusion. He must have been shot by a bullet while sleeping in his bed, it came through a window in the middle of the night and lodged in his thigh and he screamed out in pain and while he was rushed to the hospital the neighbors formed a posse—but no one was found. Not a picket fence was smudged, not a fire escape had footprints and no one heard a car, let alone the gunshot. So when tiny Rod came limping home to a bed with brand new unstained sheets—he had trouble sleeping—had frantic thoughts when he began to doze—was up all night and got cranky in school and dark circles grew under his eyes, which later proved quite sexy when shot in black and white. What else could it have been? Unless, his parents owned a restaurant in Tucson, Arizona, and little Rod used to watch the cook chop onions and cry and help old Verna fold napkins. And later he was given an apron and began to carry bus trays filled with cups with lipstick rims like blood and grizzled bits of bone and cartilage from the carcass of a prized red cow. *(He begins to turn off the machines and disconnect the tubes keeping Perry alive)* Years later when he headed for the big city, still wearing his apron and clutching his favorite ballpoint pen, he found a brave new world full of endive and cilantro and boneless filets that simply disappeared—and someone noticed how hard he worked and cared what he thought—and his boss became his friend and his friend became his equal and together they planned every detail of the dream bistro that would bind them for life. And when strange things started happening, just like in his dreams as a child, and people started dying all around him and his good friend's head started looking like an extra-large Hawaiian pizza . . . he returned the friend's many favors by wounding him fatally as he slept in his bed with a gun that would never be discovered. My final theory is that he came from back East from a prickly family with lots of dough and he moved out West with his best friend from school and he really made a pretty good life for himself. And lots of people care about him . . . and he'll be in their thoughts for a very long time . . . goodbye my friend. *(As the machines are shut down, we hear Perry's breaths get shallower. As he utters his last breath, he speaks)*

PERRY. Tequila.

Lights fade to black.

michael kearns

myron, a fairy tale in black and white

56   *Michael Kearns*

author's note

Many things inspired *Myron:* the eternal poetic power of
Edmond Rostand's *Cyrano de Bergerac;* Steve Martin's quirky
and frisky film version, *Roxanne;* my friendship with an African American man (named Myron) who, in his final stages
of AIDS, developed a "monster's arm" (his words, not mine).
Finally, these creative embers were ignited by the demise of
my lover, Philip Juwig, who died shortly after seeing the
play's first reading.

In the past decade—after having done how many theatrical endeavors involving AIDS? I've lost count—I've come to
realize that HIV/AIDS is merely another insidious way to
separate *us* from *them.* It is another "ism"—like racism, looks-
ism, sexism, classism, and homophobia. As a gay, white male
artist who is HIV positive, I seek the opportunity to explore
what *binds* us to them, not what *distances* us. It's Myron's
heart and soul which everyone falls in love with—even if you
don't like his color, his disease, his language, his politics, his
febrile queerness.

Attempting to create a black character was audacious, I
know, but I felt I could—as a queer who took a long time
to accept the beauty of being different—connect with my
hero's self-defined "ugliness." Myron's journey to self-accep-
tance provides a blueprint for any of us cursed/blessed with
being any shade of queer.

The toll of AIDS has reinforced the lesson of the Rostand
masterpiece: the capacity of the human heart is what's truly
beautiful. Hopefully, *Myron* reiterates a message which bears
repeating especially in a world which seems destined to destroy itself by punishing those who are different.

Like *Cyrano, Myron* is a love story more than it is "a gay
play" or "an AIDS play" or "an interracial triangle." It is a
play about learning to see with your soul instead of your eyes
and trusting the language of your heartbeats.

performances and productions

Myron, A Fairy Tale in Black and White opened on January 21, 1993, at Highways Performance Space in Santa Monica, with the following cast:

MYRON: Amos Cowson
REX: Jason Brooks
CHRIS: Charles Champion

Colin Martin directed; Rod Edwards produced with ARTISTS CONFRONTING AIDS; production design by Nelson Coates; original music by Darien Martus.

characters

MYRON: has AIDS; his arm is severely diseased, fortyish

REX: his buddy (from a social services agency), twenties

CHRISTOPHER: Myron's cousin, a hunky body builder, thirtysomething

---

SCENE ONE

MYRON. Why are you staring at my arm?

REX. I'm not. I'm not even looking at your arm.

MYRON. Why not? Are you afraid to look at my arm? Do you find it al*arm*ing?

REX. I'm not afraid.

MYRON. But you're not ch*arm*ed. You're somewhat dis*arm*ed.

REX. You're playing with me. Or you're picking a fight.

MYRON. It won't be much of a fight. I'm a one-man *army*.

REX. You keep doing that.

MYRON. Doing? Doing what? Believe me, it's h*arm*less. It's how I cope.

REX. Let's start over. I'm Rex. Your buddy. I want to help.

MYRON. You're very white. Well-heeled.

REX. You're very black. *(A beat)* Well-*arm*ed.

MYRON. You're not stupid. You can converse.

REX. You have a way with words. Are you a writer?

MYRON. I was a writer, past tense. But I cannot write without my write arm. You are beautiful; are you a model?

REX. Don't stereotype me, Myron. We're talking about you. What do you mean you cannot write? That's an excuse. What about a tape recorder? Forcing yourself to use your left hand?

MYRON. Maybe it has nothing to do with my arm. Maybe I've nothing to say. Maybe I'm as dried up as this crusty limb.

REX. Maybe not. Since you've gotten sick, you must have so much . . .

MYRON. Stop. Spare me your *arm*chair psychology. Contrary to what you read in the fag rags, being near death does not make you a writer. Or a performance artist. Or a painter. Life is what inspired me to write, not death. Not decaying skin, rotting flesh. Beauty was my inspiration, not ugly grotesquery. Are you here on a mission? To save the world? I don't want to be nobody's charity case, babydoll.

REX. Why do you patronize me? I'm here because I want to be. Because I've been lucky. I'm not sick; I've never lost anyone.

MYRON. *Arm*ing yourself against the future?

REX. Stop, would you?

MYRON. Did you know I was going to be black?

REX. What difference does it make? I said I didn't care. I am not a racist.

MYRON. Oh? And neither are those cops who beat up Rodney King.

REX. Your darkness, blackness, means more to you than it does to me. I'm not obsessed with it. And I'm not obsessed with your arm.

MYRON. Have you ever made love to a black man? *(Beat)* Have you ever had sex with a black man?

REX. I refuse to play twenty questions with you. I'm not as light—I'm not as white—as you're making me.

MYRON. Your face is turning pink. Your cheekbones are tinged with cherry red.

REX. You are making me angry.

MYRON. I am making you even more beautiful than you were a second ago.

REX. You are making me nervous. Do you need anything?

MYRON. I need for you to touch my arm. Just touch it. Please.

REX. I . . . I . . .

MYRON. You can't; you're afraid. You are beet red.

REX. I can't breathe. I'm hot. I need air.

MYRON. You smell my arm, oozing puss. Don't you, whiteboy? You are sniffing disease. Is this the charity work you were looking for? If you stick around, I'll probably shit in my pants.

REX. Is there a fucking window in this room? I cannot breathe.

MYRON. Wait until you get a whiff of my nigger diarrhea.

REX. A window.

MYRON. No window.

REX. Please.

MYRON. No light.

REX. Air.

MYRON. No air. No air for the airy fairy boy who wants to learn about death. Welcome to Death 101. Touch my arm, faggot. Touch my fucking arm. Please. I want to hold you in my arms. I used to be a wonderful lover. I had arms which could squeeze the cum out of you. Arms that would protect you and warm you and comfort you. Arms that would lift you to places you've never been before. Rex? Are you all right? *(Rex has fainted)*

MYRON. The help has fainted.

SCENE TWO

MYRON. *(On phone)* My pussy buddy passed out, I said, and I'm pissed off. Pussy passed out. Pissed off. Write it down and tell my fucking case worker to call me. Myron. M as in mad as hell. Y as in you-are-making-me-crazy. R as in racist. O as in obviously. N as in nellie nigger. No last name. Like Malcolm. Tell her to send me someone with balls, not another Little Mary Sunshine. Tell her I'd prefer someone black. I don't sound very black? You don't sound very smart. Yes, I'm angry. Now you're catching on, dollbaby. Listen, I don't want someone to rub my feet and read me chapters of Marianne Williamson. I need someone to change my shit-filled diapers and puss-soaked bandages. Or, as Grace Jones once said, "I need a man." Or a lesbian. Not some ingénue candy striper trying to sprout angel wings. Yes, I realize I've been through five buddies in the past month—I discard them like trick towels. Just have Missy Case Worker call me. Before six. That's right, lambchop, I won't be answering the phone after six. I have a date to play basketball with Magic Johnson.

SCENE THREE

MYRON. *(On phone)* He came back on his own—now that takes balls. Rex. His name is Rex. I couldn't believe it. He just showed up and insisted he wanted another chance. I'll admit, I thought he was just another empty pretty boy. I guess I was testing him.

CHRIS. *(On phone)* Well, I guess he passed the test.

MYRON. Phi Beta Kappa. Speaking of the test . . .

CHRIS. I'm negative. I feel guilty. Ashamed. I imagine it will be hard for you not to resent me. Do you resent Rex?

MYRON. Not consciously, no. All of my friends are either dead

or dying. I'm comforted, knowing he won't die on me. And
you, my darling, won't die on me.

CHRIS. I have to see you. These phone calls are making me
crazy. I want to see you, touch you. I want to make it real,
as crazy as that sounds.

MYRON. Well, get ready for reality, honey: I look like Miss Jane
Pittman on a bad day.

SCENE FOUR

REX. What did you write about?

MYRON. The good old days.

REX. I hate it when you guys talk about the good old days. I feel
cheated.

MYRON. Don't talk crazy. You're alive.

REX. The good old days equal death?

MYRON. Not politically correct, I know, but part of me believes
it. Part of me believes this is punishment for my hedonism.

REX. And part of you has no regrets?

MYRON. You're right. Both feelings have to live with each other,
like mismatched lovers.

REX. Is it what you did? Or how often? Or both?

MYRON. Both. Not to mention the drugs, the booze. I was a pig.
And I justified a lot of it by making it my material, my
palette. My themes were sex and drugs and rock 'n roll.
Mostly sex—in every flavor, every color, and every position.

REX. Is that why you feel you can't write now?

MYRON. You are smarter than you look. When I first got sober,
I thought I'd never write again. But eventually I did—maybe
even a little clearer. Then I got tested. Suddenly I could no
longer write about sex without . . .

REX. Without?

MYRON. Without shame and guilt and self-pity. All of which, I
feel, are useless emotions. Most people start writing when
they find out they're HIV positive; I stopped writing. Maybe
I wrote with my dick. But now I can't write with this fucking
arm. That says something, doesn't it?

REX. Myron, get real. That's an excuse. And a bit too fire and
brimstone. You can write; you've chosen not to. You don't

honestly think your arm is punishment for your sins or some
such bullshit?

MYRON. Why else would Miss God turn my arm into something
that resembles Oprah's thigh? The truth? Sometimes, yes,
sometimes. What's the opposite of coming out? Caving in.
That's what I feel like I been doin' for the past six years:
caving in.

REX. Were you ever in love?

MYRON. In love? In hate, maybe. I hated myself; I hated queers;
I hated niggers. I either wanted to be white or straight or
both. A black nellie faggot did not win popularity contests.
Straight blacks hated me because I was gay. Gay blacks hated
me because I was nellie. Straight whites hated me because I
was black. Gay whites hated me because I was black and
nellie. But there was always some dinge queen in the johns
or the bushes or the baths. However, contrary to what you
read in *Penthouse* and/or *Honcho,* not all black dudes are
hung like black stallions. The ones who thought they was
gonna get a big piecea meat got a big disappointment instead. Oh, there were flashes of being okay, glimmers of
connections. A few encounters which had meaning: the oc-
casional black man who was comfortable enough to make
love, not just have sex, with another black guy; the occa-
sional white man who really seemed not to be another racist
size-dinge queen. But mostly there were queers, black and
white, who hated themselves as much as I hated myself. We'd
engage in this tango of self-hate, acting out our racism,
playing with our homophobia. You wanna talk slave and
master? Honey, I could go both ways: I'd play Uncle Tom
one day and Diana Ross/The Boss the next. But whether I
was on top or on my knees, I thought sex would fix it. And
for a while—until about 1985—it did. In love? You've got to
be kidding.

REX. What's the most loving sex you ever had?

MYRON. Funny you should ask. I think about it a lot. It was at
the baths, probably fifteen years ago. And even though I was
probably pretty tweeked at the time, I remember it vividly.
This black kid, not pretty in that slick way but real pretty to
me, and I were making out. Kissing, passionately. In my

experience, not many queers kissed. And not many black queers kissed each other. As I said, most of them wanted some whitemeat, period. This boy—I don't remember his name—was a great kisser. Then all of a sudden, in the midst of this romantic kissing interlude, he says to me, "I want you to fist me." Even though I knew he said "fist," I acted like he said "kiss." "I want you to stick your hand inside my butt," he said, making himself perfectly clear. So I did. It was an incredibly powerful experience—one I never had the guts to write about. It was intimate and it was connected and it was all of the things those fist-fucking queens said it was. And the fact he was a black boy, giving himself to me, was part of it. It was emotional. I'd been used to all sorts of rejection from pretty black boys. So to have my hand—my arm, to be honest—inside him was amazing. But after I came, jacking myself off, watching my arm slide in and out of his ass, I felt guilt like I'd never felt before. For days, I would scrub my hands, clean my fingernails. I could smell Crisco on my arm for weeks. I was like Lady Macbeth: "Out, out, damn Crisco . . ." I've never told anyone that story. I always thought they'd think I was sick or something. But it was oddly beautiful; I know that in my heart—in spite of my shame.

REX. Was it your right arm?

MYRON. Of course, and of course, I've thought this is my divine punishment.

REX. You've got to get over that.

MYRON. Thanks, Louise Hay. Did it bother you? My story?

REX. It turned me on.

MYRON. You're pretty amazing. Thanks. You know, part of me doesn't regret it—even if this is my fucking punishment.

REX. Your *fist* fucking punishment.

MYRON. I know it isn't—unless I make it so. Do I have a fever?

REX. You do, a bit. I can't imagine why. I probably have one, too. Thanks for the story.

MYRON. Now it's your turn. Have you ever been in love? What's the most loving sex you've ever had? What's your social security number? And how many times have you seen *Lady Sings The Blues*?

REX. I've been "in sex" more than I've been "in love." I've had a lot of sex without loving and a lot of loving without sex. I've never memorized my Social Security number and I've only seen *Lady Sings The Blues* once. But I've seen *Funny Girl* more than I care to admit.

MYRON. Don't they both sing "My Man?" *(As Billie)* "Oh, my man, I love him so. He'll never know . . ."

REX. *(As Barbra)* "All my life is just despair but I don't care . . ."

BOTH. "When he takes me in his arms, the world is bright all right . . ."

MYRON. Here I come—big finish! *(He falls into Rex's arms)*

SCENE FIVE

MYRON. Is this reality enough for you? You can smell death in this room, can't you?

CHRIS. You have senses I don't have. You have words in your brain I'll never know the meaning of. You have feelings which are deeper than mine. You are more alive than I am. No, I don't smell death. I smell medicine.

MYRON. Wait until you smell Rex. He has a smell. A sweetness. And I don't mean Elizabeth Taylor's Passion. A real scent. When he's here, I no longer smell myself dying.

CHRIS. Are you dying?

MYRON. Is that what you came to find out? Are you the messenger of death? Now that you've seen me—and my disgusting arm—you can report my demise in vivid detail.

CHRIS. Myron, I came to see you because I care about you. And you know I can't do anything vivid. You, darling, are the vivid one.

MYRON. How gay of you to call me "darling," darling.

CHRIS. Myron, let's not start on the not-gay-enough routine. Not this enough, not that enough. Not black enough. I could never please you.

MYRON. It pleases me that you're here.

REX. *(Entering)* Am I interrupting anything?

CHRIS. No. I'm Christopher, Myron's cousin from Atlanta. You must be Rex?

REX. Yes. It's nice to meet you.

CHRIS. Myron hasn't stopped talking about you.

MYRON. I been tellin' him how sweet you is—for a white boy.

REX. Shut yo mouth. *(To Chris)* This has become our routine. Are you an athlete?

MYRON. Said the actress to the hunk.

CHRIS. I lift weights.

MYRON. What a line. *(To Rex)* Say something about his big, massive arms.

REX. Myron. *(To Chris)* What do you do?

MYRON. He told you, honey: he lifts weights.

REX. For a living.

CHRIS. Computers. *(Myron makes snoring sounds)* What about you?

REX. I'm trying to learn the ropes of the hotel business so I'm working as a desk clerk to get my feet wet. Eventually, I want to travel. See the world. There are hotels in every city, right? I'll always be able to get a job.

MYRON. Yes, darling, as long as there's a hotel room, you'll be able to get a job.

REX. It was nice meeting you. I just stopped by with this prescription. I'm sure you two would like to be alone.

MYRON. Don't be so sure.

CHRIS. Nice to meet you, Rex. I hope to see you before I leave.

MYRON. He's only here for the week. Maybe you two should go out and continue your fascinating conversation about weight lifting. I can stay here and lipsync to my Billie Holiday records. Seriously, Rex, call later. I don't want him to be stuck here with Eartha Kitt all day and night.

REX. I will. I'll check in with you this afternoon. Nice meeting you. *(Rex exits)*

CHRIS. He's gorgeous. He's beautiful. He's gorgeous. He's beautiful.

MYRON. And he's as white as your Calvin Klein underpants—still a prerequisite for you—even though some of us have moved into the nineties. I bet even Johnny Mathis is dating black men. Yes, he's gorgeous but he's much more than what you see. He's as beautiful on the inside as he is gorgeous on the outside. Unusual, I admit.

CHRIS. You really wouldn't mind if I went out with him?

MYRON. Mind? Moi? Why would I mind? Honey, I gave up white-meat around the same time I burned my Donna Summer albums.

CHRIS. *(Back to Rex)* Will he call?

MYRON. If he said he'll call, he'll call. He is trustworthy, honest.

CHRIS. What will I say to him?

MYRON. What do you mean?

CHRIS. I mean, what will I say? What will I say to interest him, excite him? My arms don't talk.

MYRON. But they make a great introduction.

CHRIS. WHAT AM I GOING TO SAY?

MYRON. You'll think of something. In the meantime, do some push-ups while I take a nap. Darling.

SCENE SIX

CHRIS. *(On phone, groggy)* Hello?

REX. Myron? It's Rex. I'm sorry it's so late. I must have fallen asleep.

CHRIS. It's Chris. It's okay. We wondered why you hadn't called.

REX. I'm sorry. How's Myron?

CHRIS. Dead to the world. I'm sorry, I mean: asleep.

REX. Did I wake you?

CHRIS. Yeah. I was dreaming about you.

REX. C'mon. Am I supposed to believe that?

CHRIS. It's true. I wouldn't lie to you.

REX. Well, go back to sleep.

CHRIS. No.

REX. No?

CHRIS. I want to talk to you.

REX. Well, talk. *(Long pause)* Well, talk.

CHRIS. I like you.

REX. That's nice.

CHRIS. I like you a lot.

REX. That's even nicer. *(Long pause)*

CHRIS. I don't know what to say.

REX. Say what you're feeling.

CHRIS. I like you.

REX. I got that much.

CHRIS. I need to get a drink of water.

REX. You've got to be kidding.

CHRIS. No kidding. Please hold on. Just a sec. *(Waking Myron)* Myron, wake up. Rex is on the phone. He wants me to talk about my feelings. He wants to be seduced. I'm blank. Please help. Help.

MYRON. Help? You want me to tell you what to say?

CHRIS. Rex? Are you there?

REX. Yes, Chris. What do you have to say for yourself?

CHRIS. *(To Myron)* What do I have to say for myself?

MYRON. *(Prompting now)* I miss you.

CHRIS. I miss you.

MYRON. I have thought of nothing but you since you left this afternoon.

CHRIS. I have thought of nothing but you since you left this afternoon.

REX. Go on.

CHRIS. *(To Myron)* Go on.

MYRON. I can smell your sweetness; it has permeated the room.

CHRIS. I can smell your sweetness; it has perforated the room.

MYRON. Permeated!

CHRIS. Permeated, I mean, the room. Are you there?

REX. I can smell you, too, Christopher.

CHRIS. *(To Myron)* He can smell me, too!

MYRON. How do I . . .? Give me that phone. *(On phone now)* How do I smell, Rex?

REX. You smell kinda sexy. It makes me kinda hot.

MYRON. You're making me sweat.

REX. I'd like to make love to you, taste your sweat, lick the sweat off your chest and arms.

MYRON. Tease my nipples with your tongue. Bite them just a little.

REX. I'm nibbling on your nipples.

MYRON. And I'm running my hands through your hair, caressing your ears. Your face is bright pink. I can see it turning red. You're getting hot.

REX. I lick your armpits; the hair tastes so good. I'm unbuttoning your jeans. I want you.

MYRON. I'm ripping off your gym shorts. Your butt looks so good in that jock. I want to make love to your ass. Will you give me your ass?

REX. It's yours. Kiss me first.

MYRON. I've been kissing you since you left here. Kissing you over and over again in my mind. Kissing your eyelids, your nose, your chin, your eyebrows, your forehead, your neck. Your lips. Your face is on fucking fire now. Your face is burning my tongue.

REX. Give me your tongue. Let me suck on it. Cool it. Cool your fat, fiery tongue.

MYRON. Suck it. Get it wet with your juices so I can explore your beautiful butthole with my slippery, sweaty tongue.

REX. My ass is wet. My sweat is your sweat. I need you inside me.

MYRON. Okay, baby, get that dick ready for your hungry butt. Take my throbbing cock in your wet mouth and get it nice and juicy. For your sweaty ass to suck up. Spit on my dick. Drench it with a burst of your saliva.

REX. Your dick is fucking delicious. I've never tasted one like it before. I need you to fuck me. Fuck me, Chris.

MYRON. I'm fucking you with all my heart. With all my soul. With everything I am. My strong arms are holding you tight, squeezing you as I thrust in and out, in and out, of your gorgeous butt.

REX. I'm scratching your arms. Biting your muscles. I want your arms to ache while you fuck me. Do your arms ache? Kiss me. I'm close.

MYRON. I'm kissing you. I'm shooting everything I am inside you: all my love and pain and heartache, all my sorrow and joy and longing. Can you take it?

REX. Oh, yes, yes. Give it to me. I'll devour you, all of you. Everything you are and always have been. I want all of it inside me. I'm going to cum and I'm not even touching myself.

MYRON. I'm coming, too, sweetheart. Can you feel me shooting inside you, straight to your heart? Take me. Take me. *(Cums)*

REX. I'm yours, yours, yours. *(Cums)* This was crazy, Christopher. It's not like me. Why am I so attracted to you? I'm not your average 976 queen.

MYRON. It's not like me, either. Believe me. I better get back to sleep.

REX. Chris? If you think there's any chance this would upset Myron, please don't tell him. I love Myron.

MYRON. You do?

REX. Very, very much. And I would do nothing to hurt him.

MYRON. This would not hurt him.

REX. How do you know?

MYRON. Trust me, I know. Myron wants you and I to . . .

REX. To?

MYRON. To . . . *(Gives phone to Chris)*

REX. Wants us to what?

CHRIS. I'm not sure. I'm not sure what Myron wants.

REX. You sound different somehow.

CHRIS. I'm tired, Rex. I hope to see you tomorrow?

REX. Yes. I'll need you to tell me I haven't dreamt this. Goodnight, sleep tight. Is Myron okay?

CHRIS. He's exhausted, sleeping like a baby. Goodnight, Rex.

REX. Goodnight, stud.

SCENE SEVEN

CHRIS. *(Doing push-ups)* Tonight's the night. I've run out of excuses. He knows I'm leaving tomorrow morning. What am I going to do?

MYRON. You're going to make love to him, that's what you're going to do. Stud. You're going to fulfill all his sexy black buck fantasies.

CHRIS. But what am I going to say? He's gonna want me to talk. Talk romantic. Talk sexy. I can't.

MYRON. Just be yourself.

CHRIS. It's not myself he's interested in. I'll freeze, I know it.

MYRON. What do you want me to do?

CHRIS. Help me, goddammmit. You're the sexy one.

MYRON. I'm on my deathbed; would you tell me what's sexy about that?

CHRIS. But you have your imagination.

MYRON. And that's about it, doll. I'm sorry, Chris. I can't hide inside a rubber and go along for the ride. You're on your own. You're attracted to him, aren't you?

CHRIS. Yeah.

MYRON. Yeah? Could you elaborate?

CHRIS. He's hot. I want to fuck him.

MYRON. How romantic.

CHRIS. I'm not romantic, remember?

MYRON. But you're endowed with other qualities which turn him on. It's going to work out fine. Let him do the talking.

CHRIS. I hope you're right. I really want to get in his pants. *(Finishing exercises)*

MYRON. Then I'd do another set if I were you.

SCENE EIGHT

REX. Now that I have you in person, what do you have to say for yourself?

CHRIS. About what?

REX. About us.

CHRIS. I think you're hot.

REX. Yes? And?

CHRIS. I think you're hot.

REX. You said that. And?

CHRIS. I wanna fuck you.

REX. Okay. But not so fast. What do you want to do before I let you inside me?

CHRIS. I don't know.

REX. You don't know?

CHRIS. Maybe watch some TV?

REX. You mean a hot video?

CHRIS. No, I mean *The Golden Girls.*

REX. You're putting me on, right?

CHRIS. Putting you on what?

REX. You're trying to be funny, right?

CHRIS. I think *The Golden Girls* is pretty funny.

REX. Are you telling me you came here to watch TV?

CHRIS. Watch a little TV, then fuck.

REX. Chris, c'mon, stop teasing me. Talk to me; tell me about yourself. Ever since our phone call, I've heard your voice in my head, making me want you. The anticipation has been unbearable.

CHRIS. I know what you mean.

REX. Talk to me—let me know more about you. I'm going to close my eyes. Let your voice, your thoughts, your feelings, come out. Talk to me, Chris.

CHRIS. Let's get it on.

REX. What?

CHRIS. Get it on. You know: fuck.

REX. Is that the only word you know, fuck? Where's the imaginative man with a vocabulary who seduced me on the phone?

CHRIS. I wasn't myself. I mean, I'm not myself. I'm not myself tonight. Can we just do it? I mean, fuck?

REX. No, absolutely not. I hope I didn't mislead you on the phone; I really don't think I did. I expect a little more foreplay than you seem interested in. A little more intimacy. I'd like to get to know you better: who you are. That phone call was not just about sex, was it? I sensed pain and joy and anger and humor and all sorts of colors that turned me on. If I've mislead you, I'm sorry. But I think you mislead me. You're not the same as you were on the phone.

CHRIS. You're right, I'm not. I don't know what it is. Maybe it's fear of flying.

REX. Fear of flying?

CHRIS. You know, flying—to Atlanta. Tomorrow.

REX. Don't be a wimp. I feel like I've been betrayed. Maybe you should go. You'll make it home in time to watch *The Golden Girls* with Myron.

CHRIS. I feel terrible. You're so good to Myron. You're a really good person. I didn't want to mess things up.

REX. Believe me, you can't destroy what I have going with Myron, if that's what you mean. Go. I'm sorry it didn't work out. I thought I was really attracted to you. After talking to you on the phone, I thought there was more to you than meets the eye. I was just convincing myself; I've done it a million times. I was wrong.

CHRIS. That's right. I'm not who you thought I was. I'm sorry, I really am.

REX. I'll get over it. Give my love to Myron.

SCENE NINE

REX. You're dying and I'm carrying on about some dolt who convinced me—over the phone—he was Cassanova.

MYRON.   Not Cassanova, darling, Mandingo.

REX.   At least you haven't lost your sense of humor.

MYRON.   You'd be surprised what I haven't lost.

REX.   Would I? I feel like I've lost my mind over your fucking cousin.

MYRON.   Not my fucking cousin, sugar: that's the point. My unfucking cousin.

REX.   "Let's get it on," he was saying—like some halfwit.

MYRON.   I thought you liked 'em dumb. Doesn't that fit into your black man fantasy?

REX.   Myron, I wasn't attracted to him because he's black. Anymore than I was attracted to him because he's your cousin. Those might have been factors, I'll admit, but they weren't the reasons.

MYRON.   What were you attracted to?

REX.   A voice over the phone, a voice full of energy and passion and humor and . . .

MYRON.   Go on . . .

REX.   And love, I think. This was not the first time I've confused love and sex. But there was love in his voice.

MYRON.   Yes, there was.

REX.   How do you know?

MYRON.   I'm guessing. Maybe you intimidated him in person. Maybe he's not used to feeling . . .

REX.   "Let's fuck" is not exactly loaded with emotion.

MYRON.   Maybe it's the only way he can express himself. In person. Maybe it's not over between you two. But don't you start wishin' him back here, honey. He ain't comin' back 'till I'm on the way out.

REX.   That could be years.

MYRON.   *(Indicating his arm)* Not years, and you know it. Look. It's like one of those clubs a caveman would beat his wife over the head with. And it smells like rotting meat.

REX.   Does it hurt?

MYRON.   Only when I look at it. It's oozing something, like a volcano, erupting. Do you have any opera gloves? Extra large?

REX.   Opera gloves. It reminds me of when I was a little kid. I'd get in the bathtub and take a bubble bath. You know how you'd fill the tub until it was overflowing with bubbles? Well, I'd make opera gloves with the bubbles. I must have been seven or eight years old. Tell me, would a straight little boy be making opera gloves with bubbles?

MYRON. Not likely, honey. I made elaborate headdresses. I also remember putting underpants on my head, after seeing something on TV about Nijinksy. I'd dance around the house, like a dervish, with underpants on my head.

REX. Kinky.

MYRON. I'm happy to be a faggot. I'm wearing down; I need to sleep.

REX. Thanks for listening to all my moaning about Cuz Chris. I feel better now. Sometimes I forget I'm the one who's supposed to be making you feel better.

MYRON. You do. Kiss?

REX. *(Kissing him, on the lips)* I love you, Myron. You have a little fever. Let me get you some Tylenol.

MYRON. Thanks, honey. Don't worry about Chris. I have a feeling he'll come around. How could he not be in love with you?

REX. Get some sleep.

SCENE TEN

MYRON. I spent the night sewing.

REX. Sewing?

MYRON. My quilt panel.

REX. Who's it for?

MYRON. Me. I said "my quilt panel." I didn't say Liberace's quilt panel; I didn't say Roy Cohn's quilt panel.

REX. *(Interrupting him)* You're making your own quilt panel?

MYRON. Yes, and let me tell you, girlfriend: It's a bitch tryin' to sew a thirteen-inch dildo onto a piece of gaberdine.

REX. Black or white?

MYRON. The gaberdine? A mauve color. Speaking of purple . . . There's a letter here for you.

REX. A letter? From?

MYRON. Chris. He enclosed it with a letter to me.

REX. How weird. Why is he writing to me?

MYRON. Goodness gracious, child, don't ask me.

REX. Do you mind if I come pick it up?

MYRON. Since I don't have a fax machine, that's an idea. But promise to take off your heels and put on your running shoes. Ciao.

SCENE ELEVEN

REX. *(Reading)* Dear Rex, I am writing you because I cannot get you out of my heart. My heart. That is where you've invaded and remained since I first laid eyes on you. I realize what a fool I am, even temporarily, thinking of you in sexual terms. How could I not want you sexually? But that is only a small part of the reservoir of feelings I am unable to contain. I am overflowing. You, Rex, are as beautiful on the inside as you are on the out and for me to only speak of your sexiness is unforgivable. I am sorry for being such a dolt in your presence. Such a klutz. Such a dope. It's taken time for me to realize what you really meant to me. And now I must convince you: In letters, I will prove my love for you—there, I've said it: "love for you." I will prove my love for you is not about a hot sexual connection. It is far, far deeper. I expect nothing in return. I will write—hundreds, thousands of words, whatever it takes to let you know how much you mean to me. You need not write back; in fact, you mustn't—I don't deserve it. I am trying to learn from your example: giving without requiring anything in return. I watch you caring for others—a scene I play over and over in my head and heart— I see a Rex made up of compassion and empathy and understanding and concern. All genuine. All real. So unselfish. Perhaps I can learn from you, learn how to feel with an open heart. Please accept these words as an outpouring of a growing devotion. I am yours, Christopher.

SCENE TWELVE

REX. Did you and Chris grow up together?

MYRON. Not exactly.

REX. You're so secretive about your family.

MYRON. What family? Chile, I never had no family.

REX. What's that supposed to mean?

MYRON. It means I'd've had better luck if I'd been dropped on someone's doorstep in swaddling drag. I've got this story down—from all the times I've rehearsed in twelve-step meetings. I never saw my father; I never heard my father; I never tasted my father; I never touched my father; I never smelled my father. I had no father. Father-less. I never celebrated Father's Day and I never will. I heard about my father—from my mother. Problem is, she didn't know who my father was either. He'd change with her manic-depressive moods. One day he'd be tall; the next day he'd be short. "He's a doctor," she'd say on Tuesday; "a derelict" on Wednesday. One summer she told me how handsome he was; by winter he'd turned into a dog. I learned, much like Mama did, to create my father. Mama could fantasize, I'll say that. I, of course, believed my father was Sidney Poitier—especially after I saw *To Sir With Love.*

REX. Brothers and sisters?

MYRON. Brother. Or half brother. Your guess is as good as mine.

REX. Where is he?

MYRON. Dead, but don't rush me, Miss Walters. My brother and I had little in common—if that offers any clues to his ancestry. He was a butch number. Mama loved him; her "little man," she would always say. I was, in startling contrast, her "big sissy." He played with guns; I played with dolls. Mama spent mosta her time drinking and looking for substitute daddies: a hobby I learned to perfect in my twenties. But I shouldn't jump ahead. Mama found a religious fanatic—this one prayed after he beat the shit outta her. She found God in those beatings, I guess. Even stopped drinking—probably didn't want to numb the sensation. My brother, Joey, remained her hero—even though he was a notorious gang member in our neighborhood. She was proud of him. Her pride was cut short one day when Joey was shot—in cold blood, on our front porch. I was forced, by my new "Daddy" to kneel at his side, in a pool of blood, and pray. For his "soul," Mama said. Within days, she was drinking again. Daddy Religion split. Mama drank with a vengeance. 'Til it killed her. I did not pray for her soul, any more than I prayed for my brother's. I was relieved.

REX. How old were you?

MYRON. I was in high school. I was a teenage werewolf—a good student by day and a depraved little queen who roamed the parks at night.

REX. Where did you live?

MYRON. With an aunt.

REX. Chris's mother?

MYRON. Chris isn't really my cousin, Rex. Chris is one of the guys I met in the park. He was everything I wanted to be: pretty, big, sexy. I was completely awed by him. We only tricked that one time—he musta been very horny because, believe me, I was not his type. But he liked me. I couldn't believe it when he told me he had a family, a family who loved each other. His parents were both teachers. They were a happy family—like some TV series. I could not believe his life. I wanted, more than anything, to be Chris. We became friends. I fantasized he was my cousin and began telling people he was my cousin. He didn't mind so it stuck. I practically lived at his house.

REX. What about your aunt?

MYRON. I don't think she noticed I was gone. I'm telling you: I had no relatives. No one to relate to. Only Chris and his family.

REX. Did they know you were gay? Did they know about Chris?

MYRON. I'm sure they did but it was something unspoken.

REX. Have you remained close to Chris since?

MYRON. Not *close* close. Even though we shared the slutty seventies, in Atlanta's hot spots, we grew apart. He stayed in the South and got into computers; I came to the West Coast to be a writer. He's a successful businessman; I'm a doomed artist. Two different worlds.

REX. Do you love him?

MYRON. Do you?

REX. I love his letters.

MYRON. Speaking of which . . . *(Hands him a letter)*

SCENE THIRTEEN

REX. *(Reading)* I love you. Do you believe me? You are every-where—even in my dreams, I can taste you and feel you. You are with me, like a guardian angel: protective, shielding me from life's battles. My journey is complete because of your energy, your force, your life. Do you believe me? What is belief? Is it religion? God? Spirituality? You are a power greater than myself. Is that not love? Or is it faith? My faith in you is without boundaries; there are no limits, no gates, no warnings posted. You are open, aren't you? Please accept my love—even from a distance. That is how it must be for now. I long to be closer to you, to soothe your fears as you have soothed mine. I long to be closer to you, to warm your heart as you have warmed mine. I long to be closer to you, to fill you up as you have fulfilled me. Only when I have convinced you my love is the truest love, only when I have convinced you love is not about things seen but things unseen, only when I have convinced you of my purest passion—only then will I deserve to hold you in my arms. Hold you in my arms: that is all I want from you. To hold you in my arms. I must be patient. My love for you, when it is calm, grows more euphoric. Do you believe me? Christopher.

SCENE FOURTEEN

MYRON. When I get stronger, can we go to San Francisco? I have frequent flier miles. We'll fly to the city of brotherly love. When can we go? Soon, I hope. I'll be better soon, won't I?

REX. Myron, I just don't know how soon. You're pretty run down, honey. Your nurse says you've had high fevers, uncontrollable diarrhea.

MYRON. Don't believe everything that nurse says. I don't need a nurse. I have you.

REX. Myron, I've told you: I can't be here around the clock. I wish I could but I have to work, I have to make a living.

MYRON. I don't like her changing me, cleaning me up. She's rough. When can we go to San Francisco?

REX. She's not rough, Myron. I've spoiled you—like a baby, haven't I?

MYRON. Maybe so. So spoil me and let's go to San Francisco on my frequent flier miles.

REX. When you get a little stronger.

MYRON. When will that be? When will I get stronger? Tomorrow? The next day? What if I don't get stronger?

REX. That's something we have to talk about: what if you don't get stronger. Then what?

MYRON. Then I die—that's what.

REX. Should we talk about that?

MYRON. Did they teach you this at one of your training sessions? You sound so professional, so businesslike. "Should we talk about that?" Like you're discussing a real estate deal.

REX. Myron, do you think this is easy for me?

MYRON. I'm sorry. *(Beat)* I want to go to San Francisco.

REX. What would we do in San Francisco? Tell me. Where would we go?

MYRON. I would show you my past—retrace my steps, jolt my memories, summon my ghosts. I would see heaven on earth through your uninfected eyes. There's new life there, they tell me. Oh, it's not the same as it was in the seventies but the streets are bursting with energy—love and sex and all that male brotherhood. I want you to see that. I want to see you seeing it. I want to see it again. I want to see life again. Before I die. I have frequent flier miles.

REX. Do you believe in God?

MYRON. I believe in passion.

REX. Do you believe in love?

MYRON. Only recently. Many times I mistook passion for love. Do you believe in God?

REX. Yeah, I think I do. But I don't know how to define it.

MYRON. No one does, really. God is in San Francisco.

REX. Stop.

MYRON. No, I'm serious. I saw him there once. I could introduce you—if I could find the place. It was preplague. Ten years ago. I went to this AA meeting—small, intimate, maybe twenty guys at the most. We sat in a circle and everyone told their story. I remember one guy talked about sleeping with his mother's bras and panties when she deserted him. Another guy talked about his drunk father fucking him in the ass when he was seven years old. Then there were your garden variety alkies who just drank to numb the pain—no particular pain, just plain pain. I can see the faces of those men; I can hear their voices. Some of them had beards with streaks of gray. Long, leftover hippie hair so clean you could smell it. One guy was bald, another bleached blond. There were the ones who sounded like truck drivers and the ones who sounded like movie goddesses. They were all trying to figure out what happened—what happened to us, why did we drink and drug ourselves into oblivion? Because it was the thing to do? Because we hated ourselves? Because we learned the behavior from our mommys and daddys? In that room, it didn't matter. Nothing mattered except our being together. It was the smallest, the tiniest, I ever felt in my life. And yet the most powerful. There was no competition, no resentment, no hatred, no fear. No color. At the end of this meeting, after people had thrown up their souls, we stood in a circle and held hands. I can feel the hands of the two men on either side of me. One of them had the rough, crusty hands of a construction worker, the other had the silken hands of someone who had only touched champagne glasses. This leather queen, as nellie as he was butch, led us in the Lord's Prayer. Maybe there was a candle in the room, casting shadows? I'm not sure but there was a presence—an aura?—hovering over this circle of queer men. It was shapeless but not colorless. Sometimes I remember it as golden, other times I remember red. It had to be God in that room. I began to cry, subtle tears, sneaking down my cheeks and along my neck, down my chest. I felt God. Or something. I felt something larger than I was, larger than anyone in the room, larger than mommy and daddy and all the pain in all of our lives. God was in San Francisco that night. I felt it, saw it, experienced it. Do you believe me?

REX. Of course I do. Where's that God now? When we need him?

MYRON. Good fucking question. Maybe he's being held hostage at some straight AA meeting in the Valley. By the way, I've hated that God sometimes. Most of the guys in that meeting are dead; I know that for a fact. Some of them went back out and OD'd. Most of them got It. So, yeah, it's a good question: Where is God now?

REX. Myron, should we prepare?

MYRON. For what? Miss God's arrival? I don't have a thing to wear.

REX. For the possibility you don't get better this time.

MYRON. Oh, that. You know what to do. There's a handwritten will.

REX. Handwritten? When did you do that?

MYRON. A week or so ago.

REX. Handwritten? I thought you couldn't write.

MYRON. I . . . uh . . . improvised. I did my Daniel Day Lewis impersonation.

REX. You're too much. Who should I contact? Do I get in touch with Christopher?

MYRON. Yes, call him, but only in an emergency. There's a letter for you, by the way.

REX. It seems he writes me every day.

MYRON. Every day for two months. How many letters is that?

REX. Sixty-three.

MYRON. Do you like his letters?

REX. They amuse me.

MYRON. Amuse you? That's all.

REX. Myron, I love his letters. I told you that. I want to write him—even though he told me not to.

MYRON. If he told you not to, honey, then don't. Definitely don't. He's practicing the art of unselfishness. Probably read about it in one of those Leo Buscaglia books: *Loving You, Forget About Me.* Believe me, it's a healthy improvement. She used to be soooo needy.

REX. Have I worn you out? You haven't said "San Francisco" in the past five minutes. I'm going to go. Maybe I'll check on you later tonight. I love you, Myron, you're a good friend.

MYRON. You're my best friend. Next to that frightening nurse they've assigned me.

REX. I'll tell her you said that. By the way, what are you leaving her?

MYRON. My dirty drawers.

REX. You are demented. I mean, not really . . .

MYRON. One more thing: call TWA, find out the rates. I want to take you to San Francisco. I can't die with frequent flier miles.

SCENE FIFTEEN

REX. *(Reading)* Please, my love, excuse my handwriting. I am feverish; you have rendered me lovesick. It's an exquisite pain I feel, however, knowing I have found love. You make me weak; you make me tremble. I shudder. My heart beats faster; my mouth gets dry; my entire body sweats at the thought of you. You never leave me, never. If it weren't for you, I would surely die. I hope these fevered words don't frighten you. Your happiness is all I want; your life is all that matters to me. I want to mother you, father you; be your lover, be your brother. Be my baby, be my uncle. I'll be your husband; I'll be your wife. Mistress me, mister me, parent me, sister me. Have I convinced you of my love? Have I convinced you, my love? Perhaps your kiss would calm me; perhaps your kiss would take away my fear. I mean, fever. No more than a kiss, Rex, that's all I ask. A kiss.

SCENE SIXTEEN

MYRON. *(Alone)* Rex! I want you. I want Rex. I'm ready to go. To San Francisco. There's a new arm waiting for me in San Francisco. A brand new arm. I'll be able to hug you in San Francisco. Hug the shit out of you. Where are you? I want you, Rex. Rex, fly me to San Francisco. Clean me, Rex, clean me so we can fly away. To be married. All in white. In white light. Rex! In San Francisco. Marry me, Rex. Clean white sheets, clean white towels. A new black arm. No nurse's uniforms. No blood. Clean black skin in a white tuxedo. Pure white skin in a black tuxedo. No shit. White wedding cake. Rex! Vanilla ice cream. I love you. Rex, I love you! I'm ready. Where's the white light? Rex, where are you?

SCENE SEVENTEEN

REX. I'm here, Myron, I'm here. Sleep, honey, you need to sleep. You are so tired. I am so tired. Even when I fall asleep, I dream about it. About you. About us. I had this dream: I was making love to Christopher, kissing him passionately, rubbing my hands all over his body. But we were lying in this bed, in your bed, and when I began to pull down his pants, I realized—instead the beautiful cock I've been anticipating—it was your arm. It was your arm and we were in this bed, your bed. I could not touch it. I still cannot touch your arm. I've gotten used to the smell of it; I've gotten used to the sight of it; but I cannot touch it. What's the difference between your arm and his cock? The feelings of the person who writes me those letters have nothing to do with his cock. And sometimes my feelings for the person who writes the letters gets in the way of my feelings for you. Can I love both of you at the same time? I don't know. If you were . . .

SCENE EIGHTEEN

Rex is on the phone. We hear Marvin Gaye's "Sexual Healing" and Chris' voice. If you're calling for some sexual healing, you got the right number. This is Christopher. Leave your name, your number and some vital statistics and I'll get back to you. *More "Sexual Healing."*

REX. It's Rex. Is your message some kind of a joke? Myron is going. Fast. I think you should get here as soon as possible if you want to see him. I'm looking forward to seeing you. I think.

SCENE NINETEEN

MYRON. *(He is very weak)* Rex, is that you?
CHRIS. No, I'm sorry I'm not Rex. It's Chris. Your nurse told me Rex will be here in a few minutes.
MYRON. I don't want her talking to him. You either. What are you doing here?
CHRIS. I came as soon as I heard.
MYRON. Heard?
CHRIS. The news.
MYRON. What news?
CHRIS. That you're not doing so well.
MYRON. And who told you? Who told you I'm not doing so well?
CHRIS. Rex.
MYRON. Rex? Rex told you? You spoke to him?
CHRIS. He left a message.
MYRON. Thank God.
CHRIS. What?

MYRON. Thank God you didn't speak to him. I have to admit something to you, Chris, and it's not going to be easy.

CHRIS. C'mon, Myron, you can tell me anything.

MYRON. You might get angry. Chris, you have been writing Rex every day since you left; you have written him nearly seventy-five letters. He's in love with you.

CHRIS. What are you saying? Are you crazy?

MYRON. You heard me. He fell in love with you when you were here. I've merely encouraged his love for you to grow. I said the things you would say if you could.

CHRIS. No, Myron, you said the things you would say if you could. This has nothing to do with me.

MYRON. It has everything to do with you. Do you think Rex would fall in love with an ugly dying queen with a monster's arm? He loves you. Now that you're here, you must fulfill his love by making love to him.

CHRIS. You're crazy. It's you he loves. I know you. I know how you can write; that's who he loves—the Letter Writer, not me. Not some incoherent computer queen with muscles.

MYRON. I'm diseased; I'm pathetically deformed. And I'm dying, rotting away. You and he can live happily ever after.

CHRIS. You're wrong and you know it. I'm leaving, Myron. You must tell him the truth. You must tell him who wrote the letters. You must tell him, before you die, how much you love him. I may not be very smart about a lot of things but I do know this: You owe it to yourself to tell Rex the truth. Only then will you be ready.

MYRON. Ready?

CHRIS. Ready. I love you, Myron—in my way, the best I can. And loving you, at this very moment, means leaving.

MYRON. One favor, please, before you go.

CHRIS. What?

MYRON. Hand me that pencil and paper.

SCENE TWENTY

REX. I got here as fast as I could. Myron, are you okay? The nurse said you were groggy. Are you going to talk to me? Please. I've missed you today; I've worried about you, honey.

MYRON. Thank God you're here. There is no one to clean my butt for my big death scene.

REX. The nurse is here, Your Highness.

MYRON. I do not want Ratchett to touch me. I want you.

REX. You're too much, you know.

MYRON. If I weren't too much, I wouldn't still be here. What smells worse—my arm or my shit? How can you stand me?

REX. It must be love. *(Changing subject)* I thought Chris would be here by now.

MYRON. He left.

REX. Who left? What are you talking about?

MYRON. Chris left. I guess he couldn't face the finale.

REX. What about . . .?

MYRON. What about you?

REX. That's not what I meant.

MYRON. Yes it is. He left you a letter, I believe. It's a bit crumpled and damp. Perhaps you should read it.

REX. Later. I want to talk to you. I have something to tell you.

MYRON. You must read the letter. Now. Before it's too late.

REX. I do not understand.

MYRON. Read it out loud, so I can hear.

REX. He must have written it in a panic; I can barely read it. *(Reads)* I'm running out of words. I'm running out of energy. I'm running out. You must believe . . . *(To Myron)* I can't read it.

MYRON. Let me help you. *(Reads)* You must believe how much I love you—like nothing else I've loved in the entirety of my life. You alone have taught me what love is all about. I will never be able to thank you—there aren't enough months in the year, days in the week, minutes in the hour. You have completed me, Rex. I am full of you, full of your life, your soul, your energy. But I must confess: I have not been completely honest. Please find it in your heart to forgive me. I am not sorry. I only wanted to prove my love for you. You are young, sweetheart. Know you are loved. Believe it. *(Myron has dropped the letter; he is not reading)* Do not wait for any more proof. I must leave you. I am too much for you. I am too much for this world.

REX. You are . . . you are . . . him. You are Christopher.

MYRON. *(Pretending to read)* I love you, I will love you even when I am gone. Christopher.

REX. You are Christopher. You love me.

MYRON. He loves you. *(Beat)* I love you.

REX. You love me. All along. It's been you all along. I should have known. How did I not know? The tears on this letter are your tears; the sweat is your sweat; the words are yours. It's been your passion, your heart beating on every page. Myron, honey, it's you I love. I've loved you all along.

MYRON. How could you? That is impossible for me to believe.

REX. No, Myron, love is not impossible. All love is possible—you taught me that. Myron? Myron? Don't die, Myron. Not yet. Please, do not die. Let me tell you how much I love you. Myron? Please, honey, I will write you love letters. I will try to give you all the love you have given me. Myron? You have taught me to love. Don't go. Myron, please please please. *(Rex kisses the dead man)*

Curtain.

james carroll pickett

queen of angels

a

tragical comedy or comical tragedy
full of intrigue & plenty of dancing.
angry scenes! deceptions! songs!
and arousals of love!
demons that fly across the stage
with a chorus of naked queers!

*It is hard to estimate the value of the whole drama. We are put
off by the conventional language, the short verses and glib
rhymes; we smile at the simple character motivation and the
conventions of time and space.*

*We are shocked at the bloody realism of the deaths, and amazed
at the juxtaposition of piety and comic realism. We are aware of
how far the execution falls short of the magnificent subject.*

*But we do not know how the music, the setting, the pageantry of
the procession may have lifted the performance to a higher realm.*

George R. Kernodle
Miracle Plays—The Theatre in History

Carnival:[1] *(L.* Carnelevare. Carne *= flesh* + levare *=
removal.) The putting away of flesh as food. Flesh taking. The
season immediately preceding Lent, devoted to feasting, riotous
entertainment, revelry, or indulgence.*

---

[1] A carnival should not be confused with a circus. A carnival is a much raunchier, less
elegant form of entertainment.

author's note

WHY THIS TAKES SO LONG[1]

Shortly after completion of my play *Dream Man* in 1984, I began taking notes for a new play I hoped would more directly confront AIDS. Many friends and colleagues were ill and dying, or dead, and by that time I knew I too must be ticking.[2] I approached the new project—variously titled *Hurdy-Gurdy, Feast of Fools*, and *King of Hearts*—with an odd mixture of numbing fear, raging anger, and foot-dragging dread.

Early on, I envisioned a Greek chorus set against the background of a plague, as in *Oedipus*, but the patricide and incest themes of the Oedipal myth did not work for the story I wanted to tell. A chance encounter with an out-of-print *Punch and Judy* script persuaded me that the puppet clowns' outrageous, violent, and hilarious doggerel more closely resembled my experience of the AIDS crisis than the tragic dithyrambs of Sophocles.

In 1988, I lost my friend and lover Vaughn Gepford to AIDS. That was also the year I got clean and sober and received confirmation of my own infection with the AIDS virus. I yearned for Vaughn's humor and companionship very much—still do. Mundane events would trigger grief— like passing the Jay's Jayburgers stand at the corner of Virgil and Santa Monica and remembering some stupid argument we'd had there on the sidewalk one summer afternoon. Sometimes I would actually pick up the phone to call him and report some humorous or banal event of the day before I remembered Vaughn was gone. Forever. I thought I might be losing my mind.

---

[1] This was a program note for the original production. It also served as a kind of coming out with my HIV/AIDS status—not out of a sense of bravery or matrydom, but because I was tired of wondering just how much friends and students and colleagues knew or didn't know regarding my health status. When the *L.A. Times* review referred to my HIV status (with my permission) I felt as though I had gone about as public as I could.

[2] Ticking is the wonderful image created by Paul Monette in his superb AIDS chronicle, *Borrowed Time.*

About this time, I stumbled across a translation of Gilgamesh, the ancient Sumerian myth, precursor to Orpheus, concerning the love of a king who lost his male friend to death. I had found the source for my plot.

In 1990, my creative partner, Michael Kearns, and I produced *AIDS/US II*. It was exhilarating and challenging to compile a script with the remarkable cast of persons with AIDS and their loved ones. It was also daunting to confront that company's courage and honesty in dealing with AIDS, while trying to mask my own failing health. That experience drove me to finish a first draft of *Queen of Angels* and arrange a reading at A Different Light Bookstore in Silver Lake. It was at that point I began a collaboration with composer Jon Cohen, who also helped restructure the script.

With extraordinary support *(portare)* from my friend and teacher, Milton Katselas, two readings were staged in 1991 at the Beverly Hills Playhouse. The outstanding actors who participated in all the readings made a major contribution toward further development of the play. Three hospital stays in 1991 and 1992 contributed to my sense of amusement regarding this "tragical comedy or comical tragedy."

In the spring of 1992, Philip Littell called me from San Francisco, where he was writing a new libretto for the San Francisco Opera Company. He asked what was happening with *Queen of Angels*. When I glumly reported that the Mark Taper Forum had politely turned it down for their New Works Festival, he asked if he could approach Tim Miller to arrange a production at Highways. I eagerly agreed.

Much of the credit for this play—and none of the blame for its follies—goes to Milton Katselas, Joseph Scott Kierland, Paul Monette, Richard Labonté, Michael Lassell, Jon Cohen, Philip Littell, Kerry Slattery, Neil Tucker, James Leo Herlihy, Henry Fenwick, Bella Brannan, Reza Abdoh, ACT UP/LA, Tim Miller, Richard Atcheson (who provided succor despite deep disapproval), my irreverent students, and Michael Kearns for their relentless leadership, encouragement, and support.

original performance

Queen of Angels premiered October 1992 at Highways Performance Space, Tim Miller and Linda Frye Burnham, Artistic Directors. Directed by Philip Littell. Music by Jon Cohen. Designed by Ian Falconer. Produced by Kerry Slattery.

The original Los Angeles cast, in alphabetical order:

Rob Campbell
Jerry Corona
Gil Ferrales
Gabe Gelbart
Brian Gross
Michael Hauser
Curtis Johnson
Tyr Jung-Hall
Michael Kearns
Tom Keegan
Mike Kelly
Rex Lee
Philip Littell
Davidson Lloyd
Jeff Macauley
Fred Maddux
Daniel McVey
Quentin O'Brien
Sam Pancake
Diego Tabordas
Travis Terry

acknowledgment

The author thanks the Dramatists Guild for providing emergency medical loans, and the Los Angeles Cultural Affairs

Department and the Brody Arts Fund for providing grants at a critical stage in the development of *Queen of Angels*.

characters

MAX: a poet in the throes of dementia. Around forty

QUEEN OF ANGELS: a gender-fuck drag queen. Fortysomething

TOBIAS: a wounded boy. About twenty

THE SHOWMAN: interlocutor, an entertainer. Ageless

MISTER FRIK: the Showman's Punch Show puppet, aka Punch

MISTER FRAK: the Showman's Punch Show puppet, aka Judy, Physik, Hangman, Devil

HOMER: an idiot

EL COYOTE: a scavenger, guide

COMPANY OF CLOWNS: ethnically diverse. Angels, jugglers, jesters, augustes, acrobats, and fools

place

A Doomsday Room for the terminally ill, represented as a tattered carnival tent, wherein dwell all derelict memories and dreams of the poet.

time

There ain't no time.

PROLOGUE: OUR GANG

*An open space to be filled with movement and stillness; darkness
and light; language and silence. There is a cyclorama
representing the subtle and constantly changing L.A. nighttime
canopy, hereinafter referred to as The Sky.*

The Sky is teal. Spotlight on the Queen of Angels.

QUEEN OF ANGELS.
I had a committed relationship once.
He had commitments in Puerto Vallarta.
I was committed to Ward 6-A, Queen of Angels
Our Lady of Peace and Padded Cells.
He would have broken my heart. If I'd had one.
Now? Now I am the Queen of Angels.

I sell their asses on the Boulevard.[1]
My boys they can be had for pennies on the pound.
I am the queen of sodium vapor streets.[2]
Have you seen my gang? Look Touch.   ˋ
Watch their bone white faces. See their sunken eyes.
Merely boys who bear deathmasks before their time.
Last season's angels stalking the sublime.
Sought too steep a climb.
Brought down in their prime.
Somebody's got. Somebody's not.

On the five A.M. avenues have you seen my brood?
They play in noxious fumes. Heads pound on crystal meth
On the boulevard of broken dreams
beneath the streetlamp moon.

---

[1] Santa Monica Boulevard (cruising area for hustlers, johns, the desperately seeking, and
the desperately sought). Or any other street.
[2] Sodium vapor streetlights are the common means of illumination on big city thorough-
fares. They cast a ghostly glow.

On suburban parkways have you seen my youth?
Do you know what time it is? Do you really now?
After school and TV and their little naps
Tell me, wouldn't you choose oblivion too?

These are not poor runaways, honey
They've all escaped, running for their lives.
Late at home tonight check your little ones.
No they are not there. Where oh where oh where?
Bet your life they're here.
Somebody's got. Somebody's not.

The fortunate are raped, beaten, face starvation.
Unlucky ones are shipped back home,
sentenced to probation.
Somebody's got to pay the price all right, my dear.
On expressways in cities have you seen them?
Somebody's not going to make it. Tonight.

act one: departure

SCENE ONE: THE SHOWMAN'S TUNE

A belltower clock chimes six times. The Sky is lavender. The Showman enters cranking his hurdy-gurdy.[1] Homer drags a wheeled cart that contains the Punch Show. They halt. The droning ceases. A cold wind blows. He consults a tattered notebook that he refers to throughout the play.

SHOWMAN.[2]
   Aye. Thizzle du.
   Tiz a inkompleet tayl an 1 thaz vayree ole
   but tiz a stowree I bleeve kin stil b tole.

---

[1] A stringed instrument, similar to a lute, played by turning a rosined wheel.

[2] The Showman's patois is not intended to be any particular dialect, but a broken and repatched argot, shreds of language surviving from past and future holocausts. As with any poetry, if you say the words out loud, all will be revealed. If you don't, you'll be miserable and hate the author forevermore.

At the tym o the telun twaz a tayl withowt no indun
4 the playg that wuz vizatun wuz stil desindun.
Thiz stowree thin iz kunsurnin a man
hu luvd an lawst hiz fren 2 deth.
An the lezun he lurnt wuz
that he had not the kupasitee 2 breeng hem bak.
Tiz the stowree so 2 speek o bekumun hewmun. *(He sings as
he sets up the Punch Show, which is a curtained box)*

4 thim that haz a dollur I bring 2 yu a boon;
4 thim that haz a nickul weel syng merrie 2 yur toom;
4 thim that haz a penee I poze a bleekur toon;
An 4 thim that haz haypennie dizkloze 2 yu yur doom;
But 4 thim that haz not anee the Ayngulz weep.
An may I add: Fuk yoo! *(The Punch Show curtain opens to reveal
Frik, a puppet)*

SHOWMAN AND FRIK.
Fuk yu, fuk yu! an tayke yur imtee beleez home 2 roost
Hay downe derrie derrie
Fuk yu, fuk yu! Go hayng yur nekz thayl suyn enuf b noost
With a downe derrie downe *(An offstage scream)*
Mizdur Frik . . .?

FRIK. Yez . . .

SHOWMAN. Wayr iz Mizdur Frak?

FRIK. Around . . . *(Muffled cries from below)*

SHOWMAN. Wut haz yu dun 2 hym?

FRIK. Nuddin . . . *(An offstage scream)*

SHOWMAN. Stopit! Stoopid popit. Let Mizdur Frak kum up. *(Another puppet, Frak, rises)*

SHOWMAN. Kant yu 2 behayve 4 2 minutz? Letz finush the toon.

Fuk yu fuk yu! Go way yu poor an peneeless, Vamoost!
Hay downe derrie derrie downe downe
Fuk yu, fuk yu! The Showmanz Toon iz suyn 2 b unloozt
With a downe, with a derrie
with a downe derrie derrie, downe downe.

FRIK. Too many downes.

FRAK. Not enough derries.

FRIK. We'll be playing to these faeries the rest of our days.

SHOWMAN. Laydulz N Sooptureenz, The Doktur Turn!
N witch Miztur Punch iz vizutid by a fuzishun.

Frik is Punch. Frak is the Physik.

PHYSIK. Are you dead?
PUNCH. Yes.
PHYSIK. Where's it hurt? Is it here?
PUNCH. No. Lower.
PHYSIK. Here?
PUNCH. No. Lower. Lower.
PHYSIK. Then is your handsome leg broken?
PUNCH. No! Higher. *(Punch kicks Physik. Physik returns with a stick)*
What have you got there?
PHYSIK. Physik Mister Punch.
PUNCH. I'll physik you . . .
PHYSIK. I'll show you a gnurly stave.
PUNCH. I'll show you an early grave. *(Punch kills the Physik)*
Now Doctor you may cure yourself if you can
It's only amongst Punch's good friends
his money most freely he spends
to laugh and grow fat he intends. Hee hee hee hee hee.

SCENE TWO: DOOMSDAY ROOM

*A Chorus of Clowns enters—a tribe of men, chanting,
drumming, performing an insane dance. They are angels,
inmates, jugglers, jesters, acrobats, and fools.*

CHORUS OF CLOWNS.

Recordare, Jesu, Jesu pie. Recordare, Jesu, Jesu pie
Ne me perdas illa die. Quod sum causa tuae viae, tuae viae.
Ne me perdas illa die
Oh what a boom in this doomsday room
We clock in eight A.M. working straight through Sunday
It's a veritable zoo with the traffic coming through
We admit it's a bit like a midway[1]
Patch 'em up, put 'em out, take the next one,

---

[1] Both a carnival midway and the name of a very busy AIDS hospital in L.A.

got the timing of it down to perfection
For a rush that'll blow your mind,
try your hand on this assembly line
What a thrill! (Who'd have thought!)
What a high!
(Overnight!) We've become this grand sensation
So the volunteers are shot and the faculty is stressed
Nonetheless we're the toast of the nation
So belly up, get in line, take a number
Buy a ticket to the eighth world wonder
We're the best and the rest be damned
Fastest ride this side of Dizzyland[1]

Why must you linger on here
What mystery compels you to go on
Who hears your song
When all your friends are gone?

Tonight's the night! Are you feeling sound?
Has your T-cell count been dwindling down?
Got a touch of thrush?
Step right up and put your faith in us

JACKSON. (Plato's Symposium[2]) I will die before I get that TV
series, that guest shot, that feature role at the Mark Taper
Forum, or even a decent Equity waiver swan song like that
beautiful boy in *Plato's Symposium*. I will expire doing this fag
stuff in this dingy, dark place a mile and a half from Rock
Hudson's star. But I will get my two-point-five column inches

---

1 "Disneyland" is an amusement park, reputed to be "the happiest place on earth." It is
a copyrighted registered trademark of the Walt Disney Company. This has nothing to do
with them. It would be wrong.

2 This title is taken from and intended as a tribute to the stage production by the same
name produced in Los Angeles in 1985. Jackson Hughes was a talented, beautiful performer
who died while performing his one-man show, *Our Man In Nirvana*, in the dingy, dark
Theatre/Theater on Cahuenga just north of Hollywood Boulevard, within spitting distance
of Rock Hudson's star. Jackson was closely associated with Philip Littell, a creator and
performer in *Plato's Symposium*. "That beautiful boy in Plato's Symposium" refers to com-
poser/pianist/performer Jerry Frankel. "If mom and Philip are pushy enough" refers to
Philip Littell, who coincidentally would, seven years later, direct the world premiere production of *Queen of Angels*. Unlike the character depicted here, Jackson Hughes was deeply loved
and is remembered often by many.

on the obit page (with a picture if mom and Philip are pushy enough). Oh why oh why can't I be as famous as Tab or Merv or Pee Wee, but without anybody knowing I suck and am sucked and all those other dirty things too. With all this talent with all this beauty with all this intelligence with all this graceful masquerade of not really being queer. All this effort and nobody really cares whether I am or not, and in the end it doesn't really matter does it 'cause I will be just as dead as the rest and I wasn't a movie star or even a TV series guest. I will be just another dead faerie who couldn't even enjoy those last few dozen or so dicks out of fear and denial and self-recrimination and dark secrets and then . . . that will be that. Those who knew me will remember for a little while until they are gone and then there will be no reason to recall my passage at all. They'll never know I was queer and they'll never know I was here. I will bury all the evidence.

CHORUS OF CLOWNS.

Life is a carnival run by a hangman.
Sooner or later you will have to pay the price
We'll be there waiting for you, all medical forms in hand
Sign on the X. Give us a week. Get a new lease on life.
What a rip. What a heist. What a slip on the ice.
What a plan. What a grand old plague this is.
Every hour on the dot there's another bloody lot
coming down with candidiasis.
Can a cure be found? We hope not!
It's a pretty penny all this loot we've wrought.
And the numbers show there's at least a decade left to go.
Call in the stars. Call up the press. We've got a gold mine
Come as you are. Casual dress. We'll take the next in line.
Take a gander at the wonderland inside.
We're the fastest one-way rollercoaster ride.

Here in this hospice by the sea we guarantee you're almost home free.
Climb on aboard what are you waiting for? Nothing in life is free

You got the cash. We got the time.
Next in line if you please . . .

SCENE THREE: THE FIRST COMPASSIONATE STRANGER

The flare of a match illuminates a man's face. Max, on a
hospital gurney, lights a cigarette. He is writing in the notebook
we saw the Showman with earlier. The Sky grows pink.

MAX.
    Three visitors came today. Three. All strangers.
    Ministers from the Church of Ardent Altruism.
    Compassionate Strangers. The first was a man about fifty.
    Roly-poly, thinning red hair,
    in a polyester suit with a cheerful tie.
    I thought of him as a kind of Ronald McDonald
    for the franchise of the terminally ill.
    He said he was with The Project
    and wanted to know if I knew of The Project.[1]
    "Listen, you ineffectual asswipe," I said.
    "I held the founder[2] of your Project in my arms
    just before he died in a room right down the hall there.
    And thank God he died
    before seeing what you asexual bureaucratic dwarves
    did to his Queer dream.
    Get the fuck out of here."
    "Let me know if you need anything . . ." Ronald whined.
    "I'll tell you what I need, Dickbrain. I need a good blow job.
    Send one of those around, why don't you,
    you stupid eunuch?"

SCENE FOUR: AM I LOSING MY MIND?

EL COYOTE. You're too hard on them, *mijo.*

MAX. Give me a pain shot.

EL COYOTE. You just had one.

MAX. Then fucking give me another one, Sancho. *(El Coyote*
    injects Max with Demerol)

EL COYOTE. My name's not Sancho. Asshole. They gonna be
    lettin' you out of here in the morning.

---

1 Thinly disguised reference to AIDS Project Los Angeles.

2 One of the four original founders of APLA, Max Drew, died in 1986 at the Sherman
Oaks Community Hospital in Van Nuys.

MAX. Listen. I want you to tell me something.

EL COYOTE. Of course, dude. But don't mess up the surgical greens. I just got them laundered.

MAX. You must tell me the truth.

EL COYOTE. Cross my *corazon, el mero mero.*

MAX. Am I losing my mind?

EL COYOTE. Hey. No big loss, you know what I mean?

MAX. I am losing my mind.

EL COYOTE. *Si.* Looks that way to me.

MAX. So there's not much time.

EL COYOTE. No, *señor.* There ain't no time.

MAX. It will be good to be going someplace again.

SCENE FIVE: IOWA SONG

Donald is surrounded by Clowns. Through the following, he is bound in a straitjacket, blindfolded, gagged, and carted away.

DONALD.

I had to get off that farm in Iowa.
I knew if I could just get through high school
without getting beat up too bad again,
I could make my way to the city.[1]
If I could just shut up and take it
when they taunted me with those bad names:
Sissy, fat ass, mamma's boy.
Charlie, I miss you.
My folks they made me join the 4-H Club,
thinking that might toughen me up.
But I knew, even back then,
the really rugged fellows all belonged to F.F.A.:
Future Farmers . . . Future Farmers of America.
In 4-H they had both boys and girls
and at our very first meeting
they told us we had to pick a project.
They gave us a piece of paper
with two lists of suitable activities.

---

[1] As did tens of thousands of queers to escape small-town small-mindedness.

Now one column was for boys and one column was for girls.
But I didn't know that.
Guess which one I picked? Sewing.
Everybody howled.
Anyway I got very good at sewing.
My crowning glory was a beautiful pink taffeta slip
I made for my mother.
It won a blue ribbon at the State Fair in Des Moines.
Later on in school I switched from sewing
to the care and feeding of swine.
My father finally spoke to me about my 4-H project.
But I never again won a blue ribbon.
It's taken me all these years to figure out
that chubby Iowa farm sissy I abandoned in 1953
was the best part of me.
Last week I went to Sears
and got me a brand-new sewing machine.
Big fancy deluxe model with zigzag and everything.
I'm finally getting around to making that memorial:
a quilt panel for Charlie.
I picked up three yards of pale pink taffeta
and a Butterick pattern for a size nine slip.
No darlings. Too small for me.
I'm putting it in the quilt
alongside Charlie's leather jacket.
Only him and me will know what it means.
F.F.A.: Fatass Faeries of America. Forever.

SCENE SIX: THE SHOWMAN'S SCHEME

The belltower clock chimes seven times. The Showman's Punch Show. Frik hits Frak.

FRAK. Wud you hit me for, Frik? I ain't dun nuthin' yet.
FRIK. Why wait? Now get this straight, slave: I am the king and you are the knave.
SHOWMAN. Kwyte! Donchuno wayr we r? Thayrz sik peepul prezunt. (*El Coyote begins to construct a gallows*)
FRIK. Sick people are present everywhere.

SHOWMAN. Yez. But theez heer n thiz doomzday room thayr dyun.

FRIK. Everybody in this room is dyin'?

SHOWMAN. Yez.

FRIK. This *whole* room?[1]

SHOWMAN. Thazryte.

FRIK. Sheeze . . .

SHOWMAN. Thatz y weer heer.
2 provyde sum komikul releef 2 thayr dizpayr.

FRIK. I liked it better when we played Bartholomew Faire.[2]

SHOWMAN. Thayr iz no more fayrz.
An no more publuk hangunz.
Thiz iz the sort o playce wayr we hav 2 kum
2 now 2 mayk a livun.
An tonyte Destuneez sweet lyt shynz upon uz bryt.
4 a grayt powit fawlz owr way.

FRAK. Oh the tradudjy!

FRIK. Oh the poor-me.

SHOWMAN. An if we kan sho weev sum kumpashun tu shayr
the powit heel b kweeth 2 uz hiz powetakul werk
4 sompthin lez thin the kawst o a prayr.

FRAK. That's it!? Some lousy rotten poem for us to keep.

SHOWMAN. With ownurship o thiz famuz powitz writ
kumz freedom 4 uz 2 krawl owt o thiz shit.
Weel leev thiz jipsee lyf we leed
rowmun kroz thiz terubul age
An tayk our propur playc
on the mor profitubul lajitamut stayj.[3] *(El Coyote rigs a hang-man's noose)*

FRIK. The eternal schemer's futile dream:
some dying queen's masterpiece on the cheap.

SHOWMAN. Shhhhh! Yul c. Pay atinshun now heerz wayr I got 2
du the preluminayreez.

---

[1] Meaning on this stage, and in this theater, and on this planet.

[2] An English spring solstice carnival circa late eighteenth century. The height of Punch's popularity.

[3] That the Showman refers to the legitimate stage as profitable is meant to be wildly hilarious.

FRIK. Who're you suppose to be, you pompous bag of wind?

SHOWMAN. Interlockachure. I deliver the prologz an the antilogz.
Win thayrz a lessun 2 b lurnt
tiz me hu givz the stowree a seeriuz turnt. *(Frik makes a raspberry sound)*
Myne yur manoorz elze yul ennup az amatoorz.
An now laddies an gurtlewayurz: Feer not:
we hav umblee kum an suyn enuf we shall umblee go.
Twixt the owur that doth run
weel prezent thee with owr showe.

SCENE SEVEN: THREE RIDDLES AND A PUBLIC HANGING

El Coyote leads Max on, and places a box directly beneath the hangman's noose.

SHOWMAN. Aye. Heer he kumz. Thiz iz him. The sinturmoz pursunidge in tunytes specktakul. Max. The heerow. A powit. *(El Coyote positions Max on the box, and puts the rope around his neck)*

MAX. Get it over with. Why are you stopping?

EL COYOTE. 'Cause, *zonzo*, this is where you got to give righteous answers to three riddles.

MAX. Why?

EL COYOTE. 'Cause this is a time-honored and ancient ritual, *putjo*. You don't wanna be fuckin' around with my people's sacred cultural traditions, now do you?

MAX. Go ahead. Ask. I am very good at riddles.

EL COYOTE. Okay. We start with the easy one. What is it that most satisfies desire?

MAX. Absence.

EL COYOTE. *Muy bueno. A buen hambre no hay gordas duras*, eh? Gets trickier as it goes on now. See how this riddle thing works? What spurts like flame, grows cold with apathy, but flares at the smell of conquest?

MAX. Blood.

EL COYOTE. Impressive. So here comes the ballbreaker. You

ready? Take your time. Think it over. No rush. What is born every night but dies every dawn?

MAX. Hope.

EL COYOTE. Bingo. *(He kicks away the box. Max dances grotesquely at the end of the rope for a moment, then a stark and utter stillness. The Sky is purple)*

SHOWMAN. Gorblyme! Wut a bit o badluk tymin that wuz
Pak er up Homer. . . . Weel b off then 2 anuthur town
Wayr thayrz awlwayz anuthur publuck exekuyshun
an no dowt a bigur krowd kum rown.[1]

FRIK. Ain't we gonna do the baby bit?

SHOWMAN. Not heer. Not now. Weel du it win itz tyme.

FRIK. But I love the baby bit.

FRAK. I hate it.

SHOWMAN. Hush! Show sum respeck for the newlee departed.

FRAK. Poor poor poet. Composed for only forty-two years. . .

FRIK. Yes. But now he'll de-compose forever![2]

MAX. *(Cries out)* Let me die!

SHOWMAN. Aye! Wel now itz lukin up a bit now idnit?
A hangunz 1 thyng but the hangun o a powit hu still syngz?
Thatz fantastik! Thiz orta bryngum n 4 myles awrown.
Bettur set im loose Loboze a feller kud chowk 2 deth n that
pozishun. Kum heer, Omi . . . how iz it 2 thiz kondishun yuv
kum? Juz wut iz it yur kondemd 4? *(El Coyote cuts Max free from the noose)*

MAX. Sentenced to live when all I loved are dead.

SHOWMAN. Ded! O wut?

MAX. Because they fucked.

SHOWMAN. Aye? Tiz no 1dur then that heerbowts thayrz so few
folkz afoot. Uh . . . if yur askin me? Itz a bit hevee mayte. 4
the prolatayreeayt. Now now. Git up heer sun. Tiz a long
way yit a 4 weer dun.

MAX. Let me die.

SHOWMAN. O thatz 1 wish I warrunt yule git. But thayrz bettur
wayz o duwunit than with a rowp.

---

[1] Referring to the small audience present at this performance.
[2] Heard originally as a children's joke concerning Beethoven, the composer/decomposer.

MAX. There is no hope.

SHOWMAN. Aye but yur n luk sur! Iyam the dizpinzer o hope.
4 Iyam blest with the gif 2 heelwartz.
Speerachul praktishunur with kriztul an kwartz.
Metafiziz an mystikul sloothe.
N dire eemurgunseez. I kin pul a tooth.
I, sur, stan redee 2 reveel 4 yu
the hole pajunt o hewmun slawtur!
An 4 a slytur more sum kin awlso konjur wutz 2 kum.

MAX. You can foretell the future?

SHOWMAN. Wel now I kud. . . . Yu wudun lykit.

FRIK. I see no reason to keep the suckers in suspense . . .

FRIK AND FRAK: *The queer dies!*[1]

SHOWMAN. Kwyte!

FRIK. C'mon, we seen it a million times.

MAX. What can forestall this catastrophe?

SHOWMAN. Hooo! Yu ask such thyngs o the likes o me?
Iyam but the Swatchel Omi.[2]
Tiz the heerowz task 2 tranzform hiz tyme. Not myne.
I kin 4 c a long wayz up ahed.
Alaz. Wut I kud tel aynt so pritee az the pazt.
The 1 thing I kin say iz sur the fewchur bryte
holdzs not a singul merukul n syte.
Morovur thiz playg
2 wich yu an yur frenz kuruntlee sukum
iz but the jentul kiz o kumpashunz nyte
kumpayrd 2 wutz 2 kum.

MAX. The curse was to outlive all I love.

SHOWMAN. Xsep 1.

MAX. None.

SHOWMAN. Yu hav 4got the lad hu bayrz the woond?[3]

MAX. No, I will never forget. Tobias too was doomed.

---

[1] The surprise in this should be that the queer who dies in this play is not Max, but Tobias. Most popular media until very recently felt compelled to make the homosexual suffer in the end through disease, madness, or death. It has been an ugly historical cliché. This attempts to mock the tradition.

[2] Swatchell=Punch; omi=homme (man). Punch Man.

[3] The wounded boy, prince, or king in mythology. A fatal flaw that prevents the wounded one from completing his task.

SHOWMAN. Notso sun. He dwelz neer the toom
    undur the spel o the Kween beneeth the streetlyte moon.
MAX. Then take me there!
SHOWMAN. O Iyam afrayd thatz 1 trik kanot b playt.
    4 that wikid Kween wrulz the whorl o shadowz an shaydz.
    Dont yu no tiz a relm b low she haz 4bid me go.
    Yu c, sur, I 2 hav bin hext.
    Damd 2 wawndur 1 playc 2 next
    All akroz thiz konchuz playn with no releef frum sun or rayn
    Tiz my purpechul lot 2 stay atop
    thiz kursid glowb an inturtayn.
    An the sadust trooth b 2 tel:
    I hav yet 2 figur wethur tiz hevun or hel.[1]
MAX. Tell me the way.
SHOWMAN. Wel wayt now. Wayt!
    Wut hav yu got n the mattur o pay?
    I kant purform 4 gratiz awl day.
    Bizniz iz down n thiz ayg o playg.
    Wut iz it yu du? Yur a powit thay say.
FRIK. Moon.
FRAK. Joon.
FRIK. Spoon.
FRIK AND FRAK. Buffoon!
SHOWMAN. Kramit mamitz![2]
MAX. I was a poet. Once.
SHOWMAN. I c. I c.
    So wut abowt asynin yur magnum opus 2 me?
    Juz so it kan b presurvd 4 Destunee?
    Iym runun a bit lo on songz 4 my repurtoree.
    So luk heer sun.
    Iym sur thayrz sum work o yurz I kin yuze
    with a litul editun dun. See? *(The Showman unrolls a parchment)*
    O korz yur kredut az a Man O Onur
    wil stan n good sted 4 thee.
    Win yu return frum yur visut 2 the abiz
    yul b stow yur fynul vurz on me.

---

[1] The Showman, a pragmatic man of the theater, is forever locked out of the creative, fantastic netherworld of imagination.

[2] Mammets. Devils, evil spirits, often represented as pagan images such as puppets.

If 2 thiz barturd deel yu agree
the lirukz shal b myn 4 Eturnatee.
So if yul juz syn heer
on thiz simpul kontrak o seekuratee . . .

MAX. Anything to see Tobias again.

SHOWMAN. But 1 grayv warnun, sur, juz soze yu no:
Yur visut must b by aynchun dekree restriktud tho.
It beginz in the glimur o the payl moonzs glo.
An inz at dawnzlyte with the cold kokz kro. (*Max signs the contract*)
Vayree gud! I eegurlee awayt yur return frum b lo.
So offu go. Miztur Kyotee heer noz wel the rowt 2 go
4 he iz at liburtee 2 strowl 2 an fro
twixt the payl o the livun an the shaydz o wo. (*The Showman cranks his hurdy-gurdy*)

MAX. Wait!

SHOWMAN. 2 layt! Owr spel iz spun. Yur mizadvinchur haz b gun.

FRIK. I wanna do the baby bit!

SHOWMAN. Laytur! Weel duem awl 4 thiz iz thru.
An so maydunz an dragunslayurz let the awthur reveel 2 yu
the sad an piteeful frewts o hiz laburz.

FRIK. Here we go then . . .

FRAK. What?

FRIK. More faggot nonsense![1] (*The belltower clock chimes eight times*)

SCENE EIGHT: THE PATRIOT

The Clowns are on a clown break, smoking, trying to relax.

THE GOOD GAY REPUBLICAN. I'm just sick. Sick and tired of having to see those radical demonstrators everywhere with their idiotic signs and their hideous fashions and their monstrous hairdos. Why in God's name do those smart alecks have to stick their ugly faces on the television and say such awful things about our government? Yes, as a matter of fact, I *am* better off now than four, eight, or even ten years ago.[2] Read

---

[1] A phrase used by a long-since-forgotten New York critic in his review of a gay-themed play.

[2] "Are you better off now than you were four years ago?" was a Reagan campaign phrase used to defeat incumbent Jimmy Carter.

my lips.[1] And the niggers are better behaved too, or at least they ain't misbehavin' on my block. Goddammit, if the Spics want to take jobs here, they're just going to have to learn to speak English! I'm damn fed up with going to my own neighborhood market and asking for the Ivory Liquid and being met with a vacuous stare from some brown face that doesn't habla diddly squat. Pretty soon all incentive to work will be gone and we'll all just suck off the sagging public tit. Then where will the big-spender bleeding-heart liberals be? Huh? Up the creek, that's where. Up the creek without a paddle. Well, I'm damn tired of being the paddle! Where will those crude bigmouthed demonstrators be then? Are they fools? Don't they know we have the constitutional right to secrecy? They're only making it hard on themselves and hard on the rest of us! What we do in the privacy of our own beds is nobody's business but our own! I'll tell you one thing: when some neo-Nazi wants to load my squeaky-clean ass onto some metaphorical cattle car, he'll have a devil of a time finding me. Those radical assholes will be on the first train out. And am I supposed to be sorry? I warned them. I tried to tell them. But no. They were willful and stubborn and called me bad names. Maybe if those Jews had just cooperated a little bit, tried to compromise instead of being so defiant, just maybe those camps wouldn't have been quite so crowded. Oh, silence is *not* death.[2] It stands for safety and secrets and no loud confrontation. *(The Good Gay Republican sputters and dies. All the other Clowns die)*

SCENE NINE: LIMBO

Max and El Coyote have entered Limbo. They stand amidst the dead Clowns. El Coyote anoints the dead. The Sky is mustard.

MAX. I swear I will bring Tobias home tonight or die.

EL COYOTE. *Primero dios, payaso.* But the night is very young. The season very dry.

---

[1] A catch phrase used in George Bush's campaign to defeat Michael Dukakis for the presidency. It means "I really mean it."

[2] SILENCE=DEATH is the motto for ACT UP, an effective and heroic AIDS activist organization.

MAX. Hurry! There's not much time.

EL COYOTE. But there ain't no time. Dig? That's the rule, sucker.
Wasn't me that made it. Some other motherfucker. So who
is this homeboy[1] you lookin' for so bad?

MAX. My friend Tobias. He died.
We lived and loved together, always at each other's side.
Offering courage when one was afraid.
Laughter when the other was sorrowful.
I was the singer. He was the song.
There has to be some other end to us than death.
Can't you see?

EL COYOTE. I see you are a big fool, *putjo.*
Better learn to sing solo, *mijo.* Forget him.
Your friend is gone. Soon no one will be left to remember.

MAX. I will not forget. I will be the rememberer.
For him. For me. For all the rest.
Listen. Do you hear?

EL COYOTE. I don't hear nothin.' An' you won't neither, you
know what's good for you.

SCENE TEN: AMERICA SAVE THE CHILDREN

*The Chorus of Clowns begins to sing and engage graphically in
a variety of lewd and creative sexual acts.*

CHORUS OF CLOWNS.
America save the children!
We are your fucking children, assholes.[2]
Huddled on the streets.
In doorways. Under bridges
Sleeping in cars. Begging for bread. Confused. Hopeless.
Hungry. Lonely. Terrified.
We were. We are. We always shall be.

It is the end of a hopeful era
Massive slaughter
Refugee camps

---

[1] Used here in the sense of partner, companion.

[2] As are all gay and lesbian men and women, the homeless, the mentally institutionalized,
prisoners, terrorists, etc. The "worst" of us are somebody's little boy or little girl.

Barbed wire
Poison air
Ocean sewers
Human ovens
Battered children
Derelict dreams
Abandoned decency
The world as we know it on the brink of the abyss.
We were. We are. We always shall be.

Sainthood can be had for pennies on the dollar
Martyrdom is free for the asking.
We die together, pious and pagan indiscriminately.
Our ranks depleted. Angels dropped like butchered lambs.
It took the rogues first.
The artists. Explorers. Adventurers. The fearless.
Those who had the most to teach.
We met. We fucked. We scattered.
And carried in our hearts all that each could hold.
All are innocent. None are spared.
We were. We are. We always shall be.

EL COYOTE. So hey! Got to look on the sunny side, Clyde: can't get no worse. Past this place ain't nothin' but nada. *Comprende? No mas ayer. No mas mañana.* You'd be a whole lot hipper, homey, to turn around, lick your wounds on home turf. Because past here there ain't no was. No has been. No gonna be. That's what it looks like to me. Mister Po-et-tree. It's a itsy bitsy bug, pug. So you wanna stay or you wanna chug? Up to you . . .

MAX. *Vamanos! (The Clowns crawl off into the night)*

SCENE ELEVEN: EL COYOTE TANGO

El Coyote teaches Max the tango.

EL COYOTE.
    Yo. Chill out dude. You got to get more like me.
    Go in the hunt with courage.
    Balls out, man.

Dry years like ours,[1] coyotes descend from dusty hills.
Oh I'm sniffin' for water, lookin' in birdbaths,
backyard pools, fuckin' jacuzzis, anything man
so long it's wet and don't stink like blood.
Ain't no signs of weakness allowed, dude.
Shit! Coyotes got to eat too.
How strange the call . . .
Like we sneaked into this manicured lawn. Dig?
Bared yellow teeth, lifted a hind leg,
Temptin' Junior with tales of wildass freedom
somewhere in the shaggy hills behind home.
Lobos . . . How strange the call. How strange the call.
Listen, *mi amigo,* if you wanna turn around, then go.
And on this one arid evening in this luckyfuckinhunt
under the ghost glow of a rare blue moon I seen it:
the untended child.
Fat slugbaby stuffed with Gerbersfood. Sssssssnatch!
Another lousy unwanted Keith left out to play beneath
Old Man Fate's unfuckinconcerned cold gaze.
America man. She loves her babies.
Supermarkets 'cross the country send out the call.
To find them all. To find them all.
Like these pictures on milk carton containers:
sepia impressions of happier days
photogravured on grocery bags.[2]
Fuckin' bags used after doublefuckincoupons
have been clipped to haul their stinkin' garbage away.
America loves her bargains, man.
So fuckin' dry man. So fuckin' dry. *(Max has fallen asleep)*
Look at this pathetic motherfucker.
Sleepy the Sand Man follows him like his shadow.
You want me to haul your ass to Elysium, chump,
least you could do is stay awake for the whole trip.

---

[1] Los Angeles was in the midst of a six-year drought when this was being composed. The night after our world premiere a gentle rain came to Southern California and replenished the parched landscape.

[2] Lost, missing, or kidnapped kids' photos are printed on milk carton containers and grocery bags in an appalling juxtaposition of crass sales pitches with the images of abused, misused, abandoned children.

SHOWMAN. *(Frantically searching for the notebook)* Wel the jurnee iz supoze 2 tayk a turn heer. Un4choonaytlee lashurs an gurneebayurz we hav loss the tayl kompleet. The awthur givz no klu az 2 wut if ineething he had n mind.

EL COYOTE. *(Throwing Max over his shoulder)* It's the Demerol, man. He shoots way too much of that shit.

SCENE TWELVE: THE BABY BIT

SHOWMAN. Wel it lukz lyk we may b havin a bit o a lul heer . . .
We shud ast 4 klarificayshun afore the proceedin b gets
but we onlee du the wurk o the ded powets.
Truz uz itz betur thiz way.

FRIK. Time for the baby bit!

SHOWMAN. Yez! Wut a xselunt ideer. Hefferz an Gurnzeemun:
The Baby Bit. *(The Showman cranks his hurdy-gurdy. The Punch
Show. Frik is Punch. Frak is Judy. The baby is a doll)*

PUNCH. Ladies and Gentlemen, pray how you do?
If you all happy, me all happy too.
Stop an hear my merry little play.
If me make you laugh, me need not make you pay.
Judy. . . O Judy, my sweet . . . *(A beat)* JUUUUUUUUUUDY!

JUDY. *(Offstage)* Whaaaaa!?

PUNCH. Get up here!

JUDY. Well here I am. What you want now I'm come?

PUNCH. Where is our darling baby-poo?

JUDY. Baby is asleepin.

PUNCH. Wake it so Daddykins can kiss it.

JUDY. No!

PUNCH. Go fetch the apple of my eye! *(Judy goes off. The baby is
tossed on)* Catchee catchee little baby.

BABY. WAAAAA! Get your filthy hands offa me.

PUNCH. Ha ha. Funny baby. Time for baby's walk.

BABY. I want my Mam!

PUNCH. Wheeeee, wheeeee, wheeeee, wheeeee! *(The baby farts)*
Ooooooh! Dirty thing. *(Punch shakes the baby until it cries)*
Shush! Shush, baby! Too much noise.

BABY. WAAAAAAAH!

PUNCH. *(Bangs the baby's head violently until it falls deathly silent)*
No fun . . . *(He flings the Baby away. Judy enters)*

JUDY. Where is the light o' my life?

PUNCH. Why I'm right here, my love.

JUDY. Son of a bitch! *(She beats Punch)*

PUNCH. Ugly witch!

Judy, Judy, plague of my life.

A rope would be welcomer than such a wife. *(He beats Judy until she is quite dead)*

To lose a wife is to gain a fortune.

Who'd be plagued with a wife

that could set hisself free with a rope or a knife

or a good stick like me? Hee hee hee hee hee.

SCENE THIRTEEN: ONE-TRICK PONY

Harley enters, pursued by a Clown in a skeleton suit.

HARLEY.

I've always been a sex hog.

Only met one horn dog who was a sleazier pig than me.

Coupla three years ago, now, I guess. He was a mess.

Craziest fucked up kid I ever seen.

Don't know what he was on. I was speedballing.

We did everything. It wasn't safe. We didn't give a shit.

Had a Jeep then. Black CJ-7. Laredo. Tricked out real nice.

Oversized Dick Cepek mudders[1]

mounted on fat chrome mags.

I was cruisin' Myra Avenue down below the Detour[2]

when I spotted him walkin' real slow

under the Sunset overpass

wearin' nothin' but a slinky tank top

and shredded cut-offs.

Curly blond. Swimmer's body. Nice basket.

Not usually my type.

But he had a cute little butt.

Both cheeks peekin' out beneath the fringe.

So I pulled to the curb to watch him awhile

---

[1] Cepek mudders are a brand name of very fat, macho tires, designed to crawl through swamps and heavy mud. Extremely impractical on the asphalt streets of L.A., but an effective fashion statement nevertheless.

[2] A popular gay bar in the Silver Lake district of L.A.

in my side rearview mirror.
He moved like a cat, slinkin' through the graffiti shadows
prowlin' up and down that endless row of idling cars.
The electric window lowered
when he approached the gray Seville.
He said somethin' to the driver
who was wearin' an alligator on his shirt and a bad toupee,
then the window rose silently, and the Caddy sped away.
The boy under the bridge kept on stalkin'
till he came to what it was he was lookin' for.
It was me.
When he stuck his head through the passenger window
I got a good look at his face.
Jesus! I thought my heart was gonna fuckin' stop.
He had quite a line:
wanted to know was I willin' to risk
twenty or thirty dull years of life without passion
for one night of the best fuck I was ever gonna have.
I could see why he wasn't having much luck
with the Cadillac crowd.
Asked him his name. Wouldn't give it.
"What's in a name?" he asked.
I wasn't gonna risk losin' a perfectly good hard-on
by engaging in some Gertrude Stein crap.[1]
I'm queer, not crazy.
"Get in," I said. "Drive," he said. "Where to?" "North."
So I headed up the Hollywood Freeway.
He stripped in the car.
Bare-ass naked by the time we merged with I-5.
"Pull over here," he said.
And we exited into some God-forsaken industrial park.
Warehouses. Auto Parts. Salvage yards. Thrifty Marts.
We stopped in the middle of forty acres of vacant asphalt.
Wanted me to lower the canvas top
so he could look at the sky.

---

[1] "What's in a name? That which we call a rose by any other name would smell as sweet." From Shakespeare's *Romeo and Juliet*. And lesbian writer Gertrude Stein's antiromantic response in *Sacred Emily:* "Rose is a rose is a rose."

I don't think he saw many stars
bent over the roll bar like that.
"Possess me," he whispered.
But kissing, he insisted, was out of the question.
I don't know if it was the handcuffs that did it for him
or the dog collar. But he finally came.
It was quite a load. But I took it okay.
We headed back to town
just as the sun was comin' up over the Verdugos.[1]
I asked could I see him again.
"Wouldn't be the same," he said. "I'm a one-trick pony."[2]
Wonder where that kid is at tonight.
Me? I'm clean and sober now.
Drive a little white Honda.
Always wear my rubbers.
Figure with a little luck,
I got twenty, thirty more years to remember him.

SCENE FOURTEEN: WHATEVER HAPPENED TO YOU?

El Coyote deposits Max before the Queen.

QUEEN OF ANGELS. Hello, Max. I've been expecting you.
MAX. Where am I?
QUEEN OF ANGELS. This station is known by many names.
    Not quite heaven, not quite hell.
    Those with the most to atone for have the longest to dwell.
    I like that.
    So. You here in Purgatory by the Sea to enroll,
    or merely on lookie-loo patrol?
MAX. I was wondering whatever happened to you.
QUEEN OF ANGELS. Evidently not anything nearly so tragic as
    what has happened to you, doll.
MAX. Long time no see.

---

[1] A foothill range between Glendale/Burbank and the San Gabriel Mountains.

[2] Originally a carnival term for a dog-and-pony act that was severely limited by the fact the pony could only perform one trick. Here, "trick" (a sexual partner, usually anonymous and short-lived) is used as a pun.

QUEEN OF ANGELS. Yes. Lemme see. . . . When did we last meet?
Oh, but of course! I was a shy, awkward, skinny kid.

MAX. You were a great big overgrown monster.

QUEEN OF ANGELS. I was a frightened little boy, all alone in the
big bad world.

MAX. You were a self-loathing petty little faggot. A bitch. A mess.

QUEEN OF ANGELS. I've come a long way, baby.

MAX. And I loved you desperately.

QUEEN OF ANGELS. Yeah. Well. You sure got over it fast. Ah yes.
Them was the Good Ole Days. I liked it so much better then.
Humiliation was our best friend. When the old-fashioned
homo tastefully committed suicide or died of syphilis or was
beaten into a coma by the cops or went away to live with his
stroke-ridden mother or tragically disappeared into the sunset coughing like Camille. Doesn't all this modern liberation
crap just make you wanna puke? We was so much more
fulfilled when we affirmed our oppressor's deepest darkest
desires of who we were.[1] But look. That was then, this is now.
I'm sure we're both better homosexuals for the experience.
We were the very portrait of a love affair, weren't we, Max?

MAX. Love, if you ever had an ounce of it in that fat whore's
heart, was ravaged long ago.

QUEEN OF ANGELS. Yes. By the corrosion of bitterness and barbed
wire of betrayal. But can't you see, Maxie? I've changed.

MAX. Changed?

QUEEN OF ANGELS. Yes. Ever since I started attending the meetings.

MAX. What meetings?

QUEEN OF ANGELS. Oh that don't matter, sweetie.
If it had twelve steps and served cookies, I was there.
I became positively addicted to them!
"Hello. My name is Prissy, and I'm a sissy."
I had endless chats with Missy Higher Power.
I prayed. Lordy how I prayed.

---

[1] All portrayals of gay and lesbian lives made by nongay artists, journalists, essayists, carry
the slight stench of condescension and victimhood. It takes one to know one, and we are
by far the best chroniclers of our own lives. The best of us do it with humor, pathos, and
a brutal honesty that neither condescends nor glorifies our history. The Queen is once again
being wholly ironic.

Then finally, through no will of my own,
I admitted that I was . . . I was powerless over my pussy!
"Yes, yes!" I cried. I am a lesbian.
A lesbian trapped in this cocksucker's body.
And that was the beginning of a bright new me.
See? I haven't been fucked up a single day since.
That's what I've been up to, Max, darling.
I'm sooooo glad you asked. *Et vous?*

MAX. I fell ill last August.

QUEEN OF ANGELS. Really? Nothing serious, I trust.

MAX. The usual.

QUEEN OF ANGELS. Darn. What a shame. "Easy Does It."[1]

MAX. Were you always this vile?

QUEEN OF ANGELS. I think so.

MAX. How did I ever love you?

QUEEN OF ANGELS. Beats me.

MAX. I see you still have the St. Christopher.

QUEEN OF ANGELS. Yes. It was ever so thoughtful of you to send
    me packing with the patron saint of travelers. *(She returns the
    St. Christopher to Max)* Here. You'll be needing this more
    than I. Don't regret, dear. It puts a terrible stress on your
    immune system. And don't look back, Max, you'll turn to
    salt.[2]

MAX. I've come for Tobias.

QUEEN OF ANGELS. Tobias?

MAX. I heard he was here with you.

QUEEN OF ANGELS. Ah . . . *i frutti proibiti sono i pui dulci.*

MAX. I will not leave without him.

QUEEN OF ANGELS. Maybe he got his fill of bad verse.

MAX. You seemed to like it once.

QUEEN OF ANGELS. I loathe you and your tiny success wrung
    from the souls of the dead and dying. I viewed you once as
    our greatest hope for a brave new voice. I see you now as

---

[1] A slogan used by Alchoholics Anonymous and other twelve-step recovery programs.

[2] A reference to Lot's wife, and an oblique nod towards the demise of Eurydice when she tried to leave Purgatory with Orpheus but was condemned to death once more when she turned back see whether he was still coming along with her.

you have become, a third-rate doggerel monger. You peddle your integrity to the highest bidder now, Max, and paint over the shitstink of ripe reality with the perfume of purple prose.

MAX. I'm taking Tobias back with me.

QUEEN OF ANGELS. I'm afraid that will just not be acceptable, dear. Now let's get something straight between us, Max. For a change. Unlike you, I am not in the midst of some homo midlife crisis to taste-test some fag hag's latest flavor-of-the-month cure.[1] So you can take your Buddha-of-the-White-Light love.[2] Take your affected, assimilationist, lispy affirmations.[3] Take your plain-wrap recycled Baby Jesus sermons.[4] Take your we-are-special-from-some-other-planet faerie dust justifications.[5] Take your S-and-M role-playing, tit-clamping, foreskin-piercing, bind-me-up-in-a-gag-till-I-puke rituals stolen from some other culture.[6] Take your macrobiotic holistic fascism,[7] your bitter Chinese herbs,[8] your desperate placenta implants,[9] your Pope-Pious-the-Tenth act,[10] and shove them all up deep where the sun don't shine. You stink, Max. You emit the stench of whimpering, simpering victimhood. Put your hand on the fucking radio[11] till your hair falls out by its natural organic roots if you want. But count me the fuck out. And leave Tobias alone. We plan to leave here with some integrity left, making our exit with some fucking shreds of grace and dignity intact. Tobias has been quite a

---

[1] The famous AIDS healing gurus are women. Mature, matronly, slightly disapproving though nurturing motherly types.

[2] Eastern mysticism flourishes during this plague.

[3] Refers to the silliness of "I'm Okay, You're Okay" jargon.

[4] Watered-down religions tailored to secular times: Dignity, MCC, and other homo versions of Christianity.

[5] Radical Faeries and other "tribal" spinoffs.

[6] S-and-M's dubious stretch to justify itself on the basis of ancient cultural ritual.

[7] This plague seems to have generated more than its fair share of fundamentalist zealots. The health industry is not immune.

[8] One of many over-the-counter AIDS "cures." The author has tried most of them.

[9] Michael Kearns' lover, Philip Juwig, flew to France to try this one about six months before his death.

[10] There is a fraudulent myth that those infected with the AIDS virus somehow magically achieve the status of sainthood—or suddenly become great playwrights or painters or poets or actors. The Queen is very annoyed with this bullshit.

[11] A reference to old-time radio healers such as Oral Roberts.

project but I've nearly got all your corruption out of him. He's an all-new completely postmodern queer. He's reprogrammed. He's safe. He's sexy. But not toooo sexy.[1] He's pure. He's sweet. He's squeaky clean. He is—in a word—immune again. And he is not yours to reinfect.

SCENE FIFTEEN: GLORYLAND

QUEEN OF ANGELS. And now allow me to present to you the Coming Attraction you so pathetically crave. Your Happily-Ever-After has, I'm afraid, flown home to roost. Say hello to what your future has become. The tired Old Queen is dead dead dead, dear. Long live the New King Queer! *(The bell-tower clock chimes ten times. The Sky is mauve. The Chorus of Clowns and Tobias enter)*

CHORUS OF CLOWNS.
Let me tell you something children.
Gather round and listen to me.
Do you know where Gloryland is?
Ain't no mansion in the heavens
No rollin' over Jordan River.
No pearly gates to turn you away
Now your suffering is over.
You can leave behind your sorrow
And behold this brand-new day
Open up and let the spirit fill you.
And you will dance in a bright new day.
There ain't no use for you to wander over yonder
All you need to do is open up your eyes brother
This is Gloryland. This is Paradise. This is New Jerusalem.
Can't you feel it?
This is Kingdom Come! Yes this is Paradise.

---

1 The desexualization of gay men is one of the greatest tragedies of the AIDS crisis. There continues to be great confusion between promiscuity and the transmission of the virus. Unprotected sex with just one infected partner can kill you. Safe sex with a horde of partners won't kill you. Early AIDS education exhortations to "Know Your Partner" seem bitterly ironic to those of us who have witnessed both partners of monogamous couples die. Neither piety nor Puritanism has been an effective vaccine against the AIDS virus.

Welcome to the New Millennium.
Bless the many who refused you.
Pardon those who have abused you.
And remember our friends who are gone.
Here our anger is compassion.
What was hate becomes affection.
Never forget but move on.
Open up and let the spirit fill you.
And you will sing in a brand-new day.
In our hearts we will discover our salvation
In our faces the world will see a new generation
Hail to Gloryland. Dream the dream you dare to dream
This is what they mean by Freedom. Freedom!
Praise to Gloryland. Hallelujah! Paradise.
Welcome to the New Jerusalem.

SCENE SIXTEEN: YOU ARE NO LONGER LOST

MAX. Tobias . . . is it you? Is it really? Am I awake or am I
dreaming?

TOBIAS. Max?

QUEEN OF ANGELS. Yes, dear, Max here dreams he's going to take
you for a spin on the carousel of sin and rekindle some
long-dead desire.

MAX. It's all right, Tobias, don't be afraid.
I've come to bring you home.
You are no longer lost. And neither am I.

TOBIAS. But I'm not lost, Max.
It's wonderful here. Almost heaven.
I am not your boy anymore. I see things now as a man.
A man who sees death in things.
You must get over me, please. I've gotten over you.

QUEEN OF ANGELS. Couldn't have said it better myself.

MAX. What have you done to him?

QUEEN OF ANGELS. There's a couple of minor details you failed
to take into account, *mon ami.* Tobias is mine now.

TOBIAS. Get away from here Max! It's dangerous. Get out. Fast.

QUEEN OF ANGELS. *(Snatching the St. Christopher medal from Max)*
Well. That, as they say, is the *fin de comedie.*

SCENE SEVENTEEN: THE SHOWMAN'S RIGID REFUND POLICY

SHOWMAN. Alaz dayrdevulz an debyutawnz at thiz krewshul poynt n the skrip the kreeaytur o thiz mask kumpleetlee ubandund hiz task. He wuz overtaykun by a tyde o deepreshun an lef the poor playurz 2 thayr own demizez. We havunt the fayntust ideer o wut hapunz nex. Thatz the risk yu tayk n lyv theeytur. N anticipayshun o thiz inturlood we hav mayd provizshunz an lyt refreshmunz wil b survd n the 4yur. Weel tayk a breef rezpyt thin wyl the playurz pre-payr themselvz 4 Ack 2. O. An if by chanz yu wuz konsiderun refunz o yur admishun: 2 layte Iym afrayd. Thim wut mus sufur iz thim that haz payd.

act two: return

SCENE ONE: INTERMEZZO

The Chorus of Clowns dances in the gloryholes[1] of a public restroom.

CHORUS OF CLOWNS.
I hope I recognize him when he come.
I'm sure this was the day he said he come
I'm waitin' I'm prayin', I'm waitin' I'm prayin',
I wait a little longer, I wait a little longer
Just a little while to watch a little longer.
To watch a little longer.

I know this was the time we were to meet. I'm burnin.'
I know this was the time we were to meet. I'm yearnin.'
I hope my hair looks pretty, I've waited here so long,
So long, a little longer. I wait it's been so long.
I wait it's been so long. I wait it's been so long.

---

[1] Gloryholes are drilled into partitions separating the toilet stalls so that a cock may pass through—or a tongue, or a finger, or any other tubular, erotic body part. A "watchqueen" is often posted to keep a lookout for the vice cops.

I'm sure I recognize him when he come.
I'm sure to stay beside him when he come.
I promised I'd be here, he promised he'd come get me.
O Jake . . . Tom, Dick, or Harry. O Jake . . .
Tom, Dick, or Harry. Or whatever your name is.
Whatever your name is. Whatever your name is
I'm sure this was the day you said you'd come.
I know this was the hour we were to meet.
I hope I recognize you, Sugarplum.
I stay . . . I wait . . . O Jake! I stay . . . I wait . . . O Jake!
I fear you have forgot to come my love . . .
O don't forget me, baby.

SCENE TWO: THE SECOND COMPASSIONATE STRANGER

Max, in his hospital gown, lights a cigarette, writes in his notebook.

MAX.

The second compassionate stranger to visit today
was a woman.
A rather large beast who reeked of lavender and garlic.
She wore a button this big on her ample bosom
that screamed: "YES I CAN!"[1]
She stuck her fat round face in the door and inquired,
"Hidee, Can I come in?"
"NO YOU CANNOT!" I replied.
"I just thought you might like some company," she proposed.
"I don't. And I especially don't want
that love-your-disease crap[2] contaminating this room."
"But don't you know?" she beseeched. "It's a gift."[3]
"Then it's a gift I'm returning. Call the manager. I want to
see a supervisor. The ninety-day warranty has expired. I'm

---

[1] Some slogan or other for some AIDS support group or other.

[2] A questionable premise in Louise Hay's philosophy. Ms. Hay, while claiming to be a healer and making a good deal of money for her services, has so far lost every single one of her "clients" to AIDS.

[3] Yet another half-baked New Age concept, that disease is somehow a "gift." Susan Sontag's brilliant essay, *AIDS and Its Metaphors,* explodes this stupid, dangerous superstition.

sending this piece-of-shit gift back."

"I so understand how angry you must feel," she whispered. "Angry?" I asked. "Oh why should I be angry!? My fucking body is covered with open sores oozing a constant stream of thick yellow pus. I piss all over myself at least twice a day. My ass is bloody and covered in shit. I'm numb from my knees down to my feet, and my brain is rotting away with some exotic fungus. Am I angry? . . . Naw."

"I know what it's like," she insisted. "I lost my son to this."

"Good," I yelled. "Every mother in America should lose a son to this. Then maybe somebody would wake the fuck up and do something. Get the hell out of here!"

She left without a fucking whimper. *(The belltower clock chimes twelve times. The Sky is cobalt)*

SCENE THREE: BALLET *AU NATURAL*

The Chorus of Clowns dances in. They are naked, bathed in a beautifully tasteful blue light.[1]

SHOWMAN. Howz lytz pleez . . . howz lytz! *(Exposed to the grim light, the Clowns scatter offstage)* Iyamsoree but Ive bin nformt by the mprirsayrio o thiz spektikul that I mus deelivur un2 u the fawlowun pronownzmunt. Du 2 the kurunt kool klymunt koncernun the fundun o publik nturtaynmunt thayr haz bin a bit o revishun dun 2 the fawlowun porshunz o owr show so az not 2 ofend thoz hu atend the theaytur n ordur 2 retayn konfurmayshun o beleefs awlredee helt. Nevurthelez thoz with mor frajul sensubiliteez r frum thiz poynt 4wurd kindlee 4warnd that u mus provyd yur own sensorun. N anee evint thoz porshunz o owr play that u fynd n anee way amewzun or with evun the slytust hent o redeemun soshul valyew hav mos surtunlee bin rawt thru the binevolunz o yur tax dawlurz. N partikulur the awthur bayd me xprez apreeseeayshun 2 the Kulchurl Afayrz Deepartmunt an the Brodee Artz Funt 4 withowt thayr jinuruz pekuniaree

---

[1] This scene was added a day before opening by the director and author to satisfy the advertising poster's promise "A Chorus of Naked Queers." On closing night of the world premiere run at Highways, the author joined the procession. Ticket sales were not affected.

suport he wud shurlee hav run owt o nefekshuwul medikay-
shunz long b 4 he did. Ontheuthurhan awl mpudint nsultun
dizgustun diztaystful reepugnunt obnokshush reelijuzlee-
bigutud rayshuleeprejudust kulchurleensinsutuv jindurofin-
dun kreed damungun ore karnul lude irotik obseen ore n
anee manur kontributun 2 the deelinkwensee o a mynur (an
ore pornografik pasudguz az proskrybt by stayt an lokul
standurdz o deezunzee az deeturmund by the Supreem Kort
ore anee othur kort) ar heerby an henz4th waruntud 2 hav
bin kumpozt ntyrlee an kumpleetlee on the awthurz own
purzunul an pryvut tym far far ayway frum the sukur o the
publik tit. Thayr. I think that awta jus abowt kuvur it. Awn
with the show thin . . . Wut followz iz ineebodiz gez. Lizzen
dayzeez n shovulmin we r not the awthur ownlee akturz.
Pleez not 2 blaym uz 4 thiz!

SCENE FOUR: THE JACK KETCH ROUTINE

Punch is in jail.

JACK KETCH. You must come to justice now, Mister Punch.

PUNCH. Who're you?

JACK KETCH. The hangman. My name's Ketch.

PUNCH. Ketch this, then! *(Punch hits Ketch)*

JACK KETCH. I've come to take you up.

PUNCH. And I've come to take you down. *(Punch knocks Ketch off his feet. Ketch returns with a gallows, places a ladder against the gibbet)* What's that? A tree! You're planting a tree. How sweet. Stop thief! Those apples are for me. *(Ketch brings out a coffin)* A basket for the fruit, I see.

JACK KETCH. It's time now, Mister Punch. Just come on out and take your medicine like a man.

PUNCH. But I'm not a man. See? Just a cloth puppet draped over the idiot's hand down below.

JACK KETCH. Come on now. It's time.

PUNCH. Oh you would not be so cruel . . .

JACK KETCH. Why were you so cruel as to commit so many murders?

PUNCH. Yes, but that's no reason you should be cruel too and murder me.

JACK KETCH. Now, Mister Punch, are you ready to suffer?

PUNCH. Why yes, I'm ready for supper.

JACK KETCH. Are you ready to die?

PUNCH. Why yes, I'm ready for pie.

JACK KETCH. Put on your bib then, Mister Punch. *(Punch sticks his head to one side of the noose)* No, stupid. Like this . . . *(Ketch illustrates by putting his own head through the noose. Punch pulls the rope tight, and Ketch is hanged by the neck)*

PUNCH. He's out! He's out! I've done the trick!

Jack Ketch is dead. I'm free!

I do not care now if Old Nick himself should come for me.

Hee hee hee hee hee! *(The Devil himself pokes his horned head into the proscenium. Punch squeals in terror)*

SCENE FIVE: PLEASE DON'T TOUCH ME

The Sky is olive. Max is approached by Tobias.

TOBIAS. "In the City Without Hope, despair can be the only sin."

You wrote that in a poem you gave me once.

You must not touch me.

MAX. Please. Come closer.

TOBIAS. If you are still my friend you must not touch me.

A friend is not allowed to add to grief.

Life gave me love which it knew I would lose.

Death has given you the saddest songs of the heart.

No. You must not touch me. It is forbidden now.

MAX. In the City of Misery, hope was a cruel refuge through endless nights of longing for you.

The Boulevard of Dismembered Dreams

was lit by the pale glimmer of ghosts

departed lovers, one-night stands, tricks, treats,

a hand, a mouth, an arched back, an aching prick

seized in the deep sweet darkness of anonymity.

And then one awful morning in the dim gray drizzle of dawn

I staggered alone homeward bound.

What is that awful stench? I cried.

And in the pale vespers light I realized: it was me.

Reeking of the dead men I ignited who extinguished themselves in me.

TOBIAS. I have tried to learn to love my smell.

MAX. Oh Tobias, it's so sad that you never knew the Glory Days.
When mock orange perfumed the streets of paradise.
My God! A stroll at dusk was to risk intoxication.
It was a time of jasmine nights and honeysuckle dawns.
Come back with me
and we will be locked forever in each other's embrace.

TOBIAS. I can't, Max.
My Glory Days were not to be.
My place is here.
My time is now.
Please. You must not touch me. *(They strip off their clothes and fall upon one another passionately)*

SCENE SIX: WHY THERE ARE NO DUETS IN THIS SHOW

SHOWMAN. Wel thayr wuz supozt 2 b a luvlee duwet heer. Un4chunaytlee the awthur got n a pechulunt snit an kominst 2 havun a taryubul fyte with the kumpozer. 4 sevrul krewshul weekz thay wuden evun speek 2 1 anuthur. An thay nevur did git awrown 2 repayrun the kolaburayshun.[1] Sew thay nevur finushuntit. Wut a shaym. But truzt us: if thay had it wudda bin juz bwuteeful. It wudda bin the toon yude all be humun on the way bak home 2nyte. Wel thiz iz the way I imagun it: az the 2 o thim r singin Max and Tobias kum klozur an klozur 2githur til at laz they fawl n2 an enosent luvurz embrayz. Thiz thin iz the part wayr the Kween kumz n an katchuz thim 2githur. Now the Kween iz not a wel womun 2 beegin with an thiz juz sinz her intyrlee offa deep ind. N any evint thiz iz wut hapunz aftur that.

SCENE SEVEN: THE QUEEN OF ANGELS DISCOVERS MAX AND TOBIAS *IN FLAGRANTE*

QUEEN OF ANGELS. Hello, my darling little one.
Goodness! We're looking glum.

TOBIAS. Please. I can explain . . .

---

[1] This is a cliché of the theatre. In actuality the author and composer, Jon Cohen, got along splendidly.

QUEEN OF ANGELS. Please do. I'm queer, not psychic.

You can go home now, Max. Die in your own bed.

Alone. Forgotten. Untouched.

You are no longer welcome here.

TOBIAS. Stop . . .

QUEEN OF ANGELS. No! You stop, sonny boy. I jerked you up from the debased gutters of hell. You owe your very existence to me.

TOBIAS. You're not my mother.

QUEEN OF ANGELS. No, Tobias, I am not your mommy. I am one hell of an improvement over that biological bitch. She bore you, but I chose you. When she and everyone else disdained you, I reclaimed you. I was the one picked up the pieces of you, a desperate hustler on hands and knees crawling across glittering nighttime alleys digging for diamonds.[1] But it was glass, honey! Cheap broken shards of beer bottles and shattered windshields. You were so fucked up, jacked up, cranked up, you couldn't tell the streetlight from the moon. Oh you had a birth mother all right. And she delivered unto us one very fucked up piece of damaged goods. You've been a major rehabilitation project, Tobias. Don't screw me over now.

TOBIAS. If I come with you, can you teach me how to love my smell?

MAX. Yes, Tobias. We'll teach each other.

TOBIAS. Meet me later, then. On the Boulevard beneath the streetlight moon.

MAX. When?

TOBIAS. I'll be there soon.

SCENE EIGHT: TOBIAS FLIES THE COOP

TOBIAS. I'm going home with Max.

QUEEN OF ANGELS. How sweet. And when did this change of heart come over you?

TOBIAS. I have to go back.

---

[1] Street slang for those who are on so much crystal methamphetamine that they hallucinate, searching through broken glass sparkles in the sidewalks and alleyways, hoping to find diamonds amongst the detritus.

QUEEN OF ANGELS. I see.

TOBIAS. It's not forever.

QUEEN OF ANGELS. Nothing ever is.

TOBIAS. I have to see if I can learn to love.

QUEEN OF ANGELS. Love! Love isn't nearly all it's cracked up to be.

TOBIAS. I want one last chance at it. When I come back I'll stay with you forever.

QUEEN OF ANGELS. "Forever." Where have I heard that before? Ah, yes, back before the Trojan Wars. Forever, it seems, lasts in Gay Standard Time about a fortnight.

TOBIAS. Please. He needs me.

QUEEN OF ANGELS. And what about me? Don't answer that. I couldn't possibly bear your sickening sweet sentimentality.

TOBIAS. You'll always hold a special place . . .

QUEEN AND TOBIAS. . . . in my heart.

QUEEN OF ANGELS. Quick! My insulin. You leave me no choice. If I hold you here, you'd spend your days resenting me, your nights plotting escape. In the Kingdom of Hearts there are no natural heirs, and so I must plod along here, doing the best I can with whatever trash sifts down. Go. You are free.

TOBIAS. You won't regret this, I promise.

QUEEN OF ANGELS. Right. I might have been born yesterday, darling, but I was up all night. Now pay attention. *(She gives Tobias the St. Christopher medal)* Hold on to this. It's tricky business getting past the dog who guards the gate. Max must join you just before dawn. He cannot be late. At the darkest moment, just before first light, hold his hand and pray for safe flight. And if your best-laid plans should fail, you can always come home to me. I, at least, am the very model of consistency. *(She drapes the medal around Tobias' neck)*

TOBIAS. You did love Max, didn't you? *(No answer. Tobias leaves)*

QUEEN OF ANGELS. Once upon a time. More than blood. And what about me, Tobias? *(El Coyote slouches in from the shadows)*

EL COYOTE. Arf! Arf!

QUEEN OF ANGELS. You'll never play Sandy in "Orphan Annie," fido. But at least you're true. Come along, Dingo. I've got a little job for you that only a dog would do . . . *(The Queen and El Coyote pas de deux into the night)*

SCENE NINE: PUNCH AND THE DEVIL

The Showman cranks his hurdy-gurdy. The Punch Show.

SHOWMAN. Punch an the Devul.
N witch Miztur Punch receevz hiz kumupunz.
PUNCH. Who are you?
DEVIL. I am the Devil and I've come to get my due.
PUNCH. Oh! Oh no. You must have the wrong feller.
DEVIL. Is your name Mister Punch?
PUNCH. You see? That's not my name at all.
Wrong man. Luck to you, sir. Bye bye.
DEVIL. I seen your wife Judy . . .
PUNCH. You did!? I mean . . . not my wife, sir, I assure you.
Never married.
DEVIL. She said you was a small-pricked sonofabitch who could
ne'er satisfy her in the bed.
PUNCH. Why that lying bitch!
DEVIL. You're Punch all right. *(The Devil stalks Punch with the
pitchfork)*
PUNCH. Now I hear the bell. And it's me funeral knell
And I'll see you all in hell. I hope yer frizzle well.
Damn your eyes! *(Punch goes down, down, down)*
SHOWMAN. An so inz owr komikul trajudee o Punch hu dyd 4
luv.[1] With awl the oridjunul Jokz. Fartz. Songz. Dansez.
Kickunz Etsetura. *(Punch pops up from below)*
FRIK. Hey wait a minute, man. That's no way to end the show.
SHOWMAN. Thaz wut the skrip kawlz 4.
FRIK. You stop it here and there will be rioting in the streets.
Guaranteed.
SHOWMAN. The evul he kumitz iz the evul that repayz.
FRIK. I'm not evil, man. I'm just doing what a man's got to do.
Understand? *(Frik maneuvers behind the Devil, motioning the
audience to remain quiet. He strikes the Devil from behind, wresting
his pitchfork away, and runs him through and through)*
PUNCH. That merry fellow Punchinello
dancing here you see sir

---

[1] Punch does not know the meaning of the word *love*, nor does he want to, or need to.

Whose mirth not hell itself can quell
he's ever in such glee sir.
Each jovial fellow at Punchinello
will (laughing through his tears) roar.
I'll rant and revel and play the Devil
then set all hell in an uproar. Hee hee hee hee hee!

SCENE TEN: UNDER THE STREETLAMP MOON

Tobias is alone underneath a streetlight. A ground fog curls around his feet. The Sky is black. A million stars. He cries out.

TOBIAS. Oh Max, where are you?

SCENE ELEVEN: SUCCUMBING TO THE SPICED BRINE OF LUST

The Sky is gunmetal gray. The belltower clock chimes twice. Skipper (El Coyote disguised as a Sweet Young Thing) wears a sailor's uniform as he approaches Max.

SKIPPER (EL COYOTE). Looking for a good time, Hot Stuff?
MAX. I'm lost. Actually.
SKIPPER. Gee, mister, you're never lost when you're with the Navy.
MAX. What's your name?
SKIPPER. Skip. But you can call me Skipper if you like me.
MAX. Well. Skipper. You're out kind of late for a boy your age. Aren't you?
SKIPPER. Yeah. I guess so. I'm kinda like lookin' to get laid. And when you're my age sometimes you have to troll for a real long time.
MAX. A lad with your bait shouldn't have long to wait.
SKIPPER. Hey, that rhymes, huh? So wanna hoist anchor, lick my lure, or what?
MAX. I've gotta go.
SKIPPER. So whatsamatter with me?
MAX. Look. Sorry. Have to meet somebody . . .
SKIPPER. Excuse me. Sir.
But you wanna take it from a kid who's mature for his age: A bird in the hand's worth two dozen in the bushes.

Come sail my ocean and I'll make you forget
every landlocked trick you ever had.

MAX. I don't think so . . .

SKIPPER. C'mon. Climb atop my masthead, matey.
With mainsails a'billowing
I'll take you o'er the bounding brink.
The full tide rises. And there's no guarantee
the Sea of Rapture will wait 'til the morrow.

MAX. Your voice . . . it's so familiar.

SKIPPER. Listen mister, I'm well-known on all five continents
and across the seven seas.

MAX. Oh fuck it. I know who you are. *(They clutch)*

SCENE TWELVE: THE BALLAD OF SEXUAL COMPULSION

*The Sky is scarlet. The Chorus of Clowns dances on,
surrounding Max and Skipper.*

CHORUS OF CLOWNS.
It started when we were little boys.
We played in shit; used cocks as toys.
Eventually we got caught
by mom, by dad, by the bully beat cop
We were exposed, rotten, shame shame shame.
Faggot. Fairy. Cocksucker. Mother Fucker.
But a queer is a queer is a queer by any other name.

Bart the Bull loved a boy whom he promised to be true.
I'll never be unfaithful dear, each night he'd coo
But in the evening after work at the bars
'twas down the hatch
Bart would twitch and start to itch
where only a man could scratch
He was exposed, rotten, shame shame shame.
Gonorrhea. Hepatitis. Scabies. Baby Fucker.
But a queer is a queer is a queer by any other name.

Johnny here was married once to an actual woman in fact
She bore him two delectable kids: a jill and then a jack

They dwelled a decade in the suburbs, happy as four clams
'Til catching poor John in bed
with a man's cock 'tween his hams
He was exposed, rotten, shame shame shame.
Fellatio. Pervert. Sodomizer. Father Fucker.
But a queer is a queer is a queer by any other name.

SCENE THIRTEEN: THERE AIN'T NO TIME

Max is naked in Skipper's arms. The Sky is auburn.

MAX. I love your smell. Your hair. Your tattoo . . .
Oh god, no! What time is it?
EL COYOTE. There ain't no time, dude.
Wanna make another mooring in the lagoon of doom?
MAX. Christ!
EL COYOTE. Jesus don't hear you dude. Barking up the wrong
fucking tree. The last Christian died on the rood.[1]
MAX. Damn you! Damn your soul to hell. *(Max hurries to get
dressed. El Coyote sings)*

SCENE FOURTEEN: INSIDE THE JOINT

EL COYOTE.
Too late man. I blew my soul.
Inside the joint I blew my soul.
Broke down and expressed *mi amor*
for that juicy little dinge in cell block C.
Fucking deadly.
Other inmates they give you the silent treatment
and if that don't work gang rape you till you bleed.
Ain't no signs of weakness allowed, dude.
No weakness allowed, dude. No weakness allowed
Tenderness is contraband. Eat or be eaten. Eat or be eaten.[2]
C'mon *amigo* . . . *vamanos a la reina.*
And God help the sonofapoorbitch
who threatens the big house with love

---

[1] A direct quote from Friedrich Nietzsche, El Coyote's favorite philosopher.
[2] El Coyote's second favorite philosopher, Arthur Schopenhauer.

'cause there ain't no safety in solitaire neither.
The lonesomeness eats you up in there.
Hey you fuckin' faggots don't talk to me about tough.
I been walkin' queer street all my life.
Ain't no tougher fuckin' block than this.
You askin' for pity? From me?
Shit, man. I hate the sea.
Only salt I ever taste is tears. It's like this. Dig me.
I choose to live out on the margins of your fucked up society.
Scavenging the shores of your bankrupt decency.
Hey lemme tell you sompthin' dad[1]
the hunting is *muy bueno* in a city that's dying.
Whole bunch of carcasses to be picked up.
An' you cussin' me for cleaning up your mess?
Shit man! You more fucked up than me.
I said shit man! You more fucked up than me.

SCENE FIFTEEN: WE ALL HATE THIS PART

SHOWMAN. Now thiz heer nexpart kuminup iz a bit kompleeka-
tid an mytee sketchee an . . . Wel weer juz feerful that yur
gonna hayt it. I du. Alotuv uz begd the wrytur—b 4 he xpyrd
may hiz eeturnul sowul damd 2 hel tho it may b rezdin-
peeze—we emplord hym 2 rekonsidur this sumwut
laboreeuz purpul pasudge. We tole hym 2 kutit iz wut we
did. But hiz las rekwest thatit stik wuz a finul wish we kud
not refewz. It iz ovur priddy kwik an 4 thoze o yu weeree o
awl the toonz thayrz not a bit o syngin 4 the nex 10 menutz
at leest. Weel skip ahed abit thin 2 win the Kween kumz bak
frum hur mishun. Kontinyuwinawn now with the xsytun
kunklushun o Ack 2. Kween O Ayngulz.

SCENE SIXTEEN: FIREBIRD SUITE

Max is alone for a moment. It is strangely silent. Then Tobias'
bloodied and broken body is tossed onstage. Max rocks the dead
boy in his arms. The Queen appears. The Sky is rose.

---

[1] As in the hip slang, Dadd-y-o, and also to all fathers of sons who roam the streets.

QUEEN OF ANGELS. You got to the dock a bit late, Maxie.

MAX. Who did this?

QUEEN OF ANGELS. Some punks in a Firebird. License plate: HOT-4-TWAT. *(She throws the St. Christopher medal at Max)* Here. Found this too. He won't be needing it, and I won't be going anywhere for a long long time. *(The Queen hurls down the scorched license plate: HOT-4-TWAT. The belltower clock chimes three times)* Careful, doll, still hot. . . . Don't bother thanking me. I didn't do it for you. Easiest score I ever made. Walked down that Boulevard makin' myself real conspicuous—which is a short trip for me. Shore nuff: HOT-4-TWAT slipped up beside me revvin' that Firebird's throbbing three-fifty. I waved demurely. "Hiya sport, gotta light?" I inquired. My Virginia Slim[1] was already aglow, but they got the drift. They cruised real slow round the block an' cut me off at Vista. I tried to act startled. "Oh!!" There was three of them. Blondie was drivin'. "Suck my fuckin' dick," Short Dark and Dumpy in the backseat proposed sweetly. "Well I dunno Sweetness, a sailor's got to make her rent." "Hey! You're a fuckin' queer!" Einstein, who was riding shotgun, yelled. "That don't mean I can't blow you, does it?" I pouted. "These kissers could suck the chrome offa that front bumper." They followed me down the alley behind OkiDog.[2] I was on the driver's side by then. I fondled the gold chain around his neck. "Pretty," I purred. Then I yanked it free—I hope the clasp is still okay. Blondie spat on me before I could get the top off my Mason jar. "What's that, fag? Your perfume?" But the gasoline was in his eyes by then. "Here's your fuckin' fag," I said, and flicked the burning butt through the window. It was real quiet for a second. Then . . . whooooosh! Them vinyl interiors are a regular fire trap. Ralph Nader oughta do sompthin'. There was a brief commotion. Blondie and Einstein, in the front, shut up quick. El Cholo Gordo in the back tried to claw his way through

---

[1] A cigarette marketed exclusively to women. Sponsors of professional women's sporting events such as tennis tournaments.

[2] A hot dog stand (now defunct) on Santa Monica Boulevard frequented by hustlers and whores and their clientele.

the rear window. Lemme tell ya sompthin' honey: glass don't scratch so easy.

MAX. Are the boys in the Camaro[1] dead?

QUEEN OF ANGELS. I ain't. You go figure it. Listen to me, Max. Get me straight on this one: I didn't do it for you. I didn't even do it for Tobias. I done it for every desperate fairy who ever tasted the soles of those fag stompers on the 3 A.M. streets. I done it for that desperate drunk Mexican kid outside the Detour[2] who had his face blown away for a fuckin' leather jacket. I done it for every queer who ever called the cops for help an' had his ass left twirlin' in the breeze. I done it for every little effeminate boy who takes their kinda shit at the fourth-grade recess, wets his britches in terror, then gets sent home by the principal for bein' a goddamn sissy. I done it for all the fuckin' fag jokes, all the hateful politicians who egg them on, all the baseball bats, all the gay blood spilled on the point of a queer-killing knife. I done it . . . Goddamn you! I might've done it for a fucking dog. He's only just one queer. He's expendable.[3] I done it for all them that's past, and the ones that's yet to come. And it was a Firebird, Sweetie. You gonna hang with street queers, you got to learn to tell the difference 'tween Pontiacs an' Chevys. Three little boys go up in flames in fag town. Film at eleven. Let it be a sign to punks: don't tread on our dresses, dearies: some of us ain't as pretty as we look.

Go home, Max. Sing your songs. *(The Queen departs)*

SCENE SEVENTEEN: TIME TO SING SOLO

El Coyote, once again the orderly, helps Max into a hospital gown. The Sky is tangerine.

EL COYOTE. Time to go, mister.

MAX. I have no songs to sing. I'm so dry. It is a dry season.

---

[1] A model very similar to the Pontiac Firebird, made by Chevrolet.

[2] A bar in the Silver Lake district of L.A. Based on an actual queer-killing incident.

[3] None of us are expendable, and she knows it. The Queen is once again using irony to make her point.

EL COYOTE. This drought shall end. It will always rain.

MAX. There has to be some other end to us than death!
Can't you see? Can't you see that?

EL COYOTE. I see.

I see that the messiah lies dead every Saturday night
at the corner of Sunset and Alvarado.[1]
I see that it ain't possible no more to keep
all the names of the ones we have lost.
I see the future has been ripped off
and the past is not possible to reclaim.
I see that we hurt each other at least as bad
as the motherfuckers who want us dead.[2]
I see that and I see a whole lot more. But I cannot tell.
My tongue has been torn from my head.[3]
I see that you came here to get a look. You looked.
So now you got to go back and tell.
Get up, *hermano . . . Bueno.*
I see that it is time to sing solo, *mijo. (El Coyote leaves)*

SCENE EIGHTEEN: THE THIRD COMPASSIONATE STRANGER

Max is alone. The Sky is gold. The belltower chimes six times.
He lights a cigarette.

MAX.

The third visitor was a young man.
No more than a boy really.
Coal black eyes, shoulder-length hair.
Foreign accent. East European, maybe.
He wanted to know could he give me a massage.
"Why?" I asked, always suspicious I'd have to endure some
half-baked sermon.

---

[1] A particularly violent intersection in the Echo Park District of L.A.

[2] A reference to black-on-black, brown-on-brown, queer-on-queer crime, exploitation, and self-hatred. Oppressed people turn on one another when the true oppressor is impossible to confront.

[3] Minority voices are suppressed, censored, and economically boycotted in U.S. culture, therefore El Coyote has no tongue.

"Because it helps with the healing," he said.

"You're barking up the wrong tree, boy. This is a hospital. No healing takes place here."

"No, not for you," he explained. "For me. It helps me when I touch others."

"Do you believe this disease is a blessing?" I asked.

"No," he said.

"That's one point in your favor. Are you going to counsel me on the acceptance of death?"

"No."

"Are you armed with Teddy bears, stupid cards, ugly flowers, or stuffed animals of any kind?"

"No," he laughed.

"Do you give blow jobs?" I asked.

"No," he said.

"Well you can't have everything, I guess."

"Turn over on your stomach," he suggested. Then he took a small vial of oil scented with spices, poured some into his hands, rubbing them together to warm the balm. He began with my feet, which are numb to the touch, but I could feel the heat. By the time he got to my thighs and buttocks I was crying. I don't know why. "Don't worry," he said softly. "This happens with a lot of them." And then he turned me over and stroked his thumbs over my face, blending the fragrant oil with my tears.

"May I hold you?" he asked.

"Yes," I replied. "Hold me.

God please hold me." *(Tobias enters. He is a nurse)*

TOBIAS. Good morning. You're going home today. Would you like breakfast before you go?

MAX. Some nights I still dream.

TOBIAS. That's a very good sign. *(Tobias leaves)*

MAX. Please. Come closer . . . *(Max is alone. He sings a song known only to himself, in a language only he comprehends. It is a joyful song, a song of transition into some wondrous new world. The cock crows. The Sky is white. Max disappears with the rising light)*[1]

---

[1] Max is leaving to go home, not to die. (See Showman's next speech.)

SCENE NINETEEN: EPILOGUE

The Showman holds the notebook.

SHOWMAN.

An now onurorbul baybeez an koronayreez
tiz lef 4 me 2 finush off the kronakul kumpleet.
4 tiz a fak thayrz not a ayngul lefa lyv
2 tel the frakchurd tayl.
Ovr an ovr tiz the saym storee we r tole:
Itiz the cowurdlee basturdz hu ran frum the batul
hu dun theze slawturz.[1]
Az faytz chanz wud hav it:
Max owr heerow returnd 2 the livun 4 hiz breeftym
wayr he sang minee songz n a worl wayr he wuzunt wantud.
Til fynlee az foolz an mortulz r spozd 2 du
Owr powit kaym 2 peez.
An awl the suferun that lay behynd hem pazt frum vew. *(He
holds up the tattered notebook, which is Max's script for* Queen of
Angels, *the play just presented)*
Thiz iz hiz bargayn wich he fulfild 2 me n ful.
Itz 4 sayl if u no anywun hu wantzit.
We kan kleen up the langwage if u lyk.
Mayk anee chaynjuz u want. The awthur downt kayr no mor.
4 the musik we kan git a boneefyd kumpozur frum Julyard
hu akchulee noze wut heez duwun. Hyr a reel directur huze
nevur dun postmodurn or purformunz art. We kud ast the
kritukz 2 kum bak an rekonsidur. May b nex tym thayl gitit.
Weel hyr profeshunul ackturz. The townz ful o em.
Put it n a ackchul theeaytur, not a spayze.[2]
(He holds up the scroll) The afee davee!
I hav awl the opshunz an rytes tyd up heer in thiz signed
kontrak. See me afturwurdz if yur itrestud in revizin an
movin

---

[1] Derived—if not entirely plagiarized—from Shakespeare's *Henry V.*

[2] Intended as a backhanded salute to the composer (Jon Cohen) and director (Philip Littell) of the world premiere production of *Queen of Angels,* and a tribute to Tim Miller and Highways Performance Space, which consistently presents the most interesting and daring work to be found on American stages in these troubled times for the arts.

thiz show 2 a mor profitubul lowkayshun.

An so indz owr tayle. . . . Pak er up, Homer.

FRAK. Wait a minute wait a minute wait a minute! Let's do the crocodile bit.[1]

SHOWMAN. No tym. Showz ovur.

FRAK. O Mister Frik . . . Mister Frik. Time to play. Mister Frik? Where's Mister Frik?

SHOWMAN. Miztur Frik aynt kumun no mor.

FRAK. Whadaya mean he ain't comin'. Gets paid same as me don't he? Get up here, Frik!

SHOWMAN. *(Reading from a newspaper obituary)* Sez heer: Miztur Frik xpyrd at 10-40-5 P.M. awn Saturday o wut waz reportud az nachurl cawzez relaytud 2 the sisayshun o the kardee-ovazklur siztum an jinurul faylur o limfatuk funkshunz.[2]

FRAK. Gimme a break!.

SHOWMAN. Gozon. He iz survyft by a sistur n Duluth a muthur n Livurpool an sevrul kuzinz surowndun the Graytur Paduwa ayreea.[3] Aynt that a pekuyleeayritee now? No minshun wutso evur o yu Miztur Frak.[4] Mimoreel donayshunz shud b dyrek-tud n hiz naym 2 the heturo sexshul childrunz fowndayshun n Foolertun.[5] I.e.: he be ded.

FRAK. The king is dead? The king is dead! *(He tries on Frik's hat—much too large)* The king is dead. Hey hey, ha ha, ho ho. Oh no. The king is dead . . .? It's a joke, right?

SHOWMAN. It sezso ryt heer n *The Tymz*.[6]

FRAK. Aw, c'mon. This has gone on long enough. Back to work. I'll start again. O Mister Frik . . . Mister Frik. Come out.

---

[1] A bit added in later years to the traditional Punch and Judy show, replacing the Devil so as not to offend or frighten Victorian-era children. Fortunately, children are much smarter than their authoritarian parents, and they immediately began to cheer on the beast with huge teeth, recognizing it as merely another reincarnation of ravenous Punch himself.

[2] Common euphemisms used to mask the cause of death as AIDS related.

[3] Padua was a rich breeding ground for sixteenth-century *commedia dell'arte* troupes, the ancestors of Punch. Punch has progeny all over the world.

[4] The despicable omission of male-lover survivors remains prevalent in straight newspapers and film/TV industry rags.

[5] Another technique to hide the true cause of an AIDS death is to request donations for causes that have nothing to do with AIDS or queers. Fullerton, California, is a cesspool of fundamental Christianity and neo-Nazi politics.

[6] Any *Times*, but the *L.A. Times*, "a newspaper of record," is often filled with censored obituaries, and AIDS misinformation, presented under the guise of being the gospel truth.

Time to Play. Mister Frik? C'mon. You can't leave me out here alone. Bastard. *(He tries to sing)* Hey ho the derrio. We make you laugh the merrio . . . All right! Okay okay okay. I'm nothing without you. There. Happy now? Hee hee hee hee hee! Frik! Get up here. Quick. *(Mr. Frak desperately searches for Mr. Frik)* Enough nonsense. Get up here, Frik. Please. O Mister Frik, Mister Frak wants to play. Mister Frik? *(Then Mr. Frak realizes the terrible truth)* NOOOOOOOOOOOOOOOO! *(And the hurdy-gurdy goes round and round) ted sod*

satan and simon desoto

author's note

I began writing this play after taking a workshop with Maria Irene Fornes. I knew I wanted to address the threat of censorship that was happening at the time—the Mapplethorpe/Serrano/NEA imbroglio was at its peak—and I knew I wanted to include the religious right's intolerance of homosexuality. The play is also a response to the misery of HIV infection and the odd idiosyncracies of American culture—a culture that can produce a phenomenon like Andrew Dice Clay. How the piece evolved is a mystery. Why I chose the Faust legend is related to the fact that I wanted to refute the misconception that AIDS was God's wrath upon homosexuals. I read excerpts of versions by Marlowe, Dante, Goethe, Mann, Lewis, O'Connor, and Havel, as well as other materials related to the history of Satan. I rewrote and retitled the play when I realized exactly how much of a threat the Christian extremists posed to gay and lesbian people. It seemed that everyday their attacks and propaganda against us grew more intense. I was scandalized by the idea that "Christian" people could indulge in such unconcealed hatred and bigotry and still consider themselves 'saved.' Their ignorance was and is a constant source of anger and bafflement for me. But rather than give myself an ulcer, I kept thinking that if the title character in my play was a homosexual *and* homophobic—maybe, just maybe, some of the latent homophobes in the audience would be less threatened and could ultimately really be 'saved.' In rewriting the piece, I decided to try to raise the stakes without losing any of the dark humor that had emerged, so I began by researching the issues of lying, death and dying, the family, masculinity, and stereotypical humor. I anticipate the play will change some more once it goes into rehearsal. I am, however, pleased with the version you are about to read, but as Rimbaud—or was it Cocteau?—once said: "Art is never completed—it is only abandoned."

performances and productions

Satan and Simon DeSoto has had many different incarnations. A much earlier draft entitled *Crocodile Tears* was performed as a staged reading at Seattle Group Theatre in July 1990, directed by Daniel Sullivan, Artistic Director of Seattle Repertory Theatre, and featured the author in the role of Simon. It was named a finalist in the 1991 Eugene O'Neill Theatre Center's National Playwrights' Conference; the US West New Plays Fest at the Denver Theatre Center; and the New Play Competition at the Mixed Blood Theatre Company in Minneapolis. A workshop production of that version was presented at CalArts Theatre School in Valencia, California, in April 1991. This new version has been substantially rewritten and was selected for development in Portland State University's New Plays Conference. It was a finalist in the 1993 Eugene O'Neill Theatre Center's National Playwrights' Conference; Humboldt State's New Play Season; and the Carnegie Mellon Showcase of New Plays. The author would like to thank Burke Pearson for his unyielding support in the creation of this work; the Washington State and Seattle Arts Commissions; Artist Trust; the Edward Albee Foundation; Ruben Sierra; Daniel Sullivan; and the actors whose craft has helped to shape the piece.

The writing of this play has been funded in part by the Seattle Arts Commission, Artist Trust, and the Edward Albee Foundation.

characters

SIMON DESOTO: late thirties

CARL: under thirty-five

LANA: over thirty-five

JERRY SHECKLER: late twenties

MR. CHESEBRO: over forty

time

Present

setting

Various locations in Seattle

synopsis

A gay man with HIV sells his soul to the Devil.

Author's note: The tempo is brisk. Scenes should overlap, creating a cinematic effect. Please use blackouts judiciously. The disembodied legs are meant to be literally a pair of legs that do the various stage actions called for in the script. I realize this may be impossible without seeing the body of the actor/dancer attached to the legs. If it can't be done by creating a surreal effect, I would suggest cutting it and having a super play some of the necessary roles: waiter, hospital attendant, phlebotomist, etc. The role of Carl can easily be cast with an African or Asian American actor.

act one

Simon walks towards the audience in shadow. Only his mouth is lit—then his face—then his body from the waist up.

SIMON. There's this friend of mine—he's HIV positive—it's not me—don't even begin to think I'm talking about me—and he—this friend—is a performance artist, diagonal slash, playwright, diagonal slash, citizen of the world—very New York, very next wave—very up-and-coming—we're contemporaries—and, recently, he went to have his dreams analyzed—this is not psychotherapy—it's different—and his dream analyst—her name is India or Utah, I forget—told my friend that his dreams indicate that he is completely morbid. That his every sleeping hour is filled with morbid thoughts. When he casually told me this over rice crackers and Evian the other day—I thought to myself—privately—I thought—I'm morbid all the time. Not just in my dreams. My entire thought, diagonal slash, creative, diagonal slash, emotional process is morbid with a capital M. I mean, I walk down the street—I'm on Second Avenue downtown and I see a huge construction site—skyscraper bursting into the sky—and I cross the street. I think some four thousand pound crane or mass of concrete is going to come flying down on me—like what happened to that woman in New York City years ago—do you remember?—her legs were crushed under a construction crane on the Upper East Side—and she survived! Whenever I see a construction site, I see that woman—then I see myself—then I see my legs—just my legs—*(Two legs appear)*—unattached to my body, dancing down First Avenue to the Merchant's Cafe and going in and ordering a gin and tonic to go. Then I see these same disembodied legs—they're shaped exactly like my legs and they're wearing red garters—go into the Kingdome for what appears to be a dance concert for an internationally acclaimed audience of celebrated homosexuals—Harvey Fierstein is there, Gore Vidal, Bill T. Jones, k. d. lang,

Martina—and my legs come out and do this danse maca-
bre—a dance of death—*(The legs dance)*—and all these famous homosexuals are doing this dance of death with me—
it's a very 1960s audience participation show—and the music
hits a crescendo and—bang!—this man in the audience
who's dressed like a Halloween version of Lucifer pops up
in a row way up by the scoreboard and screams: "Get off the
fucking stage, you fraud—you call yourself a performer, diagonal slash, litterateur, diagonal slash, teacher of our young
minds—but you're a homosexual with a capital H. You've
gotten away with more bullshit than any other American
artist, living or dead, and it's time someone put a stop to
it!" Well, most of the homosexuals on the stage think he's
talking to them, but I know he's really talking to me. And
he pulls out this pitchfork (that he happened to have hidden in his briefcase) and he starts to hurl it at me—well, at
my legs—and my legs go running in two different directions—*(The legs run in opposite directions and freeze)*—but the
pitchfork hits my left leg and my right leg freezes and looks
completely lost—completely lost and the entire audience
gasps—my right leg is devastated—grief-stricken—and about
to seek revenge—when this shady character with the satanic
grin starts to pull off his false face—slowly and deliberately,
he peels off one face to reveal another—and it's me. Me.

*The legs run offstage. Blackout. We hear "Fascination" being
played on the accordion. The accordion player's silhouette is
upstage. Full light. Simon is seated, staring out front. Carl is
practicing juggling and Lana is sweeping up coffee beans with a
dustbuster. The half-empty bag of coffee beans is on the table
along with some other groceries.*

SIMON. Stop it, Lana—will you? You're making me crazy with
that noise. *(A beat)* Lana, don't ignore me.
LANA. You'll fall and break your neck.
SIMON. Please leave the coffee beans where they are. You aren't
my housekeeper.
CARL. She's staying here.
LANA. I'm trying to find a place to live, Carl—I wouldn't be here
if I had a choice.

SIMON. Lana, stop . . .

LANA. I like things to be neat.

SIMON. You can deal with it later! *(Lana turns off the dustbuster and sits)* I want you to tell me everything again.

CARL. Not again!

SIMON. *(To Lana)* Start from the beginning and tell me everything. Don't omit anything . . .

LANA. I'll try.

SIMON. I want to hear every detail . . . you understand?

LANA. I understand. I came home from the office for lunch but first I went out shopping for coffee. I'm pulling the beans out of the bag—

SIMON. I was at school, right?

LANA. *(Nodding)* There must've been a hole in it—

SIMON. —Fred was in his apartment, right?

CARL. Will you let her finish the story?

SIMON. Go on, Lana, continue.

LANA. I get back from the QFC and I start to make him a sandwich. Fred is in his apartment doing whatever in God's name it is that he does up there.

CARL. He was watching movies. He always watched movies. How would you spend your day if you had AIDS?

SIMON. He didn't have AIDS—he was HIV positive.

CARL. Wake up, Simon—he had pneumocystis twice—technically, that's class four AIDS.

SIMON. That's your opinion. *(To Lana)* You made him a liverwurst sandwich, right?

LANA. No, I made myself one.

SIMON. You made yourself a liverwurst sandwich and then what?

CARL. Is there any left?

LANA. In the kitchen, go on—take it—I don't want it.

CARL. You eat it.

LANA. How can I eat it after what happened?

SIMON. Wait a minute—you made yourself a liverwurst sandwich and for him—what did you make for him?

CARL. Tuna.

LANA. He hates tuna.

SIMON. *(To Carl)* Don't interrupt, please. What did you make for him, Lana?

LANA. Mozzarella cheese.

CARL. Yum.

SIMON. *(To Carl)* Will you please be quiet!

CARL. I'm hungry.

SIMON. Then go eat!

CARL. Don't tell me what to do—you're not my mother!

SIMON. I'm not telling you what to do—I'm telling you to go eat if you're hungry! Why is that guy playing "Fascination"—doesn't he have any respect for the dead?

LANA. . . . I made him a sandwich and I called him up in his apartment—that's how he wanted me to do it. If he didn't want to be disturbed, he'd let it ring.

SIMON. You called him on the phone and he didn't answer?

CARL. He didn't answer because he jumped out the window.

SIMON. Carl, I want you to go away. I want you to take your juggling paraphernalia and go write your musical about Nancy and her pea pod or whatever.

CARL. I'm not working on *Nancy and the Pea Pod* and you know it. *(To Lana)* His work's important—mine's not . . .

LANA. *(Overlapping on "His")* . . . I let his phone ring and ring and then I figured he didn't want to be disturbed because he didn't answer—right? But after an hour, I got suspicious because he usually calls down in half an hour to chat no matter how he feels . . .

CARL. *(Overlapping on "But")* Mr. Big Deal Seattle Playwright, diagonal slash, Performer, diagonal slash, Teacher Of Our Young Minds can't get his plays produced anywhere else.

SIMON. *(To Carl)* Do you need some attention? Is that your problem?

CARL. My show *Fuzzy Wuzzy Wonderful* is a very successful children's musical in five states and the District of Columbia and you can't stand it.

SIMON. Carl, go away—go visit some of your friends at Disneyland before I strangle you.

LANA. You want the sandwich, Carl? I can wrap it in aluminum foil.

SIMON. Go on, Lana, please. Don't worry about the sandwich.

LANA. At first I hear the sirens, but I ignore them—I figure—it's just a fire—right? So I go into his apartment and I don't see anything—just the window is open and the curtain is askew.

So, I walk over to the window and I look out and the cops and the crowd are squinting up with their hands over their eyes like this. *(She illustrates)* And the building manager is pointing at the windows of Fred's apartment and I wave down like I was being friendly—only nobody responds . . .

CARL. They were in shock.

LANA. The manager's looking up at me like he just saw a train wreck and I'm waving down to him like the village idiot and then all of a sudden I see the commotion—you realize in an instant what's going on. I see the body covered up and the ambulance and I get a horrible sensation all over. *(We hear sirens and see a silhouette of the open window and the curtain askew upstage. The disembodied legs are looking out of it)*

SIMON. And then you saw the note, right?

LANA. The note was on the computer screen.

SIMON. Tell me what it said.

LANA. That he loves us all and that he was in a lot of pain and this is what he had to do to stop the pain. *(Silence. Lana picks up the dustbuster and begins sweeping again)*

SIMON. Please, please, please leave those freakin' coffee beans alone! *(Lana stops. Simon screams at his neighbor)* Will you please stop playing that goddamn song!! We're grieving over here!! *(The accordion stops. The legs and window disappear. Silence)*

LANA. *(To Carl)* My girlfriend Kitty broke her leg in three places slipping on a coffee bean.

SIMON. I don't understand. Fred was so docile—it doesn't seem possible that he would do something so gruesome—does it? I mean, he loved to garden. He loved listening to the opera . . .

CARL. Maybe that's where he got the idea from—people are always dying spectacular deaths in opera. Characters are boiled in oil; they jump into avalanches.

LANA. He was sick. He was going blind from CMV.

CARL. He walked around with his medicine in a Hefty bag.

SIMON. This is the kind of stuff that's supposed to happen in New York—not in Seattle.

LANA. What are you talking about? Seattle has one of the highest suicide rates in the country.

CARL. It's the rain.

LANA. Bullshit—it's the Scandinavians. Why don't you go to bed, Simon? I'll bring you some tea.

CARL. *(A beat. To Simon)* I'm sorry for acting like a shit before. *(No response)* I just can't handle all this repetition and stress. Simon, did you hear me?

SIMON. We should take the test, you know.

CARL. I've taken the test. You're the one who won't go.

SIMON. Just because you've taken the test doesn't mean you're negative.

CARL. Yes, it does.

SIMON. It can turn positive.

CARL. Not if you're safe.

SIMON. Even if you're safe—it can lurk around in your cells and show up twenty years later.

CARL. That's absurd! Who told you that? *(No response)* You've got to stop reading all the trash they print about this disease and get yourself tested—not being tested is just a way for you to avoid dealing with the truth. *(Simon buries his face in a pillow)* I gotta go; we've all gotta be at work early tomorrow . . .

SIMON. Who's going to make the arrangements?

CARL. What arrangements?

SIMON. Someone's got to send the body back to his family.

CARL. The medical examiner's office will take care of that.

SIMON. Will they?

CARL. Don't worry about it. Goodnight. *(Carl kisses Simon and mimes to Lana to get him to sleep. He exits. "Fascination" on the accordion. The legs walk across the stage wearing red high heels and garters. Simon stares at them. Lana picks up the coffee beans by hand)*

SIMON. Why do you think he did this, Lana?

LANA. He was sick—what would you do?

SIMON. Why didn't he say something? No "I'm in trouble"—no "Help me out"—nothing.

LANA. In some countries it's culturally acceptable—Japanese samurai were expected to commit hara-kiri if they disagreed with their superior officers and in India the noblewomen throw themselves on their husbands' funeral pyres . . .

SIMON. Fred wasn't an Indian noblewoman—

LANA. He knew what he was doing, Simon—you can't blame yourself . . .

SIMON. I'm not blaming myself.

LANA. There was no way for you to know. My mother's cousin Reva was married thirty-two years and her husband put his head in an oven. He left a note that said: "Dear Reva: I hate you. Love, Mort. P.S. The dog has to go to the vet—don't miss the appointment or you'll be charged double." She spent the rest of her life in therapy tryin' to figure it out.

Lana exits. Spotlight. Accordion music. A tango. The disembodied legs move downstage with an oversized needle and take a blood sample from Simon's arm. We hear a school bell. Simon addresses the audience as if they were in his classroom.

SIMON. In Jolene's play the father calls Doogie Howser a "fag." Why? *(Looking for a volunteer)* Jolene? Why does the father in your play call this TV character a fag? *(A beat)* Everyday, I hear you kids saying to each other: "So and so is gay"; "Oh, that's so gay"; "You're a faggot—He's a faggot—She's a faggot"—I want to know what everybody's afraid of? *(A beat)* "It's gross." *(A beat)* "It's repulsive." What's gross and repulsive about it? *(A beat)* "It's the work of the devil." *(A beat)* "It's against your religion." Mm-hmm. So what you're saying is, when two people love each other and they happen to be the same sex—that's gross and repulsive. *(A beat)* Why? *(A beat)* "Because they're fags." You're not giving me an answer. Why is it gross and repulsive when two people of the same sex love each other? *(A beat)* "Because they all have AIDS." All homosexuals have AIDS—right, Linda? That's what they teach you in health class? *(A beat)* No, that's not how it all started. They don't know how it started! *(A beat)* I know I'm raising my voice, I'm angry! *(The bell rings. Chesebro enters upstage)* Don't run out!! You have an assignment—I want you to make a list of at least three people who are either gay or lesbian and have made a significant contribution to society. *(A beat)* Yes, there are more than two. *(A beat)* No. No. I said no. *(A beat)* Because there's more examples besides Richard Simmons and Liberace. *(A beat)* Yes, they can be dead. *(A beat)* Go ask the librarian. *(A second bell rings. Sounds of kids in the hallways. Light change)*

MR. C. Can I have a word with you? *(Simon nods. Chesebro hands him a play)* I reviewed this material you're proposing to read in your classes—this is inappropriate.

SIMON. It's about a seventeen-year-old boy who doesn't want to be a virgin.

MR. C. That is not appropriate material for ninth grade students.

SIMON. Why not? The kids see the same kinda thing on TV.

MR. C. All I need is for one fundamentalist parent to complain and I've got the whole school board down my back.

SIMON. I thought we had a separation of church and state in this country?

MR. C. That's not the issue.

SIMON. Then what is?

MR. C. I just got finished telling you—it's not an appropriate choice for the classroom—

SIMON. —And you're the only one who decides what's appropriate?

MR. C. It's my responsibility to look out for the student who's not ready to read a play about sex.

SIMON. It's not about sex! It's about insecurity.

MR. C. I don't care what it's about! Now, either you choose another play or you're going to have to leave the school.

SIMON. This is very democratic. What about the parents who want their kids to read it? Don't they get a say in the matter?

MR. C. If fourteen parents said yes and two said no, we still wouldn't read it.

SIMON. Why? Just because two religious zealots want to pretend their kids never think about sex?

MR. C. Those religious zealots are paying exorbitant amounts in property taxes in order to subsidize your salary, Mr. DeSoto. *(Simon tries to interrupt)* And, incidentally, very few of them are tolerant of homosexuality, so you were completely off base to ask your students to research the names of famous gays and lesbians.

SIMON. Half the kids in this class are homophobic—

MR. C. *(Overlapping on "gays")* Most of the parents at this school want their children to be taught morality and patriotism—

they want role models who avoid idleness, profanity, and falsehoods . . .

SIMON. *(Overlapping on "patriotism")* What about artistic expression? Don't the kids ever get to express themselves creatively?

MR. C. The main function of education in this district is to teach skills in reading, writing, and mathematics in an overall context of traditional Western values . . .

SIMON. *(Overlapping on "mathematics")* Great! We'll have a generation of cultural ignoramuses!

MR. C. *(Moving away)* I'm finished, Mr. DeSoto. If you decide you want to submit your resignation, my secretary will be happy to write you a check.

SIMON. Mr. Chesebro—wait—please. *(A beat)* I'm not accustomed to having my choices challenged by the school principal—okay? So I apologize if I seem a little on edge today. But if you force me to give up this job, the only people who are going to suffer are the kids.

MR. C. . . . I've already explained my position to you. If you are unwilling to accept it, you will have to leave.

SIMON. Fine. I'll leave.

Simon stares at Chesebro. Mr. C. exits. "Teddy Bears Have A Picnic" on the accordion. Carl enters with a picnic lunch. Simon joins him.

SIMON. I went to have the test.

CARL. And?

SIMON. They said I'd have to wait three days.

CARL. And?

SIMON. Three days passed and I called.

CARL. Were you supposed to call?

SIMON. I don't remember. I was curious, so I called.

CARL. Did the doctor answer?

SIMON. No, it was the receptionist. I could feel my heart starting to pound because she said, "I don't know if the results of this test came back yet."

CARL. They're supposed to call you immediately after they hear from the lab.

SIMON. Yeah, well, I jumped the gun. I could hear this state of anxiety in her voice.

CARL. You heard that over the phone?

SIMON. I could hear this "Oh, no, here's that intense, crazy man calling again"-thing in her voice.

CARL. It's your imagination.

SIMON. Maybe it is—but I heard it.

CARL. Did the doctor get on the phone?

SIMON. I knew he was going to. First I heard him whisper, "Did you see where I put that yellow pad?" and then he said, "Hello, Simon? This is Doctor Gill. The results of your test came back positive."

CARL. You tested positive?

SIMON. Yes.

CARL. You tested positive?

SIMON. I just said yes, I tested positive and I don't want anybody else to know.

CARL. Did you tell Lana yet?

SIMON. Yesterday.

CARL. *(He comforts him)* The doctor didn't say anything else? Just "Surprise, dear—you're part of the select club"?

SIMON. He told me I should come in and do a second test so he can check the results. The first test I took was the "inexpensive" one.

CARL. The Western Blot?

SIMON. No, that's the "expensive" one—for Christ's sake, even the inexpensive one is expensive—by the time they're finished, it's gonna cost me three hundred dollars to get a death sentence . . .

CARL. I thought you said you were clean?

SIMON. I did. I never screwed around like Fred and everybody else—always having sex in every back room and bookstore . . .

CARL. Don't bring that up now.

SIMON. But I never did! Those guys were always doing it at peep shows and in the bushes and I've never even been to a fucking bathhouse . . .

CARL. You weren't as innocent as you make yourself sound.

SIMON. I haven't even turned forty yet—I'm supposed to be facing mid-life crisis, not the grim reaper . . .

CARL. Simon, you've been in mid-life crisis since you were ten.

SIMON. Is this supposed to be my entire purpose in life—to be a second-rate artist and die a miserable death in Seattle?

CARL. *(Moving in closer to him)* What if I make you an appointment with an HIV counselor at the AIDS Project—

SIMON. I've already been there. Hand me that piece of chicken—will ya?

CARL. *(He does)* What did they say?

SIMON. What do they always say? He wanted to know if I was still partnered.

CARL. And what did you say?

SIMON. What does it matter what I said?

CARL. What did you say?

SIMON. I said no. *(Carl looks away)* We're not a couple anymore, Carl—you live in your apartment, I live in mine.

CARL. And whose decision was that?

SIMON. Can we please not argue about this now?

CARL. I'm sorry—but you're always so matter-of-fact about it.

SIMON. What else am I supposed to be? It's factual. We don't live together anymore.

CARL. We don't live together anymore because you never wanted to invest the time it takes to work on a relationship—

SIMON. Why is it that whenever I tell somebody I'm HIV positive they start talking about themselves . . .

CARL. I'm not talking about myself—I'm talking about us.

SIMON. This isn't about us—it's about *me*—the Florenz Nightingale at the AIDS Project did the same goddamn thing—I walked in and he starts telling me about his mother's two bouts with leukemia and how he was flying down to San Francisco to get himself pumped up with some experimental drug . . .

CARL. He was trying to ease your pain.

SIMON. What pain??—I'm still too goddamn numb to feel any pain!! *(Silence)* There's got to be something wrong with the Catholic religion. Ever since I was a kid I've been terrified of dying—why don't they just teach us how to accept the inevitable? Instead they have these sexually repressed nuns fill our heads with all these horrific visions of eternal damnation and purgatory . . .

CARL. *(Overlapping on "damnation")* You're not supposed to be afraid of dying because you were a good soul and God will reward you.

SIMON. God—there's a Hollywood concept. We're supposed to believe in this divine higher power whose every action has some grandiose purpose behind it? Explain to me why God wants people to die a despicable, relentless death? It's a goddamn conspiracy so we won't riot in the streets.

CARL. *(A beat. Kissing him)* Move back in with me.

SIMON. Carl, don't . . .

CARL. Why not?

SIMON. I love you but I can't live with you.

CARL. You're going to need the company. What if you get sick?

SIMON. I've got Lana.

CARL. What if she moves out? What if she finally gives up on you turning straight?

SIMON. Carl—please!

CARL. Forget it.

Carl exits. Simon moves to his apartment and turns on the TV. We hear "Fascination" on the accordion and the sound of the television simultaneously. Dr. Rook is seen floating inside a TV screen upstage. The disembodied legs enter with an array of pills as if selling cigarettes in a nightclub. Simon spends part of the scene downing them with water, then moves to a sofa and reads. Lana enters with a basket of laundry and begins folding it. She does not see the legs.

LANA. Why are you taking all those pills?

SIMON. It's part of my therapy—

LANA. You're going to overdose.

SIMON. I'm not going to overdose. Dr. Rook knows what he's doing—

LANA. How can he know what he's doing? He's on public access!

SIMON. So?

LANA. I can't believe you put your trust in someone named Dr. Rook—

SIMON. He's got 270 patients from all over the United States and everyone has improved 100 percent on this treatment.

LANA. Have you talked to any of these patients?

SIMON. Lana, please don't be ridiculous.

LANA. Anybody can write up a dossier saying they've been successful, Simon—how much does all this stuff cost?

SIMON. Don't worry about it—I'm charging it on VISA.

LANA. Is this like the ozone therapy you went for?

SIMON. I've got a killer virus inside of me and I'm going to do whatever it takes to get rid of it.

LANA. Carl told me you were planning to consult the sacred powers of a Lakota Yuwipi medicine man . . .

SIMON. Western medicine is toxic and overpriced.

LANA. What the hell are you talking about?! You spent over a thousand dollars on a rectal ozone machine to blow hot air up your ass.

SIMON. It's my money—I'll go in debt any way I want!

LANA. You should be enjoying your life, Simon—If I was you, I'd go on a world-class cruise, I'd put myself on a slow boat to Tahiti.

SIMON. Ultraviolet light causes the virus to replicate.

LANA. So, go to Alaska! You're spending so much time worrying about dying, you might as well be dead.

SIMON. Part of me is dead, Lana. I can't read a book or eat a meal without contemplating the fact that I may be sick in a week.

LANA. *(Overlapping on "sick")* Simon, I want to tell you a story. When Abraham the patriarch was dying, his last thoughts were for his kids—

SIMON. *(Overlapping on "dying")* Please don't preach to me about the Old Testament now—it has absolutely no bearing on what's happening to me.

LANA. *(Overlapping on "bearing")* It has everything to do with what's happening to you—shut up and listen! When Jesus Christ got resurrected, it screwed up everybody's attitude towards death—you know why?—because nobody ever thought about the separation of the body and soul before that—it was all one thing. You lived and you died. All anybody cared about was the destiny of their clan. And that's the way I think we should still think about it. Like it was in the Old Testament. We only get one chance—we all got to die—we never come back—so have a good time while you're here and maybe your friends and your family will remember you. *(Carl enters from another room with a letter in hand)*

CARL. What is this?

SIMON. What is what, Carl? I'm not a psychic.

CARL. What is this letter? *(Reading)* "Dear Satan, I'm a student of Dr. Rook's—I find his theories about your identity fascinating—I am very interested in negotiating with you . . ."

SIMON. *(Screaming at his neighbor)* Hey! Could you please lay off with the freaking accordion already? *(The accordion stops. The upstage TV screen and the legs disappear)* There. Thank God—everyday it's like I'm in Warsaw—is that guy Polish or what?

CARL. Simon, I'm talking to you.

LANA. He's in a polka band. Let him practice.

SIMON. I feel like I'm trapped in *Love in the Afternoon*. I feel like Gary Cooper and that band of gypsies who play "Fascination" . . .

CARL. *(Overlapping on "Cooper")* I want an answer from you, Simon—what is this?

SIMON. You shouldn't be rummaging through my personal property, Carl.

CARL. It was in the magazine rack in the bathroom. Are you writing letters to Satan now?

SIMON. Yes, I am.

CARL. *(To Lana)* Aren't you concerned about this? Now he's into Satan worship.

SIMON. Carl, please don't push the panic button. I'm not conducting black masses or indulging in voodoo—I haven't cut off any chicken's heads—I simply composed a letter to Satan.

CARL. Why have you composed a letter to Satan? Is this supposed to be one of your new bogus cures?

SIMON. They're not bogus! Dr. Rook is convinced that this is a man-made virus that was deliberately placed in homosexuals by the American government.

CARL. And you've completely accepted his hypothesis?

SIMON. He's got recorded proof that somebody in a CIA laboratory combined the sheep visna virus with the bovine leukemia virus and created HIV.

LANA. I believe it.

CARL. Don't encourage him!

SIMON. I know what you're thinking, Carl—you're thinking how can anybody take this AIDS huckster seriously—but Dr. Rook's philosophy makes a lot of sense to me. He believes that a supernatural force is the only thing large enough to combat a menace of this magnitude.

CARL. And now you're writing letters to Satan like he was Dear Abby?

SIMON. His whole theory is that we've gotta give up all the stuff that's been driven into our heads about how evil the devil is—that it's an invention of monotheist religions to keep us in our place. And he's convinced that a lot of historical personalities have bargained with Satan over the years without any of the dire consequences we always read about in the Faust legends.

CARL. Like who? What historical personalities?

SIMON. Ava Gardner. Eleanor Roosevelt.

LANA. Only women? What is this Dr. Rook, a misogynist?

CARL. You expect us to believe that Eleanor Roosevelt sold her soul to the devil?

SIMON. Evidently, when she found out about FDR's affair with Lucy, her social secretary, she struck up a bargain with Satan and had him stricken with polio.

LANA. And that's not supposed to be evil?

SIMON. He was fucking around on her! It was right after he got polio that she made a life for herself. She got a job teaching, became a champion of women's rights—

CARL. You're really committed to all this, aren't you?

SIMON. You were committed to your juggling while it lasted.

CARL. I hardly think Satanism and juggling can be compared, Simon.

SIMON. This isn't Satanism! It's an alternative holistic approach to healing—

CARL. It's another obsession! You should be going for legitimate medical treatment—not fantasizing about selling your soul to some benevolent devil.

SIMON. I'm taking my herbal potions—that's enough treatment.

CARL. Vitamins aren't enough to kill the AIDS virus. You need to be on drugs.

LANA. Carl—I've already been through this with him over a hundred times . . .

CARL. Quit protecting him!

LANA. I'm not protecting him. Who's protecting him?

CARL. He's gone off the deep end and you're promoting it.

SIMON. There was a government plot in this country that wanted all of us homosexuals dead—and it got out of control—doesn't that make complete sense to you?

CARL. No, it doesn't make complete sense to me—the government wanted the homosexuals dead but not the lesbians?

SIMON. Lesbians are being infected, too.

LANA. What Carl's trying to say is, we just don't want you to put all your faith in this one doctor's ideas. Maybe you should be on AZT.

SIMON. AZT, ddI, and ddC all sound like pesticides—I'm not putting that poisonous shit into my mouth.

CARL. Then you're going to die!

SIMON. You don't understand what I'm going through, Carl—I'm the one who's Typhoid Mary—not you!

CARL. I'm trying to understand but you keep pushing me away.

SIMON. I'm not pushing you away! Everybody who gets this fucking disease winds up looking like a pain-riddled skeleton and I don't want to end up with my brains splattered all over the sidewalk like Fred did—okay?! *(Silence)*

LANA. Nobody in America can deal with death anymore. Nobody's prepared for it. When somebody died in the old days it used to happen at home—not in the hospital, or in some retirement village, or, God forbid, on the sidewalk. It's just not the same anymore—nobody wants to confront it. I spent twelve hours at home when my grandmother died—I've spent more time shopping for shoes.

CARL. Simon, I care about you.

LANA. We both do—we don't want to lose you.

CARL. Please go to see a professional and I promise I'll get off your back.

SIMON. Give me the letter. *(Carl hesitates)* Give me the letter. *(Simon takes it and rips it up)* I don't think you two understand what's going on with me. Everyday, I wake up and I wonder how much more time I have—I feel like I'm walking down this narrow hallway and there's no lights—it's completely black and somewhere out there there's no floor. I keep creeping along, inching along step by step and sooner or later I'm gonna free-fall—I'm gonna fall down this well and never come up for air.

A beat. They embrace. Supernatural sounds on the accordion. The disembodied legs walk across the stage wearing skeleton suit and high heels. Simon watches them. Carl and Lana exit the stage. Mr. Chesebro enters from the opposite side.

MR. C. I've received several messages lately saying you were anxious to chat with me.

SIMON. There must be some mistake. I've never contacted you.

MR. C. *(Taking letter out of his pocket)* Something about "a series of misfortunes in your life"; needing "assistance in turning your circumstances around."

SIMON. *(Grabbing letter)* How did you get this, Mr. Chesebro? I destroyed this letter myself.

MR. C. It was faxed to me. The underworld has a state-of-the-art communication system, Mr. DeSoto. *(A beat)* Boo.

SIMON. This isn't working out the way I expected it to.

MR. C. Who was it you were anticipating? Beelzebub on a broomstick?

SIMON. I wasn't anticipating anyone . . . I convinced myself I was being foolish.

MR. C. The important thing is that I'm here—don't you think? Why don't you sit down and tell me all about these "misfortunes" of yours.

SIMON. Just like that? I'm supposed to sit down and launch into a speech about my situation?

MR. C. I'm not a visiting psychologist, Mr. DeSoto. I've got a lot to accomplish today and I don't have time to dick around with a bunch of bullshit pleasantries.

SIMON. I want proof.

MR. C. What would you like to see me do—levitate?

SIMON. I want proof that you are who you say you are. Dr. Rook never said anything about a junior high school principal from the suburbs.

MR. C. Fine. Turn on the TV and I'll show you the video of the first time you were infected.

SIMON. *(Startled)* You have that on videotape?

MR. C. I just got finished saying I did. What makes all you artists so skeptical?

SIMON. How is that possible? How can you have an intensely private moment like that on tape?

MR. C. You're dealing with the supernatural, Mr. DeSoto—anything is possible. According to our records, you've been infected three times by two different sex partners. I have the first two trysts on tape. *(During the above, Mr. C. takes a tape out of his briefcase and puts it on. Simon watches intently. The audio is sounds of lovemaking. We see two nude male bodies in silhouette mime the action upstage)*

SIMON. I can't see any of the faces—all I can see is genitalia.

MR. C. Be patient—you'll be on in a second. Sweet little apartment you've got here—did you decorate it yourself or did you have help?

SIMON. *(Watching with increased concentration)* This isn't me. This isn't me at all. This is Fred's old place in Brooklyn Heights. *(A beat)* Wait a minute—that's Carl. That's Carl about to have sex with Fred—

MR. C. Ooops. Wrong clip. *(Ejecting it. The action upstage stops/rewinds)* I keep asking them for a better filing system. *(Going to his briefcase and getting a different tape)* Sorry about that.

SIMON. *(Overlapping on "clip")* Hold it—wait—stop—put that back on—I want to see what happens.

MR. C. I'm sorry, but that would be an invasion of Carl's privacy.

SIMON. Does this mean Carl's actually infected?

MR. C. I'm sorry, Mr. DeSoto, but I'm not allowed to answer any questions about anybody else's sexual history. *(Putting on another tape)* Here we go—this should be of you. *(We hear different lovemaking sounds on the audio. Two different silhouettes are seen)*

SIMON. *(Moving his attention to the TV)* I remember this. This is the studio Carl and I lived in in the Village.

MR. C. Recognize the guy you're with? You picked him up in a laundromat on Sixth Avenue.

SIMON. What year was this?

MR. C. Nineteen eighty-four. Carl was visiting his mother in Detroit. You suspected him of cheating on you, so you decided to have yourself a little fling.

SIMON. We're not using any protection—I don't think I want to watch this.

MR. C. Of course you're not using protection—Nobody seriously started using protection until Rock Hudson died. *(Getting excited)* Mmmm. Yum-yum—here come the poppers from under the pillowcase!

SIMON. *(Moving away)* I don't think I want to watch any more of this—this is making me feel very queasy.

MR. C. Relax!! How could you have restrained yourself? Look at him. He's very cute. He's very well built. And you're a very sensual person. I don't see how you could have resisted the temptation.

SIMON. What's this guy's name? Do you know?

MR. C. *(Reading the video case label)* Byron. Byron Kaminski. Died last April. Cryptococcal meningitis.

SIMON. Shut it off. Shut it off, please. I'm finished watching.

MR. C. When you get an itch—you've got to scratch it.

SIMON. Shut it off! *(Simon snaps off the TV. Mr. C. ejects the tape and throws it into his briefcase. A beat)* When am I supposed to die? Do you know?

MR. C. Three years from today. Lymphoma. I have some Polaroids of you in the last stages of the disease—care to see them?

SIMON. No, thank you.

MR. C. I can give you a preview of your memorial service—Lana forgets to mail the invitations—only fifteen people show up.

SIMON. I'll pass. How is it that Dr. Rook never mentions this power you have to preview the past and the future for people?

MR. C. Rook is a shill. His sole purpose is to get you to write. Once you express an interest, our organization goes out of its way to accommodate your needs.

SIMON. Organization?

MR. C. It's based loosely on the pyramid principle. You've heard of Amway? Same idea. Anyone who's benefited from our services in the past is required to assist newcomers like yourself.

SIMON. Which means what—you're only an emissary and not really Satan?

MR. C. Satan? Satan isn't a person—it's a mental image. Every attribute we assign to the devil is a human conception. Mr. DeSoto—

SIMON. *(Overlapping on "conception")* I want you to tell me why I was infected.

MR. C. Why? Because you had sex with the wrong people.

SIMON. No, that's not why—that's how—I want to know why—what the purpose is.

MR. C. You picked up a virus that's been going around forever. Call it AIDS, call it influenza—I don't care—and you were chosen to succumb to it.

SIMON. Chosen by whom?

MR. C. By yourself—who else? I believe each of us dies the death we've made for ourselves—tell me how you die and I'll tell you who you are. *(A wink)* I'm prepared to discuss a business transaction if you think you're ready to sign an agreement . . .

SIMON. I'm sorry, Mr. Chesebro—I can't go through with this—

MR. C. Why? What's the problem?

SIMON. You can't expect me to blithely invest what's left of my life in something I don't totally comprehend.

MR. C. What is it you don't comprehend? You know you're infected and you know you've got three years left to live. Either you want to die or you don't.

SIMON. And this is the only alternative I have? Either I die a hateful death or I sell my soul to the man who fired me?

MR. C. I know what you're going through, Simon. Twenty-five years ago I was an outsider just like you are now. *(A beat. We hear accordion music. A song from the '60s)* The summer before my junior year at college, my mother insisted I walk up to the home of the richest family in town and ask for a job—the butler unceremoniously slammed the door in my face. But I kept at it. Every day for three weeks I knocked at that door. Finally, they gave in and hired me to teach their kids how to sail. One of those kids, a boy about eleven, drowned in a boating accident during a terrible electrical storm. I was accused of negligence and tried for involuntary manslaughter. I had to leave school. Give up my career. It was in prison that I started to realize that Satan and the forces of the underworld were within my grasp. I wrote letters just like you did. I went to secret meetings. I talked to everyone about how my life had been altered because of an "accident." How the "accident" was something completely out of my control. People listened politely but they couldn't do anything. I was helpless. A few months later I was hitching a ride on an open stretch of highway in Massachusetts and got picked up by a woman wearing red garters. She was driving a Dodge Dart—seemed to know everything about me. She offered me an arrangement just like the one I'm offering you now. I accepted and turned my life around. It was the best thing I've ever done for myself.

SIMON. What kind of arrangement?

MR. C. *(As if by magic: a soft sell)* Here. Here's a contract. Take your time. Look it over. In the event that you are able to complete the three tasks that are mentioned in paragraph two—and that I will outline for you in minute detail—you will be free of the AIDS virus completely and you will no longer be classified as HIV positive. *(Simon peruses it. We hear "Fascination" on the accordion)*

SIMON. What are the tasks?

MR. C. It doesn't work that way. First you finish number one and then I'll tell you number two.

SIMON. You're asking me to enter into a binding agreement and I can't even know the terms?

MR. C. I'm asking you to have faith in the system. They're not my rules—I didn't make them up.

SIMON. What's the first task?

MR. C. *(Handing him a paper)* Memorize this material. Present yourself as a professional comic on Friday night at nine o'clock at Giggle's Comedy Club.

SIMON. You want me to do stand-up?

MR. C. You've been in front of an audience before—you'll do fine.

SIMON. *(Reading)* Wait a minute—these jokes aren't funny— these jokes are stupid—

MR. C. *(Retrieving the papers)* Are you telling me you don't want to enter into this agreement now?

SIMON. No.

MR. C. Then what's the obstacle? *(A beat)* What's the obstacle, Simon? *(No response)* All your life you've struggled for a little recognition, haven't you? *(Simon nods)* Has anyone important ever acknowledged your talent? *(Simon shakes his head)* And now your life is being taken over by this "accident"— this freak of nature—you've never really had a break, have you? *(Simon shakes his head)* Well, I'm offering you one now. *(Chesebro hands him a pen)* Don't agonize over it, Simon. You're going to be fabulous.

Accordion music stops. Mr. C. watches Simon as he signs the contract. We hear a voiceover announce: "Ladies and gentlemen, Giggles is proud to present—Simon DeSoto!" Drumroll. The legs run a follow spot on stage. Simon is tentative. His reaction is incredulous when the audience responds.

SIMON. Why are Chinese and black faggots so much alike? They both give "bro jobs." How come they don't hire queers at the sperm bank? Too many get caught drinkin' on the job. Is it better to be black or gay? Black. You don't have to tell your mother. What's worse than gettin' kissed by a fag with AIDS? Gettin' a blow job from a cannibal. What do you call three lesbians in bed together? A ménage à twat. How can you tell when you're in a gay bar? All the bar stools are turned upside down. Why do Negros have sex on the brain? Because their heads are covered with pubic hair. Why are Jewish kids so fucking obnoxious? Heredity. What's the ultimate Jewish dilemma? Free bacon. Why did God create women? He couldn't find a sheep to give him a blow job. Why wasn't Christ born in Mexico? They couldn't find three wise men and a virgin. What's the most popular Puerto Rican antiperspirant? Unemployment. "There once was a faggot named Fred, Who loved to get fucked in his bed. He picked up gay blades, Who were infected with AIDS—Now Fred isn't fuckin'—he's dead." *(Whistles and wild applause. Chants of "Simon, Simon!" Simon looks dazed. He runs off stage to a dressing room area. Light change. Mr. C. enters with Jerry who is dressed in L.A. chic)*

SIMON. I don't like this, Mr. C., I don't like doing this at all. I'm not cut out to be a hate comic.

MR. C. Hate comic? Who called you a hate comic?—you're not a hate comic—you're a folklorist—

SIMON. I thought I could allow myself to say these jokes, but I can't.

MR. C. What are you talking about—listen to that crowd—they're still goin' crazy!

SIMON. If this is what I have to do in order to be clean—I'm backing out.

MR. C. Hey! Everyone in that audience was with you tonight. You were spectacular! *(To Jerry)* Tell him.

JERRY. You were excellent. It's a great act—great material.

MR. C. Tell him again or he won't believe you.

JERRY. You were spectacular—it's the best show I've seen in ages.

MR. C. In all your years as a playwright—have you ever gotten such a response?

SIMON. I don't write this kind of trash.

MR. C. Trash? Why is it trash? Because the audience laughed at every line? Those jokes are funny, Simon—and jokes are the only honest art form left.

SIMON. They're funny at somebody else's expense.

MR. C. Let me tell you something—people all over this country are frustrated and would love to tell their neighbors to go get fucked but they can't—so, they're payin' you good money to do it instead.

SIMON. I can see it now. There's going to be five hundred radical fairies boycotting me outside this club tomorrow night.

MR. C. Pray that they do—it sells tickets. Right, Jerry? As a matter of fact, I'll hire some faggots to do it myself. It'll be good for business.

SIMON. What about the critics? Aren't you concerned about the critics?

MR. C. It's not the critics' mundane opinion you should be worried about—it's their ability to pinpoint the salient aspects of what you're presenting.

SIMON. What salient aspects?

MR. C. I'll explain it to you later. Simon—this is my friend and associate, Jerry Sheckler. He flew in just to catch your act.

JERRY. You were spectacular. I've never seen anything like it.

MR. C. Thank him—he just paid you a compliment.

SIMON. *(Reluctant)* Thank you. *(They shake hands. Simon stares at Jerry)* You know, you're not going to believe this—but I feel like I know you. Have you ever been on cable TV? *(Jerry cracks up)*

MR. C. Jerry's livin' in L.A. now. He wants to represent you.

SIMON. Represent me? How?

MR. C. What do you mean, how? Don't be a rube. He's an agent from L.A.

SIMON. You're an agent from L.A.? *(Jerry nods)* What agency are you with?

JERRY. C.A.A. Mike Ovitz.

SIMON. Mike Ovitz?? He's the biggest! He runs Hollywood!

JERRY. Mr. C.'s got great connections.

SIMON. Wait a minute—you're with the most powerful agency in the world and you come up to Seattle to scout for talent?

JERRY. Why not? Jimi Hendrix and Bruce Lee came out of Seattle.

MR. C. Look, what we need to do now is set up a time for you to videotape your act, then Jerry here can take it down with him to L.A. Or better yet—maybe we'll fly you down there so you can do it for Mike and the rest of the office live.

SIMON. *(To Chesebro, sotto voce)* What about the Jewish jokes? Aren't they going to be offended by the Jewish jokes?

MR. C. No! They don't give a fuck as long as it makes money. The milk and cookies with a picket fence kind of entertainment doesn't cut it anymore, Simon. Modern comics are cerebral strippers and their jokes are live grenades.

SIMON. This is happening too fast—I don't think I can keep up with this.

MR. C. It's under control—what do you think you have a manager for? C'mon, I'll take you kids out for a drink.

JERRY. Great—I'm parched. *(Winking at Simon)* All that screaming and whistling after every joke.

MR. C. *(Moving towards door)* C'mon, Simon—it'll be our treat.

SIMON. This is all part of it, isn't it?

MR. C. Part of what?

SIMON. This is all part of the moral bankruptcy I have to go through to get rich and famous.

MR. C. *(Overlapping on "have")* Part of what moral bankruptcy? What the hell are you babbling about?

SIMON. I sign a contract with you to say some hateful jokes and I get rich and famous in return.

MR. C. Simon, Simon, listen—when LBJ was president of the United States, one of his aides—Walter—*(To Jerry)*—what was his name?

JERRY. Jenkins.

MR. C. Walter Jenkins, this high-echelon aide, got busted for giving blow jobs in a D.C. men's room—in a matter of hours, gay jokes were being told all over the country—same thing happened with Jeffrey Dahmer and everytime Dan Quayle opened his mouth. People joke about what scares them. Where there's anxiety, there's laughter. You're simply offering your audience a release from their daily tensions—don't make it into such a big deal. C'mon, let's go, before I get dehydrated. *(He starts to leave)* Simon?

SIMON. I have to change my socks.

MR. C. *(Mr. C. motions for Jerry to go)* Go on, Jerry—I'll catch up with you. *(A beat. To Simon)* I want you to know that what you did up on that stage tonight was absolutely exceptional. I'm very proud of you. You're an incredibly talented man. *(A beat)* Do you believe me? *(No response)* Do you believe me?

SIMON. Sort of. I don't know.

MR. C. Jokes about certain ethnic, social or religious groups are a simple, innocuous outlet for people to express their pent-up feelings. Don't take it so personally. Hey, if you want to back out—you can back out—all right?

SIMON. All right.

MR. C. C'mon, we'll be waiting for you outside. Jerry's limo's parked on Roosevelt.

SIMON. He's got a limo?

MR. C. Of course he's got a limo. He's a high roller from L.A., what did you expect? *(He exits. Simon is alone. He repeats one of the jokes from the act. Lana and Carl walk in and catch Simon off guard)*

SIMON. Hi. *(A beat)* I already know what you're going to say—so you can spare yourself the trouble . . .

CARL. Is this supposed to be part of your black magic act or have you gone completely crazy?

SIMON. No one invited you, Carl.

CARL. What makes you think intelligent people want to hear that shit?

SIMON. I'm not doing it for intelligent people.

CARL. I thought you hated anti-gay comedians?

SIMON. I did.

CARL. What do you mean you *did?* All of a sudden it's politically acceptable?

SIMON. That was before I realized I might be able to get somewhere being one.

CARL. You expect to get somewhere spewing that sewage about gays and blacks?

LANA. What about all the stuff about women and Jews?

SIMON. It was a theatrical experiment, okay?

CARL. You're experimenting by being a racist pig?

SIMON. Lighten up—will you please? The audience thought it was funny.

LANA. The audience is all under twenty, they'd laugh at a car accident.

CARL. Tell me something, Simon—how do you intend to explain your homophobia to people?

SIMON. Carl, get off my back—you don't understand what I'm trying to achieve.

CARL. What *are* you trying to achieve? Isn't it bad enough straight people already think faggots are to blame for the whole epidemic without you fanning the fire?

LANA. *(To Carl)* Don't lump me in with the rest of the world just because I'm straight . . .

SIMON. Maybe they are.

CARL. Maybe they are *what?*

SIMON. Maybe they are to blame. That's how I got infected.

CARL. This is fucking scandalous! I should pick up the goddamn phone and get ACT UP to go crazy outside this club every night.

SIMON. Go 'head—do it—it'll be good for business.

CARL. I don't believe you! You are a self-loathing, homophobic hypocrite!

SIMON. And you're self-righteous queen, Carl. You're jealous because I had an audience laughing at me all night and you didn't . . .

CARL. *(To Lana)* Can you believe this? This is the man I was involved with for over five years—*(To Simon)* What the hell is wrong with you!?

SIMON. Nothing is wrong with me! I'm finally taking control of my life. And if you were smart you'd go back and have yourself tested again—I happen to know about your sexual exploits with Fred.

CARL. Fred who? What the fuck are you talking about?

SIMON. Don't play innocent—I have proof.

CARL. Proof of what!? Are you inventing lies about the dead now to enhance your self-deception? *(No response)* This is revolting. C'mon, Lana, I'm leaving. *(He exits)*

SIMON. Carl!—Carl, get back here—I'm not finished!!—Carl!!!— *(To Lana)*—You see how he runs away from me?—He can't stand to hear the truth—

LANA. What's this about him and Fred?

SIMON. He knows what I'm talking about—always acting holier-than-thou—he's just as hypocritical as I am—always giving me shit about everything I try.

LANA. I don't understand what this act is all about either, Simon.

SIMON. I didn't write the jokes—I only said them.

LANA. Why? Why did you say them?

SIMON. I'm gettin' paid a quarter of the door plus five hundred bucks a night if I bring in over four hundred people—that's a lotta dough, Lana. I know it's ugly shit I have to say, but how the fuck am I supposed to pay for state-of-the-art experimental treatments if I can't afford them?

LANA. Simon, there's something wrong with what you're doin' here. You got to be doin' this for more reasons than money. At first I thought, oh, he's going to make a point about how screwed up our society is, but you didn't—you just kept bringin' up stereotype after stereotype and the baboons in the audience kept on laughin' at you. I don't want to get into a feminist diatribe here but I'm watching you and I finally realized a woman would never make up any of that shit you were sayin' on stage tonight.

SIMON. I'm sorry if I offended you. I'll try to tone it down, okay?

Lana exits. We hear "Hooray for Hollywood" on the accordion as underscoring. Light change. Simon joins Mr. C. and Jerry at lunch.

MR. C. Tone it down and you renege on our deal. Look, Simon, if you're going to back out of our agreement I want to know right now—are you in or out?

SIMON. I'm in. All I'm asking is, why does it have to be so blatant? Can't it be a little bit more subtle?

MR. C. We've already discussed this. Jokes don't create society—they only reflect it. If the mirror image is ugly—why break the mirror?

JERRY. There's a deep human need to think in stereotypical terms.

SIMON. Not for everybody.

MR. C. Some stereotypical exaggeration may be false, I grant you—but it's aesthetically necessary to make the point.

SIMON. What point?

MR. C. That people need to separate themselves from the others.

SIMON. What kind of battle are we fighting here? I mean, I understand I'm supposed to do these three tasks and all—but I'm not quite sure what it is that I'm trying to accomplish for you.

MR. C. There's a fundamentalist cultural and religious conflict gearing up in this country and in some peoples' minds it's going to be the cause of the next civil war—

JERRY. Just like in Belfast or Beirut.

SIMON. And you two are associated with the fundamentalists?

MR. C. The fundamentalist population is important to us—yes.

JERRY. We make a lot of choices in Hollywood based on the religious right profile.

SIMON. And that's why you've got me telling the jokes?

JERRY. *(Nodding)* Negative stereotypes of the enemy enhance a sense of moral righteousness—we've done our research.

SIMON. Who's the enemy—people of color and queers?

MR. C. Anybody who isn't like them. Here's the waiter—decide what you're eating for lunch. *(The disembodied legs approach the table as if they were the waiter serving drinks. We hear a Muzak version of "Fascination")*

SIMON. *(To legs)* I'll have the black cod and a glass of fume blanc. I still don't understand, Mr. C. Why did you choose me to be associated with these particular people?

MR. C. Every set of tasks is specifically designed to test the person who's requested help from our organization.

JERRY. We involved the fundamentalists in your case because it seemed like the perfect match.

SIMON. You know what they're trying to do? They're trying to pass hate bills in states all over the country . . .

MR. C. We know all about it. That's part of your challenge.

JERRY. You can't allow yourself to be overwhelmed by self-righteous indignation everytime you complete one of these tasks, Simon.

MR. C. You've got to stop caring about the artistic value of your work.

SIMON. This isn't about the artistic value of my work! I should be fighting these people—these people you've got me proselytizing for want all of us queers to be obliterated.

MR. C. I'm not going to waste any more of my time or Jerry's, if you can't be 100 percent committed to this contract.

SIMON. I'm committed—it just seems perverse to be working for the opposite side . . .

MR. C. I'm asking you for the last time—are you in or out?

SIMON. I'm in. I'm in. I can do it. I was just trying to understand *why* you were asking me to say those things.

MR. C. Good. *(A beat)* Jerry sent the tape down to L.A. and Ovitz loved it. He thinks we can get a cable deal or a series on Fox . . .

SIMON. He loved it?

MR. C. Of course he loved it. Lesson number one—stop demeaning yourself.

JERRY. He watched it twice—that's unheard of.

MR. C. The power brokers made a few observations about your performance.

JERRY. They think we need to soften your face and butch up your voice.

SIMON. What's wrong with my voice?

JERRY. Ovitz says it comes over "light."

SIMON. Light?

MR. C. Queer.

SIMON. I am a queer—that's probably why.

MR. C. You've got to work on it. It makes people nervous. A traditional audience expects men to behave in formulaic ways—tough, aggressive, cutthroat and so on . . .

JERRY. Male performers have to embrace behavior associated with domination, competition, and violence. Tenderness, emotional intimacy, self-disclosure are all connected with women.

SIMON. Should I be taking notes?

MR. C. Jerry's recording the session—we'll give you a cassette after lunch.

JERRY. They've also decided you have to change your name.

SIMON. To what?

JERRY. Simon Seyz. S-E-Y-Z.

SIMON. What's wrong with DeSoto?

MR. C. This keeps them guessing about your background. Why do you think Andrew Dice Clay changed his name from Silverstein?

JERRY. And they want you to get married.

SIMON. Married? Why?

JERRY. Everybody working in L.A. needs a cover.

SIMON. But I'm not going to be in L.A.

MR. C. You don't know that for sure.

JERRY. Your life is going to be under intense scrutiny. Don't give the tabloids any fodder.

SIMON. Is this supposed to be one of my tasks?

MR. C. This is number two. You'll be halfway there.

SIMON. I don't think I can manage this one, Mr. Chesebro.

JERRY. It's not as difficult as it sounds.

MR. C. Listen to what Jerry has to say—he had to do it himself.

SIMON. *(To Jerry)* That means you're gay, right?

MR. C. Simon! You don't ask somebody from L.A. a personal question like that.

SIMON. Why not? I thought we were having a personal conversation.

JERRY. It's all right, Mr. C. *(To Simon, sotto voce)* I like to keep my private life private. If the cable deal goes through you're going to be in a highly visible position. You've got to learn how to protect yourself. We want you to be regarded as strictly heterosexual.

SIMON. What for?

MR. C. Don't be naive. American culture puts homosexuals down.

JERRY. You don't want to be labeled a fag. If you're labeled a fag, you won't be able to compete inside the power structure.

SIMON. Who am I supposed to marry? I haven't been with a woman since the high school prom.

MR. C. Jerry and I think you should approach your friend Lana.

SIMON. *(Incredulous)* You want me to marry Lana?

MR. C. Hasn't she had a soft spot for you ever since you met her at college?

SIMON. Yeah, but she'll know I'm being dishonest—

MR. C. So what? This is about your survival, Simon—survival alone counts—what you've got going here is a battle against your own personal extinction and you've got to learn how to lie.

JERRY. It worked for me.

MR. C. I want you to think of yourself as both your own lawyer and client. You know why? Because the main function of a lawyer is to lie for his client. Besides, society is already in a state of collapse and your lying to Lana isn't going to add to the chaos, believe me.

JERRY. My wife was employed as a parking attendant at the Getty Museum when I approached her—she's never once questioned my motives.

MR. C. *(A beat)* Personally, I don't understand this whole gay thing. I don't see how you could choose to find somebody else's cock appealing.

SIMON. It's not something you choose, Mr. C.

MR. C. That can be debated. I've read all the theories about what makes people gay—genetics, prenatal factors, variations in brain structure—and I'll tell you from firsthand experience—this is not bias—my brother was gay—and he wasn't treated any differently than I was when we were growing up. The reason he was gay was because he chose to evade responsibility. Left two beautiful kids and a wife for a traffic cop in Marina Del Ray. Then died of AIDS—one of the first. As far as I'm concerned, homosexuality is a form of arrested adolescence.

SIMON. *(A beat)* Can I ask you something about our deal? *(Mr. C. and Jerry nod)* If I were to get Lana to marry me, we'd be able to have an ordinary sex life just like any two typical straight people—right?

MR. C. Right.

SIMON. *(To Jerry)* Do you have sex with your wife?

JERRY. As often as she likes.

SIMON. So basically you're straight now?

JERRY. Basically, yes.

SIMON. How do you control your urges?

MR. C. He doesn't give into them. It's just misinformed lust, Simon.

SIMON. You don't ever want to have sex with men?

JERRY. Of course I do, but I'd rather control those urges. It's a very powerful feeling.

MR. C. Being a man is a powerful feeling. You're both relearning how to be men.

JERRY. When I found out I was HIV positive, I gave up sex for over a year. When I started up again with my wife—it was like finding an oasis in the Mojave.

SIMON. You tested positive?

JERRY. Once upon a time. I'm clean now. I fulfilled my three tasks.

SIMON. Was one of them becoming an agent?

MR. C. Simon!

SIMON. Sorry. *(To Jerry)* I didn't realize that's how you became a part of Mr. C.'s organization.

MR. C. Jerry's a superstar—he's living proof that you can make it happen for yourself.

JERRY. No one has to leave their death to fate, Simon—I learned that from being sick as a dog in a hospital with a collapsed lung. I dragged myself out of that black tunnel I was trapped in and I started to breath again. I refused to die. All these frauds who talk to us about the calm and serenity of death are talking out of their own fears—I crossed over that threshold and I'm telling you the happily-ever-after scene that they describe is a fantasy. *(Lana enters with an ironing board and iron and starts working as the legs enter with a tray of food and begin serving Chesebro, etc.)*

SIMON. *(To Chesebro)* What about Carl? How am I supposed to explain marrying Lana to him?

MR. C. Carl's a liability. He doesn't care for what you're doing and he's very vocal about it. As far as I'm concerned, Carl's expendable.

SIMON. He's not expendable—

JERRY. Friends in show business are motivated by one thing—envy.

MR. C. We think you should spend some quality time with your friend Lana today—bring up the notion of getting married.

SIMON. Out of the blue?

MR. C. Woo her. You're a performer. Flatter her. Promise her fidelity. Renounce your past. Talk about love—mention love often but don't gush. Talk to her about a family . . .

SIMON. How can I have children? I'm still infected.

MR. C. You won't be forever.

JERRY. Play on her sympathy. Talk about how the virus has changed your life.

MR. C. Stay focused on her face and occasionally let your eyes stray to her breasts and down the length of her body.

SIMON. I never look at Lana that way.

MR. C. That's why I'm suggesting that you do. A woman appreciates being flirted with and desired. You can't be half-hearted about this, Simon. You've got to be 100 percent committed to getting her to say yes or it's never going to work. Questions?

Simon looks across stage to Lana. Light change. Simon crosses to Lana. Mr. C. and Jerry continue to eat.

LANA. Gary FTD'd me those flowers today—he still feels shitty about leaving me. Sometimes I think I should have cut him off completely. If I had cut him off I would be remarried by now instead of being a fag hag.

SIMON. Why do you call yourself that?

LANA. It's true—I've always been a fag hag—I admit it. When I was fat, gay men were the only ones who would ever pay attention to me. They treated me with respect.

SIMON. Were you attracted to me the first time we met?

LANA. Who can remember—that was a millennium ago.

SIMON. It wasn't that long ago—why can't you tell me?

LANA. What are we playing "Truth or Consequences" for? Did somebody reject you?

SIMON. No. It's important and I need to know.

LANA. Yeah, I was attracted. I'm attracted to all the queer play-wrights I meet—how else am I supposed to get cast?

SIMON. What was it that attracted you?

LANA. Your body.

SIMON. Be serious.

LANA. I don't know—it was probably your passion. You're a madman.

SIMON. Am I still the same passionate person you knew back then?

LANA. I'm not going to accept the trash you're doing at that comedy club, Simon—so don't ask me to!

SIMON. I'm not asking you to—I'm asking you if you still find me attractive?

LANA. You're gay.

SIMON. Maybe.

LANA. What the hell are you talking about—maybe?

SIMON. I think I might've had a change of heart. Lana, come here and sit down—you're not my maid.

LANA. I like to iron—it keeps my hands out of the Häagen Dazs.

SIMON. Sit down—will you please?! I need to talk to you.

LANA. *(Sitting)* I've watched you drool over every good-looking man we've ever seen together and now you're telling me you're not gay?

SIMON. It doesn't mean I can't reform.

LANA. Reform how? What are you trying to become—a born-again Christian?

SIMON. In a way.

LANA. In what way? You're gonna go fundamentalist now so you can cure yourself of the virus? This is too much—Carl needs to hear this. *(Moving to phone)*

SIMON. Don't call him over here! I'll tell him myself—I've got nothing to hide.

LANA. This is pretty comic, you asking me about my intimate feelings for you and then acting as if you're an available straight man.

SIMON. I'm interested. I've always been interested. I've just sublimated it.

LANA. Sublimated it to what—a dick?

SIMON. I want you to take me seriously, Lana! I've been attracted to you for years and I just started to realize it. Ever since I broke up with Carl, I've been trying to find somebody to love and it's like I haven't even seen the one person in front of me who's worth getting involved with.

LANA. Has the virus affected your brain? It's me you're talking to—Lana—remember?

SIMON. I know! Maybe this is going to sound weird to you, but finding out I was positive taught me how important it is to appreciate people while you've still got them. It's made me want to say things that I haven't been able to say before.

LANA. Like what?

SIMON. Like I'm tired of living my life the old way. Like I want to settle down—Carl and I will never be able to resolve our differences and I don't want to waste anymore of the time that I have. *(A beat. Simon looks at her chest)* I need you, Lana. I think about you all the time. I think about how we could be good for each other.

LANA. Why do you keep staring at my chest like that?

SIMON. *(A beat)* I was just thinking how sensual your breasts are.

LANA. *(She covers herself)* Simon, please don't play games with me!

SIMON. I'm not—I'm being sincere!

LANA. You know how many guys I've fallen in love with and had my heart broken by? The list is too long. I'm not interested in making it any longer.

SIMON. I'm telling you the truth! You're sexy, you're pretty, you're funny, you're honest, you're intelligent. You're a very attractive woman. *(A beat)* What would you say if I told you I wanted to marry you?

LANA. Marry me!? No, no—this is insanity—you're a friggin' h-mo, for God's sake—I can't marry you!

SIMON. Why not?

LANA. Because!! This is like one of those horror stories you read about of old men like Leonard Bernstein gettin' married so they won't be accused of being gay . . .

SIMON. I'm not doing that, I swear!

LANA. Then what *are* you doing?

SIMON. I'm telling you that you're beautiful and I want to make love to you.

LANA. Make love to me how?

SIMON. With my body. With my soul. With myself.

LANA. You mean as in sex? *(Simon nods)* We can't have sex—what about your situation?

SIMON. We'll use protection.

LANA. *(A beat)* This is very scary. I'm standing here considering having sex with a man I've known to be gay for fifteen years. Not only is he gay, he's HIV positive.

SIMON. But you are considering it?

LANA. Simon, it's been so long I'd fuck myself if it was possible.

SIMON. We can use a rubber and spermicide—we can use two rubbers. And if we get married I can have a vasectomy. *(We hear "Fascination" on the accordion)*

LANA. *(Staring at him)* This is very spooky. Do you know how many times I've daydreamed about this happening? I can't begin to tell you how many times I've watched you work at your desk or be on stage and thought, "If only he was straight—if only he was straight"—it was my mantra for God's sake—and now to have you waltz in here and announce that you want to marry me? I don't know how to deal with this.

SIMON. *(Moving closer)* Dance with me.

LANA. *(Overlapping on "with")* No—I've got to iron—I'm busy.

SIMON. Dance with me—please. You're my best friend—you're the only person I've ever felt comfortable with—

LANA. No, Simon! I've got to work.

SIMON. Please, Lana—please. I'm pleading with you. I need this to happen.

LANA. *(Overlapping)* Why are you doing this? Why are you doing this to me? *(Simon grabs hold of her hands and kisses her forehead. Stopping him)* Stop that!! How can I believe you? You've been acting so strange lately?

SIMON. I love you. I've always loved you. I've just been afraid to show it. *(We hear a lush orchestral version of "Fascination." They dance. The song ends. Simon and Lana kiss. They kiss again. Carl walks in wearing an eye patch and watches them)*

CARL. What are you guys rehearsing?

SIMON. We're not rehearsing—we're kissing.

CARL. What for? Are you doing research?

SIMON. No, we're kissing because we like it.

CARL. That was a romantic kiss, not a friendly kiss.

LANA. We know—we were being romantic. What's wrong with your eye?

CARL. They don't know—they're running tests. *(To Lana)* What do you mean you were being romantic—Simon's gay.

SIMON. I don't think I am gay.

CARL. You're gay, Simon. I should know, we slept in the same bed for five years.

LANA. Those kisses he just gave me weren't gay.

CARL. What the hell is that supposed to mean? How can you tell if a kiss is gay or not?

LANA. There was definite purpose in his kisses.

CARL. Are you two both high?

SIMON/LANA. No.

CARL. Then what's going on here?

SIMON. Is the doctor going to retest you for HIV? I told you to get retested weeks ago.

CARL. This isn't AIDS, Simon. Answer my question.

LANA. Why do you have to wear that eye patch?

CARL. I told you, I have an infection—I wish you two would stop avoiding me!

LANA. We're not avoiding you—we're interested in your well-being.

SIMON. It could be CMV—did you ask them about that?

CARL. It's not CMV. The doctor would know if it was CMV.

SIMON. Not if he wasn't looking for it.

CARL. I'm not going blind and I don't have AIDS. Talk about misery loves company . . .

LANA. That's a terrible thing to say.

SIMON. Let him alone. He's envious.

CARL. Envious of what? *(To Simon)* I shouldn't even be talking to you as it is.

LANA. Carl, don't act like that. Will you please?

CARL. You two give me the willies. What the hell are you doing kissing one another like that!?

LANA. It's not what you think. I can explain.

CARL. Explain what? That you've been diddling around behind my back. For how many years? What are you trying to cast me as here, Lana—the other woman?

SIMON. This isn't behind your back, Carl. Get over yourself—

CARL. I'm talking to her. *(To Lana)* What is this—you finally got him to go to bed with you after umpteen years of carrying the torch?

LANA. It just happened today—

SIMON. Let her alone. I'm the one who initiated it.

CARL. But she's the one who wanted it to happen—why do you think she followed us all the way to Seattle?

SIMON. Carl—go home!

LANA. You caught us in a personal moment—if you'd learn how to knock for a change, embarrassing scenes like this could be avoided.

CARL. You want me to knock—here, I'll fuckin' knock—I'll knock all you want! *(He kicks a wall or door or piece of furniture and exits)*

LANA. *(Running after him)* Carl! Carl, wait—will you please? Carl, you're acting like a two-year-old!

SIMON. *(Following her)* Let him go. He'll be back.

LANA. I don't want him to think I engineered this.

SIMON. He won't. I'll take care of it.

LANA. He thinks I'm the one who made this happen.

SIMON. I'll take care of it, I said. Dance with me. Dance with me.

LANA. *(Keeping him at bay)* If I do this—if I do make love to you—no more playing around with the boys—is that clear?

SIMON. I won't. I swear.

LANA. You can only be in love with one person at a time, Simon—and if I do this, that person has to be me.

"Fascination" refrains. Lana and Simon fall into another kiss as the lights fade. The disembodied legs enter from the opposite side and throw rice. Blackout.

act two

We hear the "Wedding March" on the accordion. As the lights come up, Simon is offstage getting dressed and Jerry, Mr. C., and the disembodied legs are drinking cocktails. Mr. C. is on his way to being sloppy. We see a silhouette of Lana ironing upstage.

MR. C. *(Yelling off stage to Simon)* Jerry's talking to HBO about shooting a comedy special—

SIMON. How much of a percentage am I gettin'?

MR. C. What are you worried about, Simon—you'll get what you deserve.

SIMON. I read in *Vanity Fair* where Nicholson made almost sixty million on *Batman* because he negotiated for a percentage.

MR. C. *(Overlapping on* Batman*)* Nicholson's a name—you're still a nobody. Just make sure you deliver the goods if it's a go—

JERRY. If the special takes off, we might be able to get a sweetheart deal with one of the networks . . .

SIMON. *(Entering with tux on hanger, to Jerry)* Help me with these cuff links. My heart feels like it's in a fuckin' cement mixer. I don't know what's more nerve-racking—gettin' married or doin' an HBO special.

JERRY. Breathe. You look great. Where'd you get the tux?

SIMON. I don't know, Lana took care of it—*(To Chesebro, sotto voce)* What happens if I feel the urge to go back to my old life-style? How am I supposed to deal with those feelings if they come up?

MR. C. Don't worry—they won't. If they do, we'll send you to transformational ministries.

SIMON. Transformational ministries?

JERRY. They've converted over five hundred gays in Washington state alone.

MR. C. You're not going to backslide on this, Simon—this is no time to be a faggot—the stakes are too high—keep telling yourself that.

JERRY. Anytime you feel any pressure, come and visit me—we'll start our own group called Homosexuals Anonymous.

SIMON. It's a deal. *(Getting dressed)* Where the hell are the pants? There's no pants with this tux. Lana!

JERRY. It's okay. She's pressing them.

SIMON. Lana! Do you have my pants?

LANA. *(Offstage)* Two minutes and I'll be there!

MR. C. Sit down. Relax. *(He does)* The best thing you ever did for yourself was to disown your past—people today don't have any sympathy for homosexuals—they think they're better off hidden away like the Kennedys hid that sister of theirs—what was her name?

JERRY. Rosemary.

MR. C. Out of sight—out of mind. Queers in this country are equated with insane people, child molesters, and murderers—you know why? Because they constantly get bad press.

JERRY. They don't have any power—everytime they get a state to give them civil rights—some citizen's group collects 120,000 signatures so they can take them away.

MR. C. Those people don't need discrimination laws—they need a press agent.

JERRY. There's a lot of hatred towards queers in this country— we're lucky we're not part of that scene anymore.

SIMON. I worry about getting caught, you know? People could find out about my background very easily—what if they talk to Carl?

MR. C. We're workin' on it.

JERRY. The C.A.A. publicist made up a great fake bio for you— high school jock, Navy, big family—mother died when you were nine—always wanted to be an entertainer . . .

SIMON. *(Overlapping on "jock")* Wait—wait—wait—you're gonna try to convince people I was a high school jock?

JERRY. Why not?

SIMON. It's preposterous! I can't even throw a Frisbee.

MR. C. Simon—you know what your problem is? You never got your masculinity validated. Didn't you ever bond with the men in your family?

SIMON. No—I was too busy redecorating the kitchen.

MR. C. We need to come up with a hard-core masculine identity for you.

SIMON. You can't just transform somebody into being more masculine, Mr. C.

MR. C. That's what you think—look what they did for Rock Hudson. *(A beat)* What do you say, Jerry? Should we teach him the golden rules of manhood before he jumps into the abyss of matrimony?

SIMON. Why do you call it the abyss? You make it sound so wretched. *(Yelling)* Lana—my pants!

LANA. *(Offstage)* Shut up!

MR. C. Of course it's wretched. It's completely antithetical to human nature. Mankind isn't designed to share—it's meant to be selfish.

SIMON. You're the ones who convinced me to do this—now you're telling me not to?

MR. C. We're not telling you not to—we're telling you it's a necessary evil. Just like the devil. Right, Jerry?

JERRY. Right. *(To Simon)* You signed a prenuptial agreement? *(Simon nods)* Then there's nothing to worry about.

SIMON. How many times have you been married, Mr. C.?

MR. C. Two times too many—I hate fuckin' women—they're inscrutable. Frank Sinatra got it right when he said a woman was like a bank. You lose interest after you take out your assets.

SIMON. Is Frank Sinatra supposed to be an expert?

MR. C. He was married to Ava Gardner, wasn't he? Make me another drink, will ya, Jerry?

JERRY. You want one, Simon?

SIMON. No, it makes me puke.

MR. C. Drink one—you won't be pissin' in your pants when you hear the wedding march . . .

JERRY. I'll get you some scotch.

SIMON. So tell me—what are these golden rules?

MR. C. You sure you want to hear them now?

SIMON. Yeah, I want to hear them. I want to be prepared.

MR. C. Mr. C's golden rules of manhood are never to be broken and I give them to you as a heartfelt wedding gift. One: Thou shalt not love in ways that are confidential or sharing. Men don't disclose personal information because then people won't be able to control their behavior. You follow? Two: Thou shalt not commit public fury. You got to learn emotional coolness, Simon. Men are less empathetic, more task oriented. Three: Thou shalt do unto others before they do unto you. *(Jerry hands them both drinks)* Don't ever trust anybody—no matter who they are—the minute you let down your guard, they'll fuck you and your wife.

LANA. *(Entering, wearing her wedding dress)* Don't be listening to him, Simon, he's bitter.

MR. C. What are you letting him see you dressed for? Aren't you superstitious like the rest of your clan?

LANA. What clan would that be, Mr. C.—the Jews or the inferior sex? *(As she throws them to Simon)* Here's you pants, darling—next time iron them yourself.

SIMON. *(Putting them on)* There's a double crease—

LANA. If you don't like them, don't wear them.

MR. C. They're off to a great start.

LANA. *(To Chesebro and Jerry)* What are you filling his head with that chauvinistic rubbish for? I don't want him tryin' to live up to your warped image of hypermasculinity.

MR. C. *(Overlapping on "chauvinistic")* Hey—hey—hey! Who you callin' chauvinistic? I adore women. Women are God's most glorious creatures. They're the most gracious, intelligent beings on earth and I cherish everything about them.

LANA. I bet you do. *(Taking his drink)* Simon, I don't want you drinking—it's not good for your condition.

MR. C. Don't let her give you orders like that!

LANA. *(To Chesebro and Jerry)* And make sure you and Jerry clean up your own mess—I don't have a colored maid to pick up after you. *(To Simon)* Did you talk to Carl yet?

SIMON. I left fifteen messages—he won't return my calls.

MR. C. Fuck him if he can't take a joke.

LANA. He's our friend.

JERRY. He was your friend.

MR. C. If he was your friend, he'd be coming to the wedding—don't you think?

LANA. Do you mind? I'm trying to have a private conversation with my husband-to-be here.

MR. C. Yeah, I do mind—this is my domain. Carl's gone public with his feelings about the act and it could have a negative affect on Simon's popularity.

LANA. *(A beat. To Simon)* Did you talk to any of the teachers at his school?

SIMON. They all say the same thing—he doesn't want to have anything to do with us.

MR. C. Then why is he boycotting you?

JERRY. He stands outside the club picketing from dawn to dusk—

LANA. Why don't you talk to him then?

SIMON. I've tried—he ignores me.

LANA. Has he been diagnosed? *(Simon nods)* How are his eyes?

SIMON. From the looks of it—worse.

MR. C. Give him some time—he can't hold a grudge forever.

JERRY. You're looking beautiful, Lana. How do you feel?

LANA. Like I'm jumpin' head first into Mount Kiluea. Somebody needs to help me put the flowers in the car. Simon? *(She exits)*

JERRY. I'll do it. *(To Simon, as he exits)* Your hair needs to be brushed.

MR. C. *(Looking after Lana)* You better watch out for her—she's feisty.

SIMON. *(Brushing his hair)* She's smart—she can take care of herself.

MR. C. If she was smart she'd know that intellect in a woman is unbecoming.

SIMON. That's ridiculous, Mr. C. How can it be unbecoming?

MR. C. A man wants his wife to be physically attractive first and foremost. Warmth, ladylike behavior, and femininity are what men desire in women—not assertiveness or intellect. Mark my words, a woman who reduces her husband's insecurity by verifying his manhood is a true intellectual.

LANA. *(Offstage)* Simon—hurry up!

MR. C. Listen, before you walk the plank, I need to talk to you about something—you're ex-companion Carl is becoming a real pain-in-the-ass.

SIMON. I thought you said you and Jerry had it covered.

MR. C. He's already started yakkin' to people—he told two reporters from the *Gay News* you used to be lovers.

SIMON. Jesus, fuck—now what!? Is this gonna ruin everything?

MR. C. Don't worry, I fixed it. But I want you to extend an olive branch.

SIMON. He's not going to listen to me—he's stubborn.

MR. C. This is important to you, Simon—you've invested a lot of energy in this agreement—you don't want it botched by some mouthy faggot with an overblown sense of himself.

SIMON. Why do I have to be the one to confront him—isn't there somebody else that can do it?

MR. C. No! The golden rules—remember? Get him to understand that you've given up your old life-style before he tells anybody else. But use emotional coolness. You're dealing with an enemy here and enemies will go to absurd lengths to make their adversaries look less human.

We hear a whistle. Light change. Mr. C. exits. Carl enters from the opposite side. Carl is wearing sunglasses, blowing a whistle, and carrying a placard which reads "Boycott Simon Seyz."
Simon watches him.

CARL. *(Chanting)* "Racist, sexist, anti-gay; Simon Seyz, go away! Racist, sexist, anti-gay; Simon Seyz, go away!" *(He sees Simon and moves away)*

SIMON. Hey, Carl—I've come to make you a peace offering. *(No response, Carl resumes chanting, throughout)* Carl, you look pretty lonely doing this all by yourself—where are the rest of your ACT UP buddies, did they abandon you?

CARL. AIDS is not a joke! Simon Seyz is a hatemonger! Boycott Simon Seyz. "Racist, sexist, anti-gay . . ."

SIMON. Carl, I know you're angry at me 'cause you don't like the material in the show—but I promise you, after they air the special—I'll play around with some of your suggestions.

CARL. Don't patronize hate—boycott Simon Seyz!!! *(He repeats the chant)*

SIMON. Carl—nobody's listening to you—people are driving by

starin' at you like you're demented. *(A timer goes off, Carl moves to a bag, takes out a vial of pills and takes several. He removes his sunglasses and we see he is still wearing an eye patch)* Why don't you come work for us—you could work part-time and get medical insurance for those pills you've been poppin.'

CARL. You're a pig.

SIMON. That's right, I'm a soon-to-be-famous-and-wealthy-with-his-own-HBO-special pig. And you'd do the same goddamn thing if you had the chance.

CARL. I don't need to be in the limelight at the expense of makin' people hate.

SIMON. Hey, I just tell the jokes, pal—I don't force anybody to laugh at them.

CARL. I can't believe you're so fucking deluded you can't see how ugly what you've been doing here is.

SIMON. How is it ugly? Because I'm living my life to the fullest? Because I'm trying to take care of myself?

CARL. What are you doing with the money you're making? Are you contributing to AIDS research? Are you fighting these assholes who want people like us put into quarantine camps? No! You're on their fucking side, for God's sake! I don't get you, Simon—I don't get this pathetic make-believe-I'm-straight charade.

SIMON. This isn't a charade, Carl. This is for real—get that through your thick head. I don't have to deal with the bullshit of bein' queer anymore—

CARL. You think you can snap your fingers and magically become straight?

SIMON. Lana doesn't seem to have any complaints.

CARL. It just goes to show you how desperate she is!

SIMON. You know, this goes way beyond you bein' politically correct—you got a goddamn axe to grind because you can't stand the fact that I dumped you.

CARL. You never "dumped" me. We decided to split up together.

SIMON. Is that why you've been haunting me to get back with you ever since? Un-un, Carl, I'm sorry—this is some sick revenge trip you've got going on here—

CARL. *(Overlapping on "trip")* That's right, go on—delude yourself some more—convince yourself it's something personal . . .

SIMON. Whatever I did with you is over and I renounce it. I have a whole new life and I'm asking you politely to please leave it alone. If you weren't so fuckin' possessed by the fact that I left you, you wouldn't be harassing me like this.

CARL. I'd like to know how you ever found it in your heart to say that you loved me—or was that a charade, too? Explain it to me, Simon—how can you forget five years of intimacy with someone you said you loved over and over—or did you happen to be straight then?

SIMON. I don't have any more time to waste on you . . .

CARL. Maybe I do have a personal axe to grind—but it's not for the reasons you think. It's because you lie. You lied to me then and you're lying to me now. You're a fuckin' two-faced fraud and I want to know how you can live with yourself.

SIMON. You don't want to listen to what I have to say—fine—we don't have to speak to each other ever again. (*Starts to walk away*)

CARL. Roy Cohn thought he was straight, too!

SIMON. (*Grabbing the placard and destroying it*) Here. Here's what I think of your fuckin' boycott! Take that fuckin' placard and stuff it up your ass!

CARL. You're the one who likes foreign objects up his ass.

SIMON. Fuck you, faggot! (*Simon exits*)

CARL. Everytime you say one of those scummy jokes you give somebody permission to hit a faggot over the head. (*Carl resumes chanting: "Racist, sexist, anti-gay; Simon Seyz, go away!"*)

The lights fade on Carl. We hear a burst of laughter, cheers and whistles. Simon is in the middle of his act. There's been a transformation of sorts. He's more relaxed.

SIMON. I was walking on Capitol Hill the other day—you know, the Swish Alps—and I ran into these faggots who all had moustaches—now I thought to myself—what the hell are these guys wearin' moustaches for?—doesn't it get in the way of the lipstick—and I finally figured it out—they're all hidin' the stretch marks. (*Laughter*) Faggots—my favorite people— the only people I like better are blacks. I'm serious—what are you laughin' at? I love my fellow brothers. I especially love them when they break into my car and steal my CD player. Fuckin' coons! Hey, don't get me wrong—if we didn't have the black race there wouldn't be any professional sports—am I right? How do you keep five black dudes from rapin' your wife—throw them a basketball—*(Mimes lay-up. Laughter)*—bawooosh! I recently got married—anybody here married? Why didn't you warn me? I should have given her a muzzle instead of an engagement ring. Anybody here know why women like to have their nipples licked? It brings out their best points. *(Laughter)* "There once was a woman named Lana, Who liked to give head in the sauna. The steam was so thick, She bit off a dick. Now they call her the human piranha." *(Applause and cheers. Simon moves to the dressing room area and begins getting changed. Mr. C. and Jerry are waiting for him)*

MR. C. Who wrote the limerick?

SIMON. I did.

JERRY. Your marriage is inspiring you to poetry.

SIMON. I got tired of doin' the one about AIDS.

MR. C. Do them both.

SIMON. Somebody tell Frank to turn on the fuckin' air conditioner! It's a hundred and twenty-four degrees out there.

MR. C. He likes it hot—the customers buy more to drink.

SIMON. Why should I be sweatin' like a dick all night, if I'm not gettin' a percentage of the bar sales?

MR. C. What's the matter, Simon—you got a complaint?

SIMON. I gotta list. I want you to get rid of him outside the club. I'm sick of seein' his face out there every night—

JERRY. Use the back door.

SIMON. No! I want him gone. I don't want to take anymore chances of him talking about me to people.

MR. C. Don't waste your energy over it—he can't last forever—he's losin' his eyesight. Nobody pays any attention to him anyway—they think he's a bag person.

SIMON. *(Overlapping on "anyway")* Pay him off, shut him up, I don't care—I want him out of here—he's like a fuckin' lost dog.

MR. C. Fine. We'll deal with it. What else?

SIMON. I feel like I'm bein' jerked around by you two. More and more people are coming to see the show. I never complain about bein' married. I got the Simon Seyz act down but I'm still not clean—when is it gonna happen?

MR. C. It's coming.

SIMON. No—you don't seem to understand—I can't wait any-more—I want to do my third task now before I get sick.

MR. C. You're not gonna get sick—you're healthy . . .

SIMON. Can you guarantee that? I don't want to be going blind like he is.

MR. C. You won't.

SIMON. That's not good enough. I want to do the third task *now.*

MR. C. Simon—you want me to level with you?

SIMON. Just tell me when I get to do it—all I want is to hear a date.

MR. C. You're not ready. You're not ready to do the third task. We're working on a whole persona here and some people in the organization think you still got a way to go.

SIMON. What do you mean I'm not ready?! I'm ready to get married and tell your feeble fuckin' jokes every night—but I'm not ready to be clean—I've got a contract with you people . . .

MR. C. I realize it must be a disappointment for you, but this is what they decided—

SIMON. I don't fuckin' care what "they" decided—I'm negotiating with you, not them . . .

MR. C. Hey!! What are you bellyachin' like a teenager who can't have the car keys for? So some people still don't trust you—they'll come around. You've got six months' worth of club dates lined up all over the Northwest—enjoy them.

JERRY. The agency is still negotiating with Fox, Simon—there could be a TV series in the works.

SIMON. I don't fuckin' care about a TV series—don't you two understand?—I want to do my third task and get it over with!

MR. C. You will. Trust me. I know it's frustrating, but it takes time—that's the way the organization works. Jerry and I don't have any control over it. We're not your adversaries in this, Simon—we've bent over backwards to make this an easy ride for you—show a little consideration for some other people for a change. *(Silence)* In the meantime, Jerry and I have a special assignment for you to do.

SIMON. What? You want me to sign autographs outside the Southcenter mall again?

MR. C. Don't be a wise ass.

SIMON. Maybe you want me to dress up like Homer Simpson this time and hand out flyers for the show . . .

JERRY. Your audiences double when you make a personal appearance.

MR. C. There's a dinner party tonight in Redmond for the Oregon Citizens Alliance . . .

SIMON. No way—fuck that . . . I'm not doin' that. I'm sick of spending time with those imbecile nitwits—

MR. C. Will you let me finish! There's going to be a couple school administrators there and I want their permission for you to talk to the kids on career day—

SIMON. You want me to do this act for junior high school now?

MR. C. Don't be dense! We'll hand out flyers with a dollar off coupon. *(Simon responds vocally)* The kids take the flyers home to the parents—the parents go see the show and bring the message back to the kids—

JERRY. It's the figure eight effect.

SIMON. You guys are fuckin' relentless.

MR. C. We're not doing this for ourselves, Simon—I hope you can grasp that.

JERRY. Here's the address—they're expecting you and Lana for cocktails at 7:30.

SIMON. *(Taking a slip a paper from him)* I'm supposed to drag Lana with me to this happy horseshit?

MR. C. It makes a good impression when you go with your wife.

SIMON. You know how she hates going to those affairs.

MR. C. I don't care what she hates. Her function is to support you.

SIMON. Then why don't you come over to the house and explain that to her.

MR. C. That's your job—not mine. You better learn how to put her in her place—I don't want her spreadin' any of her pro-choice, pro-gay manure at that affair tonight.

SIMON. I'm not dealing with some Geisha dishrag from the

fifties here, Mr. C. She's not gonna play the dutiful wife just because you want her to.

MR. C. Why don't you get off her strap? She'll bungle everything you've been working for.

JERRY. Mr. C.'s right, Simon. Your wife's an acquired taste.

SIMON. Thanks for the news flash, Jerry. You're the ones who fuckin' chose her for me. *(He starts to leave)*

MR. C. Hey, come back here—come back here—give me back the address—I don't want you going to any party with that rotten attitude—give it to me—give it to me! *(He does)* You want to call off the fuckin' deal, Simon?—let's call off the deal. C'mon, Simon, put your money where your bombast is. *(No response)* You know why you won't call off the deal? Because you're full of shit! *(A beat)* We have a business agreement here, my friend—and you should be acting like a businessman—not like a toddler. Understand? *(No response)* I think you owe Jerry and me an apology.

SIMON. *(After a silence)* I apologize. *(A beat)* I just want to be clean—okay?

MR. C. I don't ever want to see that kind of infantile behavior again—if you don't have faith in our judgment it's not going to work out.

SIMON. I'm sorry. What don't they like about what I'm doing?

MR. C. Never mind. Go on—go home—forget it.

SIMON. Do you still want me to go to the party?

MR. C. We'll see. Go on. I'll call you.

Light change. Lana enters in evening clothes from the opposite side of the stage. Simon crosses to her. Mr. C. and Jerry watch the scene, then disappear.

LANA. Why do you bother to drag me to these goddamn affairs if you're only going to humiliate me?

SIMON. You act like a sow.

LANA. Maybe it's because I'm married to you. You bring out the best in me.

SIMON. Talking with your mouth full like you never heard of a napkin. You're disgusting.

LANA. Simon—the man next to me was going on about how he didn't think the Holocaust ever really happened—that it was some sort of publicity stunt—I wasn't going to wait until I finished chewing to let him know he's a fuckin' moron.

SIMON. What do you care about the Holocaust? It happened fifty years ago.

LANA. I don't care if it happened yesterday—this man is a social studies teacher for Christ's sake. It's grotesque—

SIMON. He was from Centralia.

LANA. And that makes it excusable? Unzip me. *(He does)* They are so goddamn smug with their hate.

SIMON. Mr. C.'s always telling me not to let you go overboard when we're at one of these events.

LANA. I don't care what Mr. C. says—he's your manager, not mine. Can't you smell what's happening out there—

SIMON. Mr. C. knows what's best for my image and he doesn't want you actin' like a pushy broad in front of people who can't handle that kind of woman.

LANA. What kind of woman?

SIMON. Lana, you talk too much and you've got too many opinions.

LANA. How can anybody have too many opinions? You want to live with somebody stupid, marry a Barbie doll.

SIMON. I got a big day tomorrow—I don't need you raggin' on me all night.

LANA. I'm not raggin' on you—we've got to settle this.

SIMON. There's nothing to settle—you got to stop actin' like an obnoxious Jew, then maybe people will start listening to you.

LANA. *(Overlapping on "Jew")* Whoa—wait—this isn't Giggle's Comedy Club you're playin' at here—I'm your wife, remember? You don't call me an obnoxious Jew unless you want me to hit you over the head with a cinder block.

SIMON. I tried to tell you the same thing fifteen other ways and you didn't hear it. You want me to stop insulting you? Start acting like a wife's supposed to act.

LANA. And how is a wife supposed to act, Simon? Did your beloved Mr. C. give you a how-to manual? I'm not gonna sit here and pretend like my life revolves around you if that's what you mean.

SIMON. Why not? What have you got better to do?

LANA. You're a goddamn megalomaniac.

SIMON. That's right—I got people callin' me, offering me work for the next six months. If you were smart you'd get behind me and give me some support.

LANA. Simon, stop sleepwalkin'! Mr. C. and Jerry are usin' you, they don't care about your success—you're just a mouthpiece so they can collect their lousy fifteen percent.

SIMON. They've gotten things to happen. . . .

LANA. Like what—the phantom HBO special?

SIMON. *(Pouring himself a drink)* Mr. C. and Jerry have plans for me. They're workin' on a series deal with Fox and they've promised me the positive thing will clear up in a matter of months.

LANA. How? How is it gonna clear up? You're gonna get miraculously cured by doing a TV series?

SIMON. I'm not at liberty to talk about it.

LANA. You're not at liberty to talk about it because it's a fairy tale.

SIMON. Why do you insist on draggin' me down!? Can't you see it's holding me back?!! Mr. C. says—

LANA. Mr. C. says, Mr. C. says—whatever those sleazebags are fillin' your head up with is garbage, Simon. If they're promising you the moon, you better make sure they can deliver it.

SIMON. I trust them. Good night. *(He starts to exit)*

LANA. I take it this means you're not going to sleep with me again tonight?

SIMON. Lana, please—if you're horny, go get yourself a lover.

LANA. I don't want a lover—I want my husband. That's why I married you.

SIMON. You're fuckin' insatiable. I can't do it tonight. Maybe tomorrow.

LANA. Are you screwin' around with the guys again?

SIMON. NO! That's over—that's over with completely—don't ever ask me about that again! *(Silence. Simon regards his arm closely. Lana starts to exit)* Jesus, fuck . . . what the fuck is this now—a rash? *(Lana studies his arm)*

LANA. I don't know—it looks like the hives.

SIMON. Is it a rash or isn't it?

LANA. I don't know! Go to the doctor and find out. It's probably something you ate at that neo-Nazi dinner party.

SIMON. Will you stop acting like a jerk! You know how I get when this shit happens.

LANA. What are you getting so upset for? It's probably only an allergic reaction to something. *(He starts to scratch it. She exits and returns with a jar of cream)*

SIMON. I hate when this stuff happens! *(Starts searching his body for other rashes)* This could be the beginning of some fuckin' infection . . .

LANA. You're fixating on it, Simon—leave it alone—I'm sure it doesn't have anything to do with the virus! *(She starts to apply a cream. Silence. They regard each other)* Simon, I can't argue with you about this act or your illness anymore—it's killing us. I can't live like this. I'm here to comfort you if you need me—

SIMON. I don't want any comfort.

LANA. Then what the hell did you marry me for?

SIMON. You keep on pushing me, Lana—I need some space.

LANA. Space? What does that mean—space? Are you asking me for a divorce—is that what you want?

SIMON. No.

LANA. Is there something wrong with me? Tell me, Simon, is there something wrong with me? How is it that I always attach myself to these men who are chameleons—

SIMON. It's not you. It's not your fault. Just let it alone—okay? *(A standoff. Silence)*

LANA. Carl's brother called twice this morning.

SIMON. I don't want to hear about it.

LANA. They took him to the hospital yesterday. He wants to see you.

SIMON. Hospitals are temples of doom—I'm not goin' in one.

LANA. Simon—take five minutes and go visit him—you'll regret it if you don't.

SIMON. I can't be in one those fuckin' places—I can't be around sick people—*(He exits)*

LANA. This isn't just another sick person—it's Carl.

Lana exits after him. Light change. The disembodied legs push Carl onstage in a wheelchair. He is wearing a hospital gown and is nearly blind. Silence. Simon enters and studies him.

SIMON. Carl?

CARL. I'm okay.

SIMON. It's Simon.

CARL. I know.

SIMON. Lana's been on my back—she says you've been askin' to see me.

CARL. How are things at the club?

SIMON. Crazy—madness. I keep expecting to see you outside.

CARL. Don't have the energy—can hardly see anymore.

SIMON. What are the doctors doing for you?

CARL. They want me to go back on Ganciclovir.

SIMON. Why don't you?

CARL. It doesn't do any good.

SIMON. Listen to them. They know what they're talking about.

CARL. I don't want to be here. I'd rather be in my apartment with my stuff.

SIMON. Do you need any money? You want me to write you a check? *(Carl shakes his head)*

CARL. I wanted to apologize to you, Simon.

SIMON. Apologize? For what?

CARL. You've found someone new to love and that's what's important—not what I think about it.

SIMON. What about the act?

CARL. I don't understand the act. The act is ugly. You can't say those things in public and expect people to have compassion.

SIMON. *(After a beat)* I should probably apologize to you, too, Carl. I suspected you would get sick and I never told you.

CARL. You suspected? How did you suspect?

SIMON. I found out about you and Fred.

CARL. What about me and Fred? *(A beat)* Fred's been gone over a year now, hasn't he? *(Another beat)* You know I'm going to die soon? *(No response)* Simon?

SIMON. I'm here.

CARL. I want you to hold my hand.

SIMON. I can't. I gotta go.

CARL. Just hold my hand for a while, okay? *(He does)* Do you remember that children's book I tried to write about the little boy who's a sissy and goes to a wizard so he can be like the other boys? *(Simon shakes his head)* Everybody said it would never get published because the boy's mother in it says she doesn't care if her son grows up gay because then she'll have somebody to go shopping with her in her old age. See, this little boy goes to this grand wizard—who's kinda swishy himself—you know, like Cyril Ritchard in *Peter Pan*—and the wizard gives him a magic potion to drink so he'll be interested in sports and want to play army instead of wanting to play house with the neighborhood girls. Only the potion makes him violent and he starts beating up everybody and stealing and calling other kids names. The wizard realizes he's created a monster and he has to give him the antidote because the whole village is being terrorized by this mutant macho kid—but before he does—he makes all the townspeople swear they'll never make fun of a sissy ever again. I wrote about that little boy because of you. I always felt like you would have done anything not to have been born a sissy. I always thought you were really ashamed of being gay and that you'd do anything to be somebody else—is that true? Is that true, Simon?

SIMON. Sometimes. Not all the time.

CARL. Didn't you ever enjoy it?

SIMON. When I was with you, I did. Do you want me to take that blanket?

CARL. No, I like it. It's fine. This morning—before you got here—I got very light-headed—I didn't see anything real like a car or a book—but I saw all these patterns and shapes—I was lying on the bed but my mind was in a whole other place. Then I heard you call my name. I knew you weren't with me, but it was as if you were right here in the room. Then I noticed you were crying. You said, "I want to be with you, but I can't." *(A beat)* When I die, it's going to be a wonderful adventure—I keep telling myself my spirit is going to grow and develop and be somewhere else and maybe I'll get to meet L. Frank Baum's spirit and Bessie Smith's spirit and Cole Porter's.

SIMON. Why are you talking like this? You make it sound like you're already dead . . .

CARL. I'm sick, Simon . . . I can feel my insides breaking down. *(A beat)* They say when L. Frank Baum died his last words were, "Now I can cross the shifting sands"—the shifting sands are the desert region just outside the Emerald City. I was thinking that maybe that's what I'd like my last words to be—"now I can cross the shifting sands." Either that or "Nurse—I need the bedpan." Everybody on this floor talks about what happens after you die and whether or not there's an afterlife. I was thinking if there is an afterlife—I really want it to be like Oz—God knows I hope it doesn't look like Detroit.

SIMON. I'm sorry, Carl—I really got to go. *(He starts to exit)*

CARL. Simon, please don't run away from me—I need you to be here. *(A beat)* It's funny. I'm learning to love me and the people around me and this whole AIDS situation is the reason. It's tested me—it's tested my strength.

SIMON. You don't have to die like this if you don't want to. I know someone who can help you.

CARL. I love you, Simon. *(No response)* I'm sorry if I ever hurt you.

SIMON. *(Overlapping on "hurt")* Did you hear what I said? You don't have to die, Carl.

CARL. I don't have a choice.

SIMON. Yes, you do.

CARL. I'm not afraid.

SIMON. Don't you want me to help you? Because I will. You don't have to die, Carl. I can take care of it.

Mr. C. enters with a briefcase from the opposite side of the stage. Simon moves over to him. Lights fade on Carl as the legs wheel him offstage.

SIMON. Carl's very ill.

MR. C. Makes sense. He's dying.

SIMON. I was wondering if there was something you could do for him? Isn't there some sort of arrangement we can make?

MR. C. I thought you said you wanted us to get rid of him?

SIMON. He's really in bad shape, Mr. C. I was hoping you'd consider helping him out.

MR. C. That's an odd request. You're the reason he's sick.

SIMON. How am I the reason? I thought you said Fred infected Carl?

MR. C. I never said that—you decided that when you saw the tape.

SIMON. If Fred didn't infect him—who did?

MR. C. I did. I altered his status from negative to positive. He's your third task.

SIMON. This doesn't make any sense. How can he be a task?

MR. C. It's an even exchange. If you want to live—Carl has to die.

SIMON. Why did you pick him? Why does it have to be Carl that dies?

MR. C. Would it be any easier if it was a stranger?

SIMON. No.

MR. C. Then forget it—don't torment yourself over it.

SIMON. I can't forget it. You're telling me that I'm the reason Carl has to die? You didn't prepare me for this—I'm not prepared to deal with this . . .

MR. C. You have been studiously prepared for everything, Simon. You knew he was going to have to die sooner or later.

SIMON. Not like this. Not because of me.

MR. C. I'm sorry, but this is what the organization decided you needed to do. *(Handing him some papers)* Here's the jokes for this weekend's show. I'll drop by the club Saturday night. *(He prepares to leave)*

SIMON. No, wait, Mr. C., please—this isn't something I can do—this is not a do-able thing—we've got to talk about this.

MR. C. There's nothing to talk about—

SIMON. I realize you and Jerry say you don't have any control over the decisions the organization makes and all, but you've gotta ask them for an exception in this case . . .

MR. C. It's too late, Simon—you've signed the agreement—there's no other alternative.

SIMON. You tricked me—you never told me that Carl was going to have to die in my place.

MR. C. If I had, it wouldn't be a task—now, would it? Jerry and I have taken great pains to educate you about staying alive, so it would be Carl sitting in that hospital room and not you. You've got to move on—you've got to suppress this mawkishness you're feeling . . .

SIMON. I can't do this! He's my friend. I can't give you my permission for Carl to die in my place.

MR. C. In extreme threats to man's survival, human choices are restricted.

SIMON. Why are you doing this to him? He never asked to be involved in this. Please, Mr. C. Please. I don't want him to have to die because of me.

MR. C. It's a very magnanimous gesture on your part—Carl's lucky to have such a devoted friend.

SIMON. What you want me to do? Do you want me to get on my knees and beg? Is that what you want? Because I will. I'll get on my knees and beg. *(He does)* Please. Please, Mr. C. I don't want Carl to have to die because of me!

MR. C. Save the crocodile tears for somebody more impressionable, Simon.

SIMON. *(A beat)* You're a bastard. You're a despicable bastard.

MR. C. What are you cursing me for? You're the one who put these wheels into motion.

SIMON. This is not what I want!

MR. C. I'm not concerned with what you want.

Lights fade on Mr. C. We hear "Fascination" on the accordion. Jerry enters from the opposite side. Simon moves to his apartment and frantically starts packing a suitcase.

JERRY. *(A beat)* You can't run away from it, Simon—

SIMON. Get out of my apartment, Jerry.

JERRY. The organization has saved both our lives and you know it.

SIMON. How many people did they infect to let you live?

JERRY. I had to infect them myself. It was part of my contract.

SIMON. If you've deliberately infected someone, you've murdered them.

JERRY. I'm not a murderer—I'm a survivor. Just like you.

SIMON. Don't try to compare us—we are not alike—

JERRY. *(Overlapping on "are")* This is the hardest part—you've got to believe in what you're doing—after this it's all a smooth ride—

SIMON. I am not some twisted demon who casually dispenses death sentences . . .

JERRY. You've come this far—what are you giving up now for?

SIMON. Because it's unscrupulous—

JERRY. What do you care about scruples? What are you going to do? Go back to being a nonentity faggot who dies like a

leper? You fancy the idea of people avoiding you—running
away because they're terrified they'll get your disease?

SIMON. Some people can be compassionate.

JERRY. Not when it comes to queers. Don't let your emotions
get the better of you, pal—take advantage of the gift you've
been given.

SIMON. I am not capable of being the monster you and Mr. C.
want to make me into—

JERRY. *(Overlapping on "and")* You don't know what it's like to
have your body fall apart—who's going to be around to take
care of you when you get sick?

SIMON. Lana will. Carl will.

JERRY. You're not taking care of Carl—what makes you think
he'll want to take care of you?

SIMON. You and Mr. C. put my back up against a wall so I
wouldn't have any other choice. You've been filling my head
with all this shit about being a queer and what it takes to be
a man and I've been lappin' it up like some sick puppy. *(Jerry
tries to interrupt)* Un-un, I'm not gonna let you two get away
with this—I'm not gonna let this happen.

*He finishes packing. Silence. Jerry exits. Simon watches him
leave. We hear a voiceover announce: "Ladies and gentlemen,
Giggles is proud to present—Simon Seyz!" Drumroll. Spotlight.
Simon moves to the microphone with his suitcase. He speaks
rapidly, tripping over the words. During the monologue, he
unpacks and puts on a skeleton suit.*

SIMON. Did you hear the one about the faggot who sold his soul
to the devil? See, there was this faggot named Simon—yeah,
me—you didn't know I was a queer, did ya?—well, I am—
surprise!—and one morning I woke up and decided to go
for an HIV test because faggots of a certain age live in
perpetual fear that they're going to get sucked into the black
lagoon of death called AIDS—so I go for the test and guess
what?—it turns out I got it—I got the bug, the fever, the
germ—the sickness—now, most folks at this point would
start making peace with the concept of eternal peace—only
this faggot decides—fuck, no—I ain't dyin' like every other
queer I've seen—no way, man, I'm going to save myself—this

was an accident—this was an event beyond my control and I'm gonna get in touch with the devil. So, I write a few letters and the devil shows up in a blue suit and a red tie and the first thing he has me do is sign a contract—he says all I have to do is three simple tasks and I'll be clean again. Only I can't do the tasks—oh, I can do the first two all right—those two are easy—tellin' jokes about the people you all love to hate and pretending I'm no longer a faggot—but when it comes to the third one—forget it—I just can't do it. You know why? Because I'm not ruthless enough. Because I don't hate enough. Because I still have love in me. So I tell the devil to go fuck himself—I say, I'll take my medicine without the sugar coat thank you very much and I wait to die. I come here to the club and I come out of the closet and then I go home and wait to die.

Prerecorded sounds of the audience reacting negatively to Simon's act. Simon moves to the dressing room area and begins changing. Mr. C. and Jerry are waiting.

MR. C. How would you like me to explain what you just did to the people who paid to get in here tonight?

SIMON. Tell them whatever you want—I don't give a fuck.

MR. C. You better start givin' a fuck—you've got a contract to honor.

SIMON. I'm not playing this game anymore, Mr. Chesebro—I'm not doing what you tell me to do.

MR. C. You think you're shrewd, don't you?

JERRY. You're making a mistake, Simon.

SIMON. It won't be the first time.

MR. C. You're going to have to retract that statement about being a faggot.

SIMON. I'm not doing your act anymore—I'm not staying married to Lana and I'm not giving permission for Carl to die in my place.

MR. C. Carl's already dead. Carl's been dead since yesterday. *(Simon is visibly shaken)* Are you going to shed some more of your crocodile tears for us, Mr. DeSoto?

SIMON. You're a sadistic fuckhead.

MR. C. That's right. I'm a fuckhead and you're indebted to me. As far as your plans to give up the act are concerned—it's not possible. You're gonna be doin' this act 'til the day you die. And as long as I'm your manager, you're going to be married—whether it's to Lana or somebody else—you're gonna fake your way through being straight. Problems? *(No response)* Good. *(Opening his briefcase)* Learn this for next week's show.

JERRY. Please accept our condolences about your friend. *(Mr. C. and Jerry leave. Simon crumples the paper he was handed. Lana enters from the opposite side. Silence)*

LANA. You heard about Carl? *(Simon nods)* His brother said he was alert right up 'til the end.

SIMON. I want to give up doing the act.

LANA. What about your contract?

SIMON. I'm going to try to break it.

LANA. What about us?

SIMON. I've been lying to you. I asked you to marry me so I could please Mr. C.

LANA. And every time you told me you loved me it was a lie?

SIMON. I love you, Lana, but not like a husband—

LANA. No, you don't. You don't love anybody but yourself.

SIMON. Lana—

LANA. No, I'm not going to let you con your way out of this one. When you said you loved me and you wanted to marry me, I knew in my bones it was a lie because I know you—I know you like my family—I was stupid—I wanted you to want me and mean it, so I ignored the truth.

SIMON. Lana, I need you to be with me—

LANA. Why couldn't you just choose some stranger for your little dance, Simon? Why couldn't you just tell some other boob that you loved her, so I wouldn't be standing here feeling like I was beat up by my best friend?

SIMON. I'm sorry, Lana.

LANA. No, you're not. You got what you wanted. You misused me and I'm not interested in being around you anymore.

She stares at him and exits. We hear "Fascination." A silhouette of a man playing the accordion is upstage. The legs enter. As the scene progresses, the legs are revealed to be attached to Carl's ghost.

SIMON. Were you afraid?

CARL. Mmm-hmm. Soiled my sheets just like they say you do.

SIMON. *(Getting closer to him)* Will you tell me what it was like?

CARL. *(Moving away)* There's nothing to tell—besides, you'll find out soon enough.

SIMON. Did you see the white light everybody talks about?

CARL. There is no light.

SIMON. But I thought—

CARL. Simon—you can't ignore what happened between us. You bargained my life away.

SIMON. But I didn't know. I didn't know that's what was going to happen—

CARL. Mmm-hmm. What's next?

SIMON. I don't know. I'm not sure.

CARL. Are you clean now?

SIMON. Clean? I don't feel clean.

CARL. What if you are—what if you are 'clean,' Simon—it'll be because I died—you realize that, don't you?

SIMON. I was trying to stay alive, Carl. I'm sorry—I never wanted it to happen like this.

CARL. Yeah, right—I'm sorry, too.

SIMON. *(A beat)* Will you forgive me, Carl?

CARL. No. I won't.

Carl disappears. Mr. Chesebro comes from behind the screen with the accordion and continues to play "Fascination." The house lights come up. Spotlight on Simon. We hear: "Ladies and Gentlemen—Simon Seyz!" Simon hesitantly moves toward the front of the stage, picks up the paper he was handed earlier by Mr. C., and begins telling the jokes to the audience. Blackout.

wendell jones/david stanley
music by robert berg

AIDS! the musical!

authors' notes

AIDS! The Musical! It's a head-turning title, offensive to some, but not chosen exclusively for cheap attention. The show *is* about AIDS and it *is* a musical. But yes, the title is flip, and deliberately so—we were taking a cue from *Diseased Pariah News* and David Feinberg and all the other angry queer jokesters who emerged after the "seriousness" of AIDS itself became deadly. We didn't want to contribute another tired tired tired boring tragic AIDS play. It was 1990 when we began writing and our world had been transformed since the first AIDS plays emerged in the mid-1980s; the subsequent plays, films, and TV movies, in general, were not reflecting this. "Transformed" doesn't necessarily mean for the better since the AIDS death and infection rate increases by the second, but it describes the way queers have scrambled to survive, changing themselves and their communities, creating new subcultures with new ways of thinking, dressing, and expressing themselves; our consciousness shifted: we formed ACT UP chapters to make life hell for politicians and drug companies, looked within for healing in groups like Louise Hay's Hayride and the Radical Faeries, raised money or volunteered our time to help the sick and dying, made art, joked, and tried to make the erotic safe, all while fighting against the overwhelming grief and sense of hopelessness. Being part of and witness to this transformation—and because we're fags—we couldn't help but chronicle and musicalize it, taste be damned. And again, this is not trying to sound merely flip—if we hadn't injected some humor into it, we wouldn't have honored those who never let anything, including AIDS, get in the way of a good one-liner or a sick joke.

When we finally got our show up, the very people who inspired us and whom we wrote about came in droves to see themselves up on stage. This has been very gratifying for us as playwrights because that magic relationship between art and community doesn't happen very often and we have been very thankful to be part of it.

performances and productions

The workshop production premiered on August 1, 1991, at Highways Performance Space in Santa Monica, California. We managed to sell out every performance of our two-week run, got great reaction from our audiences, and lots of great reviews and press. The show was produced by The Sodomy Players, directed by Alan Pulner with choreography by Antony Balcena, musical direction by Robert Berg, lights by Lawrence Oberman, sets/costumes by Cara Hoepner, and production chores/publicity by David Stanley. The cast included Theresa Ambronn, Maury Bernstein, J. Evan Dunlap, John Ellis, Wendell Jones, Daniel McVey, Ron Mesa, David Nichols, Janice Porter-Moffitt, and Kirk Wilson.

The full production of *AIDS! The Musical!* premiered on March 20, 1993, at the Skylight Theatre, a ninety-nine-seat theatre in Los Angeles, California, for a five-week run. Again, we got great reaction from audiences and the press. This production was produced by About Productions/Criminal Space Productions, directed and choreographed by Antony Balcena, with musical direction by Timothy Johnson, sets by Stuart Baur, lights by Lawrence Oberman, and costumes by Jansen Matsumura and Dawn Levy. The cast included Robert Almodovar, Theresa Ambronn, Oscar Arce, Saadia Billman, Craig Carson, Charley Geary, Julie Stout, David Holladay, Juan Monsanto, David Nichols, Antonio Pulido, Annette Sanders, and Kirk Wilson.

characters

THOMAS: young gay man

BOB: faerie

LUIS: AIDS activist

CHRISTIAN: New Age AIDS caregiver

LISA: ex-ERA activist

PENNY: Lisa's ex

DICK DIAL: game show host

MANNA WAR: game show hostess

KARPOSIS SARCOMA AND RETINITIS: dancing opportunistic infections

VANESSA: nurse

THOMAS' BOSS

MRS. RANDOLPH: Thomas' landlady

LURLEEN DEVEREAUX: East Texas New Age AIDS activist transsexual

LOUISE HAY AUDIENCE MEMBERS 1 AND 2

CARLOS: person with AIDS

ACT UP MEMBERS 1, 2, AND 3

BAR PATRON

BEN: patron of the Flesh Pit, a sex club

JACK, KAREN, PAT, FAERIE 1, 2, AND 3: radical faeries

TALENT SCOUT

VOICE ON LOUDSPEAKER

act one

SCENE ONE

Bob's bedroom. Bob, dying of AIDS, is coughing in bed. Thomas, who also looks sick, washes Bob's face and strokes his body. Bob sits up, suddenly.

THOMAS. Just lie back, Bob.

BOB. But . . . he's here again. Don't leave, okay? I love you.

THOMAS. I love you, too. Try to get some sleep. *(Luis enters)*

LUIS. *(To Thomas)* Where were you? I waited over an hour! *(Thomas shushes him. Luis takes Bob's hand)*

LUIS. I'm sorry.

THOMAS. He's been hallucinating all day. *(Christian rushes in)*

CHRISTIAN. *(Whispering to Luis)* It's my fault Thomas missed the demonstration. I was supposed to stay with Bob this morning, but my AIDS buddy needed a grocery pickup so I left Thomas here stranded.

LUIS. *(To Thomas)* You could have called at least.

CHRISTIAN. Bob has no insurance and he needs watching twenty-four hours a day. There's only us and Lisa and we're all getting a little frayed. You take shorter shifts than any of us, so you're going to have to deal with it if we get tired and forget to give you a call. At least we're willing to make sure he doesn't die alone.

LUIS. I'm sick of your condescending tone. We have an AIDS ward at County Hospital because people like me took the time to demonstrate. You never get your hands dirty with politics. You just sit deathwatch with one AIDS buddy after another. What's going to happen when we have a hundred thousand AIDS patients in this city? Are you going to go rushing from bed to bed like some angelic vampire, helping them all move into the light? The four of us aren't enough to nurse every AIDS patient in this town. *(Lisa enters)*

LISA. There aren't going to be four of us after this week.

CHRISTIAN. Lisa, are you all right?

LISA. No, I am not all right. As soon as we get Bob in a hospice,

I'm out of here. I'm done with smog, freeways, drive-by shootings, queer bashings, and a town full of ass-kissing lipstick lesbians. I'm going back to the land, the woman's commune in North Hampton. *(Penny enters)*

PENNY. You've got to take responsibility for what's happened to our relationship.

LISA. Okay, that's it! I spend seven years with you and every night it's the same thing: you want to know how I felt when you told me you felt angry when I said I felt confused when you asked me how I felt.

PENNY. But that's part of my program!

LISA. We went to that seminar for Adult Lesbian Children of Alcoholics that teaches you how to express your feelings. You had some sort of breakthrough. You expressed every emotion under the sun and then some. You opened up. You shared. You talked so damned much half the women in the place wanted their money back. But that damned facilitator said you were a model for us all, said she never saw a woman who could share so much in her life. I was ready to strangle her.

PENNY. Don't blame Barbara either.

LISA. Oh, no, you're both angels! Penny's moving in with that self-centered dressed-for-success, thank-you-for-sharing yuppie lesbian and they're opening up their own private counseling service. Both of you just better stay out of my way or I'll share more feelings than either of you ever imagined in your worse nightmares.

PENNY. I'm not the villain here!

THOMAS. Would you argue somewhere else! *(Penny exits)*

BOB. *(To Thomas)* You're so beautiful. You glow. There's a man here, trying to take me away. Mama, Denise, are you there?

CHRISTIAN. Tell him they're in the other room.

LUIS. No way. It's time he faces facts. They've deserted him.

LISA. Shhh! Just tell him you're here.

BOB. You're all driving me nuts. What a tawdry setting for a death. I wanted something more majestic. I'm a theatre queen. I always wanted death to be like a big musical with angels and songs. *(Chorus enters for dance number)*

CHORUS. *(Singing)*

Look up and see, what a great rainbow,
Look up and see, all the clouds part.
Look up and see, thousands of bluebirds,
Everything's gonna be fine.
(Lisa, Luis, Christian, and Thomas join in)
We'll dance that old soft shoe again,
Stay up late again, watching Rin Tin Tin.
You're dying of AIDS, my dear old friend,
We've got no more time, we've got no more time,
To stay up late only drinking wine,
We've got no more time, n-n-n-no more time.
Everything's gonna be,
You'll see how it will be,
Everything's gonna be fine!

LISA.
  Sewers! We're all living our lives in a sewer!
  We need clean skies, but we breath manure—
  This city's so sick there's no cure!
  It's a sewer!
  Forests! I was dreaming of life in the trees.
  Leaves! There were women behind all the leaves,
  With kayaks and backpacks
  And mohawks and freedom,
  Bare-breasted Rhine Maidens on horses ride bareback
  The baked bread smells fragrant
  They don't have to pay rent
  And everything's going to be,
  You'll see how it will be,
  Everything's going to be . . .

LUIS.
  Pain! They'll bulldoze it and what will remain?
  There's no safe space. Life's full of pain!
  Straight men's power is just too ingrained!
  Life is pain!
  Power! Together we cannot be beat.
  Streets! I can see us all out in the street.
  I see gym boys and pierced dykes
  And old fags and crazed queers
  Exploding with such rage.

We chase politicians.
Those creeps we elected must face the infected!
And everything's going to be,
You'll see how it will be,
Everything's going to be . . .

CHRISTIAN.

Soul! What's the point of our pain without soul?
We need love if we're going to be whole.
Deep inside is the ultimate goal.
Free your soul!
What's the point in running madly from our fears!
When we're finished screaming who will heal the tears?
And it's love,
That we need.
And it's love,
And everything's going to be,
You'll see how it will be,
Everything's going to be . . .

THOMAS.

Fun! Life was simple, and yes it was fun—
Parties, restaurants, clubs on the run,
It's my turn, damn it all, I'm still young.
Life was fun!
Painting late at sunset, coffee with a friend,
Dreaming of a lover, rendezvous with men
Life was fun!
IT'S NOT DONE!
LIFE IS FUN!
And everything's going to be,
You'll see how it will be,
Everything's going to be . . .

COMPANY.

Look up and see, what a great rainbow,
Look up and see, all the clouds part.
Look up and see, thousands of bluebirds,
Everything's gonna be fine.

BOB AND COMPANY.

Look up and see (what a great rainbow),
Look up and see (all the clouds part),

Look up and see (thousands of bluebirds),
(Everything's going to be fine.)
Look up and see . . . *(Chorus exits, Bob dies, and Thomas falls
to his knees coughing)*
CHRISTIAN. Thomas!

SCENE TWO

*The emergency room of the county hospital. Thomas sits in a
wheelchair, coughing. Bob enters.*

BOB. Thomas, oh, Thomas!
THOMAS. Bob? You've come back. You're alive?
BOB. Not last time I checked.
THOMAS. Then you're a ghost?
BOB. I'm no stupid ghost. I'm a faerie, can't you tell?
THOMAS. Faeries, you told me about faeries. I hate all that re-
ligious stuff.
BOB. Faeries have to do with spirituality, not religion. There's a
big difference.
THOMAS. I know, I know. Bob, why can't everything be the way
it was? Just you and me in the tree house by the lake, alone,
with no other care in the world?
BOB. That wasn't bliss, Thomas; that was denial.
THOMAS. Some forms of denial are good. What about all the
stories you made up about faraway lands and witches and
trolls?
BOB. Anything to get us away from our biological families and
the Church.
THOMAS. That's how we survived.
BOB. But, Thomas, what did we do in that tree house? Drown
our sorrows in flat root beer and comic books.
THOMAS. Until that one drunk night.
BOB. Then all you ever wanted was sex. But you wouldn't talk
about it and you wouldn't let me hold you afterwards either.
THOMAS. Well, you know how I was. I wanted so much to believe
God was good and that good guys always won and that we
were part of the greatest nation on earth, liberating the

oppressed with golden showers of compassion and goodness. You used to make fun of me.

BOB. Only when you really needed it.

THOMAS. Bob, who do I need to kill to get it all back? Which writer do I need to sleep with to get this script changed so we all live happily ever after?

BOB. Stop being so melodramatic! You've got to get ready for the Big Spin to see if you're going to live or die. Now, if you live, I want you to see some faeries. They wear skirts and dance and sing and worship the earth. They were a wonderful part of my life—a part you didn't want to hear about. It's time. Oh, and you'll need these. *(Bob puts a bead necklace around Thomas' neck)*

THOMAS. What's this Big Spin?

BOB. You'll see. And good luck! *(Bob exits)*

"AIDS! The Game Show!" theme plays as "AIDS! The Game Show!" sign descends. The host, Dick Dial, enters through curtains.

DICK. Well, welcome to "AIDS! The Game Show!," the only game show for people with and affected by AIDS. All right! Now, I want you to meet our lovely hostess—Manna War! *(Manna War enters)*

MANNA. *(Singing)*
Your body is covered with Karposis Sarcoma
And everyone knows from L.A. to Sonoma
You've learned about AIDS, so here's your diploma
And now welcome to "AIDS! The Game Show!"

DICK. Isn't she lovely? And what a figure! That sudden weight loss sure looks good on you.

MANNA. Thanks, Dick.

DICK. Now, let's meet the contestants! Who will live and who will die today on "AIDS! The Game Show!"?

MANNA. Our first contestant is Thomas, our tortured but good-natured lead character. *(Manna wheels Thomas over)*

DICK. Well, Thomas. Tell us about yourself. *(Thomas just coughs)* Well, good for you. Manna, our next contestant?

MANNA. Luis, our hunky but aggressive ACT UP member. *(Luis enters)*

DICK. Luis, welcome. What's your story?

LUIS. People are dying, Dick!

DICK. Thank you, Luis! Manna?

MANNA. Our next contestant is Christian, caring but conservative. *(Christian enters)*

DICK. Welcome, Christian.

CHRISTIAN. I love myself and I'm not ashamed to say it!

DICK. I'm so glad for you. Now, contestants, you know the rules. Let's play "AIDS! The Game Show!" First question: What is the biggest obstacle in stopping AIDS today?

LUIS. Gay assimilationist pigs!

DICK. Wrong! Christian?

CHRISTIAN. Ourselves!

DICK. Wrong again! *(Luis and Christian exit)* Thomas? *(Thomas coughs. Manna puts her ear to Thomas' mouth to hear his whisper)*

MANNA. Homophobia and the government!

DICK. That's right. You win! *("AIDS! The Game Show!" theme plays. Manna wheels Thomas center stage, where Dick Dial joins him)* Now, Thomas, you're ready for the Big Spin! Aren't you excited? Manna, show Thomas what he could win!

MANNA. One of three fabulous prizes. Thomas, the first prize is a Cure for AIDS! *(Applause. Manna brings out processed cheese food)* Yes, our spy cameras have just discovered that a researcher has inadvertently dropped a bottle of Cheez Whiz on his lunch and the resulting mixture, it turns out, can destroy the AIDS virus.

DICK. Wow, what a prize! Can you top that Manna?

MANNA. Sure can! With our second prize, Thomas, you will win a fabulous, fun-filled life as a Diseased Pariah! First, you'll survive this bout of pneumocystis but find that your immune system is destroyed. Thus, you'll play host to a number of fabulous, fun-filled diseases, and along the way, you may even discover a few that nobody has heard of before but that are just as deadly. Here are some now! The wonderful Karposis Sarcoma! And let's not forget Retinitis! I'm sorry Thrush couldn't be here. She's working overtime at County General. Spin, girls, spin! *(The diseases parade and spin as Manna announces them)* Let's give a big hand to our guest diseases!

DICK. Boy, they sure look like a lot of fun! What's our third prize?

MANNA. Death. Thomas, you will become just another statistic.

DICK. Very, very nice! Now that you've seen what you could win, it's time for the Big Spin! Manna, bring out that wheel! *(Manna brings out the wheel, which has three sections—CURE, LIFE AS A DISEASED PARIAH, DEATH—and a needle. Thomas tries to spin it but doesn't have the strength)*

MANNA. I'll help you! *(She spins it and it lands on CURE)*

DICK. You hit the jackpot! Lucky you! *(One of the diseases comes out and goes over to Dick)* Hold on. *(The disease whispers in his ear)* Uh oh, Thomas. I've just learned that our Cheez Whiz mixture will not make enough money for the drug companies so the formula must remain a secret.

MANNA. Tough break! I'll spin for you again.

THOMAS. No! Please, no! *(It lands on LIFE AS A DISEASED PARIAH)*

DICK. Life as a Diseased Pariah! Well, well! Aren't you a lucky fellow? Enjoy yourself and have a good life, whatever's left of it! This has been Dick Dial for "AIDS! The Game Show!"

DICK AND MANNA. *(Singing)*
Your body is covered with Karposis Sarcoma
And everyone knows from L.A. to Sonoma
You've learned about AIDS, and here's your diploma
So goodbye from "AIDS! The Game Show!"

The game show sign disappears, leaving Thomas hysterical in his hospital bed. Lisa rushes to him.

LISA. Thomas!

THOMAS. Where am I?

LISA. You're in the hospital, kiddo, and you're going to have to take it real easy. You just lost two days and from the way you were just jumping around in bed, I'd guess you've been in some pretty wild places.

THOMAS. I had the strangest dream. There was a game show and drag queens and diseases—

LISA. Look girl—I'm sorry but we gotta get serious quick. I've been watching these assholes. As soon as they see you put two sentences together, they'll show you the street.

THOMAS. Wait a second! What are you doing here? I thought you'd be out with a bevy of dykes growing wheat grass and sprouts on the land.

LISA. It seems a certain friend of mine passed out with a raging case of pnuemocystis. If you had tested and taken proper care of yourself, you might never have been sick at all. So, my friend, today we start facing facts. First off, you don't have any insurance.

THOMAS. That's ridiculous. I've never missed a payment.

LISA. Yeah, well, they canceled you. They claim you had a preexisting condition. You can appeal it, but that takes time. In the meantime, you got no coverage.

THOMAS. Then where am I? How did I get into this hospital?

LISA. You're here at County USC Hospital as an emergency. It's going to be at least six months before you get through the waiting list to receive ongoing treatment.

THOMAS. Six months!

VANESSA. *(Enters)* If you can hold on for six months, we can get you plugged into outpatient services.

THOMAS. Who are you?

VANESSA. I'm your nurse, Vanessa. Your body's in good shape. With a little preventative medicine, you have a good chance of staying well. It's good to see you up and talking.

LISA. And as soon as his fever's down, you'll send him out of here with no treatment. How can you work in this place? Don't you take vows to heal the sick or something?

VANESSA. Half the women in my graduating class went to work at Cedars Sinai. They get paid more money than me and don't have to clean vomit from the people in wheelchairs waiting for a bed in the AIDS ward. God knows why I chose to be here, but I did. As for the staffing shortages, I'm not responsible for them and I don't appreciate being blamed.

LISA. I've got an unusually big mouth. I'm really sorry. I just feel so hopeless these days.

VANESSA. *(Turning to Thomas)* That's one thing I can offer you. There is hope. There are groups that work with people, there are spiritual groups that . . .

THOMAS. Oh, please. I was raised by very religious people. They sent me for "aversion" therapy when I was sixteen to heal my "constant sadness." The shrink insisted the "sadness" would go away as soon as I could fuck a girl.

VANESSA. Hey, I understand. I was raised by atheists and I never thought I'd see the day I'd be sending people to meditation groups. But when my brother was sick, he started going to Louise Hay meetings and when he was depressed, these people helped him. When he needed a better doctor, they found him one.

THOMAS. I'm glad they helped him but I don't think it's for me.

VANESSA. It's not your only option. I spend most of my spare time working on demonstrations to demand better health care for people with AIDS. Ever hear of ACT UP/Los Angeles?

LISA. Do you really think they accomplish anything?

VANESSA. What's your problem? You've been chewing my butt ever since I came in. Wait a second. I know you. You're Lisa Diamond. You spoke at that huge ERA rally in Washington, D.C. There were thousands of women there. You were the guest speaker, the youngest woman on the stage, just a little older than me. I used to see your picture in the paper all the time. You told us you could never live in a society that refused equal rights for women. I never would've expected you to blame lowly nurses for the entire health care crisis. *I'm* here in the trenches. What are *you* doing these days, Lisa?

SCENE THREE

Stage is black. A spotlight on Thomas.

BOSS. I'm sorry you've been so tired lately, Thomas. You've been free-lancing for us for over four years now.

MRS. RANDOLPH. This is a three-day notice to pay rent or quit.

BOSS. You're too slow, Thomas, and you look tired. You just got out of the hospital. You need a rest. A long rest. This is really the best option.

MRS. RANDOLPH. But you're sick now.

BOSS. Think of it as an extended vacation.

MRS. RANDOLPH. Perhaps your parents could take you in? You have spoken to your parents about this, haven't you?

THOMAS. Mother, there's something I have to tell you. I have AIDS and I'm dying. No, no, too dramatic and desperate for sympathy. Mom, remember when it was time for me to go on my mission and I didn't and you kept asking why I was so sad and you kept saying it was all real queer to you that I was leaving the Mormon church? Well it was real queer and now I have a queer disease and . . . no, no, too indirect. Look, I know I've always been a big disappointment to you. I was never a good Mormon. And I can't even get a socially acceptable disease. Uh uh, too hostile!

Scene change. Christian's living room. Luis is on the phone. Lisa looks offstage, out the front door, to Vanessa.

VANESSA. *(Offstage)* You haven't seen anything yet. See you to-night. *(Lisa closes the front door. Christian enters from the kitchen offstage)*

LISA. I haven't had such a good time in years!

CHRISTIAN. There is still some justice in this world. You go to the hospital to help your friend, you meet a nurse, and you fall in love! Yes! So I guess you've given up on moving to the women's commune?

LISA. All my life I've wanted to spend some time just with women growing plants and watching the cycle of seasons. And this women's collective is politically active. It's where I belong.

CHRISTIAN. So why haven't you left yet?

LISA. Because something is happening that I can't explain. Vanessa is so wild. Last week, she took me to this benefit. All these hot women from this great magazine: leather, candle wax, handcuffs, piercings! I've never been so politically incorrect. And Christian, guess what?

CHRISTIAN. What?

LISA. Vanessa wears lipstick!

BOTH. Yes!

LUIS. *(Hangs up the phone)* Good news! That new collective house where Vanessa's friends live has a cheap room open. Thomas can move in right away.

CHRISTIAN. Luis, I know you think Thomas would be happiest living with a group of AIDS activists, but he's never been to a meeting in his life. I told him last night he's welcome to stay here with me as long as he likes. Besides, I'm taking him to his first Louise Hay meeting tomorrow night.

LUIS. So you've got his life all figured out for him.

THOMAS. *(Enters, depressed and tired, and looks at group)* Oh, hi. Let me put this stuff up. *(Goes to his bedroom, offstage)*

CHRISTIAN. *(Whispering to the others)* His mom's visiting town for his sister's engagement party. He was supposed to give her the news. No grandchildren, homosexuality, AIDS. It's quite a bombshell for ten minutes between meeting the new in-laws.

LISA. And the last thing he needs is to hear the two of you fighting over him.

CHRISTIAN. Oh, Lisa, quit protecting everybody. Luis and I love each other. I just scare him. He's afraid when he burns out on politics he'll be just like me without the good looks.

LUIS. Can you imagine having to go to all those New Age gatherings without enough good looks to pick up anyone? That would be torture.

THOMAS. Where do you go to trade in your parents?

CHRISTIAN. Maybe Luis could organize political relocation camps for unsupportive heterosexual parents.

LUIS. That is not fair. I'm an anarchist, not a Stalinist. I don't support reeducation for anyone.

THOMAS. I never even got around to AIDS. As soon as my mother found I was definitely homosexual, she was trying to call up that doctor that gave me the "homo cure." My sister was crying and saying it was inhuman and that all we needed to do was pray together. My future brother-in-law took me out for a guy-to-guy talk and told me that if I marry a nice girl like my sister, everything'll be fine.

LISA. Oooh, that's an original idea! You can marry your sister! Incest as a cure for queers. Film at eleven.

THOMAS. I didn't think it would ever end. *(Singing)*
How could you hurt us?
I've got a weak heart

This is gonna haunt us
All of our lives

You have betrayed us
Start your repentance
You can't repay us
Not even begin

Down on your knees and start begging us please.
We won't turn away it is hardly our way.

They've got me twisting and turning about
I want to hurt them, they're really devout
They need a shock so they'll wake up and finally see

It's eating away at my heart and my soul
Driving me crazy is really their goal
They've got to love me and not what they want me to be!

And it's always
And I love you
And I love you
And I love you
And I love you
And I love you
And I love you but . . .

Just don't talk about it,
We don't want to hear it.

LUIS. You think your family is weird! My family was so dysfunctional I had to come out to them three times.

LISA. You always have to exaggerate to make your point.

LUIS. No! It's true! Each time I came out to them they got so drunk they forgot the next morning.

THOMAS. You mean you had to get the nerve up three different times to tell them their darling boy was a homo?

CHRISTIAN. How did you ever get them to remember?

LUIS. I tried everything, but it was the dress that finally worked.

LISA. Dress?

LUIS. *(Singing)*
Mother and father they kicked my ass out
I had to teach them what gay is about
They didn't argue
But they were not all that impressed

Father was crying and mother was drunk
They didn't notice my boyfriend the hunk
They finally woke up when I came home in pumps and a dress!

And it's always
And I love you
And I love you
And I love you
And I love you
And I love you
And I love you but . . .

Just don't talk about it
We don't want to hear it.

(Spoken) It helped, too, that I locked up all the booze in the house and strolled in after all the liquor stores were closed. I wish I had your parents, Lisa. You tell them everything.

LISA. Are you kidding? Liberal parents are the worst.

THOMAS. But your parents are communists. Didn't they understand your oppression?

CHRISTIAN. Communists? I thought your parents were Jewish.

LISA. You can be Jewish and communist too. One's a religion, the other's an obsession. I guess I was lucky the communist party hated homosexuals so much. If they hadn't been communists I would have probably joined that fossil party and spent my life defending the Authoritarians in Russia. I just couldn't join a party that was that homophobic.

THOMAS. Boy, a party right now sounds really good.

CHRISTIAN. You know you can't keep going night and day like

you used to. *(To Lisa)* So how'd you get your parents to come around?

LISA. Years of tears, guilt, and endless discussion. *(Singing)*
You can't be a dyke and a communist too
There's no way the masses could understand you
You know revolution can cure this
So why won't you try?

I loved a pussy and firm dripping thighs
They set me up with these dull Marxist guys
It took a while but my grandmother made them get wise

And it's always
And I love you
And I love you
And I love you
And I love you
And I love you
And I love you but . . .

Just don't talk about it
We don't want to hear it

CHRISTIAN. Your grandmother?

LISA. My extremely Jewish grandmother kept threatening to die of a broken heart if we didn't unite her family. When my sister produced babies to keep the family going my parents gave up.

LUIS. So, Christian. What was it like when you came out to your parents?

CHRISTIAN. Me?

LUIS. Yeah, you.

CHRISTIAN. I don't think my mother really knows what a homosexual is.

LUIS, LISA, AND THOMAS. What? *(Singing)*
And it's always
And I love you
And I love you
And I love you

And I love you
And I love you
And I love you but . . .

Just don't talk about it
We don't want to hear it. *(Blackout)*

SCENE FOUR

During the blackout, New Age music starts and the chorus is heard singing:

GROUP 1. *Life is always changing, change is only living.*
GROUP 2. *Holding on to now, always letting go.*
GROUP 3. *Now is all I have, all I have is now.*

Lurleen Devereaux recites a New Age meditation. As she finishes, the lights come up to reveal Lurleen, Thomas, and Christian, Audience Members 1 and 2, and other chorus members sitting on the floor of a large meeting room. It is a Louise Hay group meeting (a "Hayride") for people with AIDS.

LURLEEN. I'm sorry to announce that Louise won't be here tonight. She's having extensive dental surgery and she's not up to sharing. In her place, we have someone you know and love very well. Lurleen Devereaux! Hi, girlfriends. I'm so excited to be here tonight. I wanted to talk to you all about love. You know Louise says there are only two emotions, love and fear. Now, the first time I heard this, I thought, what is that girl talking about? I was scared when it came time for them to cut my cock off but I was feeling so many emotions. Like I was real excited because I was gonna be a woman and I was pissed at my mama and all those nasty things she said to me when I told her I was gettin' the surgery done. I mean, she had the nerve to say to me if God had meant you to be a girl, you would have been born with a big pair of titties. But no woman was born with titties, she has to grow them, just like I did. But when I started thinking about it, my mama sounded nasty because she was scared she was gonna lose me. And I got all mad at her because I was scared she wasn't going to love me anymore. You know, every time you see someone get mean and nasty, it comes down to the same thing, that queen is scared! Fear is so powerful it grabs your cock and your pussy and it won't let go. And the next thing you know, you do all kinds of things you never meant to in the first place. Now, I'm sure you all have questions tonight about love and fear. So let's see some hands.

AUDIENCE MEMBER 1. I feel like you're discounting my feelings. I get pissed every time I see what the government's doing to us. People are dying because they're not getting medications and that makes me mad, not scared.

LURLEEN. But you are scared and you have good reason. You're scared that those dirty fuckers are going to get away with it and if you're not scared, you ought to be. That's why I myself work as an AIDS activist. You may have heard of the AIDS Coalition To Unleash Power. ACT UP/Los Angeles! And the one thing we know is that there is something stronger than fear and that's love. That's what Louise taught me. And I love my fellow AIDS activists, which is why we're going to win this war and stop AIDS now.

AUDIENCE MEMBER 2. Wait a minute. We've manifested AIDS because of our own self-hate. Our anger against society is a reflection of how we haven't accepted ourselves. It's making us sick. And demonstrating with a lot of angry people is just going to make us sicker.

LURLEEN. Honey, it is true that if you have a lot of problems or a whole lotta hate, you may make yourself more open to getting sick. But sickness is not a punishment and if you really love yourself, you'll have the guts to demand decent health care for all people who are sick.

THOMAS. Hi, Lurleen? My name is Thomas. This is my first time at one of these meetings. And I'm real nervous, but I've got something I'd like to share. *(Music starts)*

LURLEEN. Oh, good, a song! I just love it when we sing. I just zone right out.

THOMAS. *(Singing)*

I don't know how to say this, where do I begin?
There is no place now in my church, they say that I have sinned
From you I hear the same words, love will set me free
But love can be a weapon against those who disagree.

I was always so good, always so devout
Never did I question, never did I doubt

Now they've turned against me, in my hour of need
I know what they're scared of because I'm afraid of me

LURLEEN. *(Singing)*

I'm very scared for this world, it's very scared of me
They look into the mirror, and hate is all they see
Here you'll find no judgments, no voices from above
It binds us all together, unconditional love

I was never that good, pious or devout,
Always did I question, always did I doubt

Don't know what they're scared of cuz I'm at peace with me
When you really love yourself, that love can set you free!

THOMAS.

I keep it all inside me, and never let it show

LURLEEN.

It's time to let the pain out, let your feelings flow

THOMAS.

But that is what I'm scared of, the anger deep inside

LURLEEN.

When you give love to yourself, there's nothing left to hide

THOMAS.	LURLEEN.
I was always so good	I was never that good
Always so devout	Pious or devout
Never did I question	Always did I question
Never did I doubt	Always did I doubt

LURLEEN.

Come into my arms now, you are safe with me

BOTH.

When you really love yourself, the truth can set you free,
The truth can set you free!

CHORUS.

> I'm not afraid of this world, it's not afraid of me . . . *(The line is repeated as the scene fades to black)*

SCENE FIVE

Carlos' bedroom. Carlos is in his bed. Christian walks in with goods/groceries.

CHRISTIAN. Hi, Carlos, it's me. I've got your milk and some of that fresh broccoli you like, potatoes, and oh, they had some real nice creamed honey. *(Christian empties the bags, some in the kitchen, offstage, some in a dresser)*

CARLOS. Did you get the gun?

CHRISTIAN. No, I did not. You're not getting a gun, sweetheart. Have you finished the SSI forms?

CARLOS. No. And I'm not going to either.

CHRISTIAN. If we don't get these forms processed, you aren't going to be getting any more medication. Your counselor knows a guy at Social Security that can get this processed in six weeks if we just finish the goddamn forms.

CARLOS. We could do it a lot quicker if I had a gun. Just go to the welfare office. When they explain how long it all takes, bam! You just blow the caseworker away. The next person would process you so quick!

CHRISTIAN. Right, and then we could shoot it out with the SWAT team. I always thought it would be great to die in a totally senseless shoot-out in the County Welfare Office.

CARLOS. You're so literal. I'm a poet. And I promise only to shoot people who really deserve it, like the president. I would really like to shoot George Bush.

CHRISTIAN. Carlos, George Bush isn't president anymore.

CARLOS. *(Gags)* President Quale?

CHRISTIAN. No, we have a new president: Clinton. Clinton.

CARLOS. All presidents should be shot. It teaches humility. And think of the tension it would release. *(Mimes shooting)* I hate queers, bam! People with AIDS make me nervous, bam! It's God's will, bam!

CHRISTIAN. Would you please stop with the guns already? Could we talk about something else? Anything else?

CARLOS. Sure, I shit myself. You wanna clean it up?

CHRISTIAN. That's what I'm here for.

CARLOS. You're so good. *(Christian puts on gloves, removes Carlos' pants, takes off large diaper. Throws it away. Begins wiping Carlos' rear end. Carlos tries to muffle his screams)*

CHRISTIAN. I'm sorry, I'm going to have to put some ointment on this. *(Christian applies ointment. Carlos tries harder to hold in his screams. Christian finishes and puts a new diaper on Carlos)* I got that Twenty-Fifth Anniversary Edition of *Valley of the Dolls* that you asked for. And *The Women.* You'll be getting cable TV in this week. I'll be back with the medicine later. Is that nun coming in this afternoon?

CARLOS. Yeah. She's cool. She's a dyke.

CHRISTIAN. Anything else you need?

CARLOS. Just a gun. *(Christian kisses Carlos and exits)* I'll bet that nun could get me a gun. *(Singing)*
Momma, I need a gun for my birthday.
Momma, I'm sure it could blow this tension far far away.
You say I'm not responsible now,
And that you simply can not see how,
I'll pick the folks who have to scream "OWW!"
When I shoot them with my gun POW!

Momma, I need a gun for my birthday.
Momma, I'm sure a gun could blow this tension away.
This world is filled with sorrow and pain,
I find it harder each day to maintain.
I'm sure a gun could help me regain,
The strength I need to help me stay sane.

Momma, I need a gun for my birthday.

Momma, Momma, Momma

SCENE SIX

Christian's living room, Thomas sits on the couch reading Louise Hay's book Heal Your Life. *Christian enters.*

THOMAS. How's Carlos?

CHRISTIAN. I don't know anymore. Don't ask. How do you like Louise's book?

THOMAS. It's a little strange for me. Kind of embarrassing, too.

CHRISTIAN. I know what you mean. I was wary of saying things like "I love myself." But I got over that and I say it freely now. "I love myself, I love myself, I am beautiful!"

THOMAS. She's right in saying I don't love myself, but I don't think it gave me AIDS.

CHRISTIAN. Forget what that guy in the meeting said. He's got Louise all wrong. She's not saying anything that mechanistic. Believe me, if she knew of a way to cure AIDS, we'd be the first to know. *(The phone rings, and Thomas picks it up)*

THOMAS. Hi. Great! Yeah, I'll be here. Okay, see you.

CHRISTIAN. Luis?

THOMAS. He's coming over.

CHRISTIAN. Well, I'm heading out.

THOMAS. Oh, come on. You just got here. Luis just gets defensive around you and sounds more militant than he really is.

CHRISTIAN. I know. And I get pretty shrill around him, too. We're a lot alike. You know, Louise Hay says that if I have a problem with someone, it's because they're reflecting a part of me that I haven't accepted yet. So I'm trying very hard to love and be in harmony with Luis.

THOMAS. This I'd like to see.

CHRISTIAN. *(Rising)* I said I'm working on it. I really do have a lot of errands to run. Need anything?

THOMAS. No, thanks. Be home around—

CHRISTIAN. Ten or so. Bye. *(Thomas returns to reading Louise. Then he throws the book down)*

THOMAS. There's something I don't understand.

BOB. *(Popping up from nowhere)* Tell me all your problems.

THOMAS. I've been reading Louise and she says that if we truly love and forgive ourselves, the outside world will follow.

BOB. Ha!

THOMAS. Does that mean that all the homophobes out there will change? Will they stop bashing us and start dating us? Even if they did, how could I ever forgive someone like Jesse Helms or Lou Sheldon? I think that if I really do love myself, I'm not going to put up with their shit. You know, the more

I learn, the angrier I get. Sometimes I feel the way Carlos does—I'd like to blow someone away.

BOB. Uh, uh. Faeries do not judge who deserves to get blown away. That doesn't mean we take any shit either. It's really very simple, except when it gets complex. See, anger is useful. Rage can take you a long way. You have to deal with your psyche. Your soul, doll. But not like straight men. That's your problem. You still think like a heterosexual and I've got news, love. We're something else altogether.

THOMAS. What do you mean? Oh, this metaphysical babble is spinning around in my head and making me dizzy. I don't know what to think anymore. And on top of that, Luis is coming over.

BOB. He's been getting pretty friendly, hasn't he?

THOMAS. Yes, sitting next to me, touching me, hugging me a little too long when we say goodbye. And I'm convinced that he's coming over now so we can finally do it!

BOB. Fabulous!

THOMAS. But I can't do it with him. I know all about safe sex, but I'm still paranoid. What if I breathe on him and give him AIDS? And there's all those thoughts—I know it's not politically correct—but I feel it's my fault for getting it in the first place and I don't ever want to put anyone in danger. Plus, what about the germs he could give me!

BOB. You are dizzy. Look, I already had Luis and I can tell you, he's safe as they come.

THOMAS. No!

BOB. He has great fingertips. *(Bob begins molesting Thomas)* He traveled up and down my shrunken body, giving me light kisses and telling me how beautiful I was. My hand swept over that beautiful skin of his, across that chest, down his stomach and further. I think I wore a condom on every finger—no, it wasn't that bad. I didn't end up coming—I didn't need to. His touch was enough. *(Thomas gulps. There's a knock at the door)*

THOMAS. It's Luis!

BOB. Quick, look sexy. And remember, the concept of sin was invented as a political tool to keep the weak in line. Repeat it.

THOMAS. The concept of sin was invented as a political tool to keep the weak in line. Wait, how do I find these faerie friends of yours?

BOB. They're not in the Pink Yellow Pages. You'll find them when it's time.

THOMAS. That's so cliché! *(Bob exits. Thomas lets Luis in)*

LUIS. Hi. How are you? You look good, much better, great in fact. *(Luis tries to hug Thomas but Thomas pulls away and sits on couch)*

THOMAS. Thanks. *(Luis moves behind the couch, behind Thomas)*

LUIS. Reading Louise? Christian take you?

THOMAS. Yeah. Let me ask you something. When are ACT UP meetings?

LUIS. Mondays at 7:30. You thinking about going?

THOMAS. Yeah, I thought I would. I'm a little scared, though. *(Luis begins massaging Thomas)*

LUIS. Don't worry, I'll hold your hand through the first meeting if you want. ACT UP people aren't hostile to newcomers— just to each other. *(Luis' hands begin moving down over Thomas' body)* All of us are grieving and pissed off and trying to figure out how to stop this epidemic. Things get dramatic and some people don't need the stress—especially if they're sick. For all the screaming, we do a lot of good and we try to balance things out with fun things like dances and benefit jack-off parties. *(Luis goes for Thomas' crotch)*

THOMAS. *(Jumps up to escape Luis)* I could help! I did high school dances in the gym! And I do great things with crepe paper!

LUIS. What's the matter? I'm practically irresistible and you can't wait to get out of here!

THOMAS. I'm feeling guilty because I waited so long to get up and do something. I waited until I got sick.

LUIS. Doesn't Louise talk about guilt being a useless emotion that holds us back?

THOMAS. You read Louise?

LUIS. Yes, and she's right about that. *(Luis starts to kiss Thomas)*

THOMAS. Wait. I don't know. Ummn, we got to talk.

LUIS. I'll be careful and slow and hard. I've got rubbers!

THOMAS. No, I'm worried about this. I'm HIV positive and I don't want to—

LUIS. I'm HIV positive, too. *(Singing, as he and Thomas prepare a bed on the floor and start undressing each other)*
The clock on the wall says
The hour is growing quite late
My time is running out
I don't think I can wait

The tensions growing high
My body starts to sigh
I look at your body and all of me wants to cry

I want to be in your body with you
To see God in your body with you
I want to come in your body with you
And nobody's body but your body's going to do.
THOMAS.
My dreams keep whispering
The whole world's turned inside out
When I'm alone with you
Passion ends all the doubt

I start to feel the heat
The pain is turning so sweet
I look at your body and I don't want to be so discreet
THOMAS AND LUIS.
I want to be in your body with you
To see God in your body with you
I want to come in your body with you
And nobody's body but your body's going to do.

In your body with you
In your body with you . . . *(Lights fade)*

SCENE SEVEN

A large meeting hall; it's an ACT UP meeting. As each person enters the meeting, among them ACT UP Members 1, 2, and 3, Carlos, Christian, Lisa, Luis, Lurleen, Thomas, Vanessa, and the chorus, they sing:

Act Up, Fight Back, Stop AIDS . . . we're Acting Up
Act Up, Fight Back, Stop AIDS . . . we're Fighting Back
Act Up, Fight Back, Stop AIDS . . . we're Stopping AIDS.

THOMAS. Lurleen, I don't think I can do this. I've never chaired a meeting in my life, much less something this political.

LURLEEN. It's not that hard, shug'. You just write down the names as people raise their hands. I'll direct the discussion.

LUIS. We've got a huge fight coming up and you're new to the group. You're not on one side or the other.

ACT UP MEMBER 1. Lurleen, I need to ask you something before this meeting starts. Is Thomas sleeping with Luis?

LURLEEN. I don't have the vaguest idea how that could be any of your business.

ACT UP MEMBER 1. Every time we have a controversial issue on the floor, someone Luis is sleeping with ends up chairing the meeting!

THOMAS. I *am* sleeping with Luis. You want me to step out, I would only be too happy.

LURLEEN. No way! Thomas is on the waiting list to get into County Hospital and he still has three months left before he can get any health care. That's what we're discussing tonight. No one has more right than he does to chair this meeting.

LUIS. Besides, he's only writing down names.

ACT UP MEMBER 1. Okay, but we'll be watching you!

LURLEEN. Okay, let's get this meeting started. (*Everyone sits and Lurleen addresses the group*) Welcome to the AIDS Coalition To Unleash Power, ACT UP/LA!

ALL. (*Singing*)
We're here, we're queer, we're everything you fear
We're fags, we're dykes, we're not ladylike
The church, the state, we're going to demonstrate.
Don't wait, hesitate, come out it's not too late

Act Up, Fight Back, Stop AIDS . . . we're Acting Up
Act Up, Fight Back, Stop AIDS . . . we're Fighting Back
Act Up, Fight Back, Stop AIDS . . . we're Stopping AIDS.

LURLEEN. For you new members, we have a committee that's

negotiating with County to get proper funding for the AIDS ward. They have a huge demonstration planned. Can we hear the report?

ACT UP MEMBER 2. *(Singing)*

Imagine a city,
A city of people,
Of all of the people who're still locked outside,
A vigil of people, the sick and the wounded,
The ones who refuse to be one more who died.
We'll stay through the morning,
We'll camp through the night,
We're telling the hospital
Health care's a right.

VANESSA.

I hear what you're saying

ALL.

Stop the murder, Act Up!

VANESSA.

Tell me now you're crying

ALL.

Health care funding, Fight Back!
HEALTH CARE FUNDING . . . STOP AIDS

VANESSA.

Sing me now, what you're shouting

ALL.

Homophobes off our backs!

VANESSA.

One more time, I want to hear it

ALL.

A chance to live, Act Up!
A CHANCE TO LIVE . . . ACT UP

LUIS.

Let's wake up this whole damned city,
The men in power, they got no pity.
We've planned this massive demonstration,
Shake them up with agitation.
We can make them meet every demand,
Or we'll close them down so fast, understand?
We can negotiate justice—
Fund us properly or we'll act up, trust us!

ACT UP MEMBER 3. Trust you? Trust you? You plan to call off our demonstration if they make some bargain with us? *(Singing)*

I'm here to tell your committee,
something stinks and it don't smell pretty.
You want to trade our demonstration,
for a scrap of compensation.
If they meet a few of our demands,
we'll jump up and down to their commands.
We don't negotiate silence,
we always stand up and fight their violence.

ACT UP MEMBER 3.	LUIS.
You don't trust me!	You disgust me!
Immature!	Horse Manure!
Traitor!	Turncoat!
Sell out!	Lies

ALL.

You keep yakking, everyone dies!

ACT UP MEMEBER 3.	LUIS.
Sleazy!	Slimy!
Scumball!	Worm!

Listening to you makes me squirm!

ALL. AHHHHHHHHHHHHH!!!!!!!!!!!!!!! *(All freeze. Carlos steps out)*

CARLOS. *(Singing)*

Oh, the tedium, as I rub my bum, these agendas are the death of me.
I lose where we are, then I'm growing hard, what a waste of first-class meat.
But look out over there, with the spiky hair, I feel like such a lech.
He's so lickable, but despicable, his politics make me wretch.

AIDS, the spectacle, it's not so wonderful, will I ever see the end?
People who we love, are dying left and right, so many wounds to mend. *(Carlos sits. The rest unfreeze. Thomas, Luis, Lisa, and Vanessa huddle)*

THOMAS. Everyone's fighting. How can we possibly pull off a major demonstration?

LUIS. We have to do something to get everyone's attention, to wake up every gay person in this city. Something that will unite all of us.

LISA. We'll paint over every office that refuses to help us with bloody handprints, just like you did in the beginning of ACT UP. *(Singing)*
We'll wake up the people,
The people who're sleeping,
The people who're sleeping while so many die.
We'll poster the city while people are sleeping
When you turn around, it's right there in your eye.
We'll spray paint each evening,
We'll work through the night
We're telling the city that health care's a right.

LISA. Are you with me?

THOMAS. A lot of people won't like this. It can't be ACT UP/Los Angeles doing this. But we need to do it.

LISA. We have to do it!

LUIS. We're going to do it!

ALL. Yes!

VANESSA. *(Singing)*
I hear what you're saying

ALL.
Stop the murder, Act Up!

VANESSA.
Tell me now you're crying

ALL.
Health care funding, Fight Back!
HEALTH CARE FUNDING . . . STOP AIDS

VANESSA.
Sing me now, what you're shouting

ALL.
Homophobes off our backs!

VANESSA.
One more time, I want to hear it

ALL.
A chance to live, Act Up!
A CHANCE TO LIVE . . . ACT UP!

LURLEEN. People, we're already an hour late on our agenda now and we have fifty-seven items left!

act two

LURLEEN. *(Addressing the audience)* Hi! My name is Lurleen Devereaux. You know, a lot of people have been asking us, "Why don't you have any straight people in your show?" The answer is really very simple, "Because we don't have to." Other people wonder, "Why don't you have some cute little children with AIDS in your show?" The media in this country have ignored homosexuals for years. This show is about that community. But for those of you who insist, this is Abigail. *(Holds up a maimed baby doll)* Isn't she cute? She is an innocent child with AIDS. She did not ask for this disease, nor did she want it. *(Holds baby doll out to audience member)* Could you hold her please? Here's her bottle. Thank you, and now, Act Two of *AIDS! The Musical!*

SCENE ONE

Action switches between Christian's living room and the street. Christian is clearing up piles of flyers and position papers from the ACT UP meeting. Thomas is on the phone with Vanessa.

THOMAS. Okay, Vanessa, this is the deal. We've decided to hit a supposed health clinic run by right-wing fundamentalists. They're lobbying to end special funding for the AIDS ward and to have more money given to private, that is religious, hospitals. That's right. They're the same people trying to close the women's health clinics because of abortions. You still in? Whoops, gotta go. I'll see you later.

CHRISTIAN. *(Discovers a can of red paint, buckets, and brushes)* What is all this?

THOMAS. Paint.

CHRISTIAN. I know what it is. What are you doing with cans of bright red paint?

THOMAS. *(Sarcastically)* If you sniff it regular it's great for your immune system.

CHRISTIAN. That's not funny. You're getting ready to go out God knows where and vandalize the city. Do you really think anyone hears what you say when you do that? No one at the hospice where I work understands it. They just get more convinced that you're crazy. Why can't you work within the system?

THOMAS. Fuck the system! The last time we had a vigil, the media refused to cover anything we did until the painting started. Then suddenly they couldn't get enough of us.

CHRISTIAN. And what did that get you?

THOMAS. An AIDS ward. In three months we're going to have every major AIDS group in the city at another huge vigil demanding funding for the AIDS ward, and we're *going* to have the media there.

CHRISTIAN. Boy, you're getting to sound as political and preachy as Luis. He must be so proud. *(Door ding-dongs)* Speak of the she-devil.

THOMAS. *(Opens the door. It's Luis)* Hi, honey. *(Kisses him)*

CHRISTIAN. Oh, don't let me disturb you.

LUIS. We were just leaving.

CHRISTIAN. You just take good care of Thomas. Or *else. (He exits)*

THOMAS. *(To Luis)* Don't mind her.

LUIS. Trust me, I don't. Geez, I can't believe Lisa went and invited Vanessa to come with us. That's what happens when girls fall in love.

THOMAS. You are so sexist sometimes. The only reason I got invited out is because we're going together. If you need to worry about someone, worry about me. My knees are shaking. *(Now they're on the street. Vanessa and Lisa enter)*

LISA. We better all be really careful. These people are hard-core right-wingers. If they catch us they'll beat the shit out of us first and then call the police.

LUIS. Write this number on your arm: 666–6969. If we get separated and someone gets arrested, call it and Clair will alert legal support. *(They begin "painting" the signs, the street, the walls, everything)*

VANESSA. *(Looking down the street)* Careful, it's the cops.

LUIS. Quick, hide everything!

VANESSA. Chill out. They're turning. Look, I scoped the place earlier and I think we can paint the whole west window. It's in the dark right now, but it'll show up great in the morning.

THOMAS. I think I'm gonna puke.

LUIS. Take a breath and calm down. Look, all of you. If we do get caught the worst we're up against is some minor misdemeanor charge. It's no big deal.

ALL. *(Singing)*

Paint the city, gonna paint the city, paint the city till it's dripping red.

Paint for all of the walking wounded, paint for my friends who're dead.

Paint, paint, paint
Paint the city
Paint, paint, paint
Paint the city red

THOMAS. Oh no, someone's coming. Quick, let's get out of here.

LISA. We haven't finished the slogans yet.

LUIS. It's okay, they're gone. *(Singing)*

Paint for Larry, gonna paint for George, paint for Henry, gonna paint for you.

Cover this city in pain and anger, paint the truth to get our message through!

Paint, paint, paint
Paint the city
Paint, paint, paint
Paint the city red *(They finish painting)*

THOMAS. It's gorgeous.

LISA. We did it!

LUIS. Let's get out of here. *(Scene shifts to Christian's living room)*

CHRISTIAN. What do you mean you're going to a movie? It's nearly 11:00 P.M. And you don't go to movies anymore because Luis doesn't like them! *(Back onto the street)*

THOMAS. Ready? *(They continue painting)*

ALL. *(Singing)*

Paint this city for the ACT UP vigil, politicians, gonna wake you now

Staff the AIDS ward, we demand it, you're gonna fund it and we don't care how

Paint, paint, paint
Paint the city
Paint, paint, paint
Paint the city red

LUIS. Isn't that enough? We've put out over a hundred posters advertising the fund-raiser for the vigil!

THOMAS. We've got twenty-five more to go.

VANESSA. We've already been stopped by the cops once tonight. It's a miracle we got off!

LISA. Aren't you having fun? This is neat. This entire neighborhood will be covered tomorrow! *(Scene shifts to Christian's living room)*

CHRISTIAN. *(Waves newspaper at Thomas)* You told me you would never desecrate a church!

THOMAS. And I never have. That was painted on a wall next to the church.

CHRISTIAN. Do you think anyone in the real world will make that distinction? I suppose Luis was real proud of you.

THOMAS. Oh God. Luis—he's going to be pissed when he finds out. *(Back to the streets)*

LUIS. You can't get arrested tonight. We don't have any lawyer ready to get you out.

LISA. We can do anything we have to do. I'm not afraid of spending the night in jail. Are you, Thomas?

THOMAS. Don't worry. We won't get arrested. We'll block the doors just like last time and as soon as the cops come, we'll move out of the way.

ALL. *(Singing)*

Paint this city for the ACT UP vigil, politicians, gonna wake you now
Staff the AIDS ward, we demand it, you're gonna fund it, we don't care how

Paint for Larry, gonna paint for George, paint for Henry, gonna paint for you.
Cover this city in pain and anger, paint the truth to get our message through!

Paint, paint, paint
Paint the city

Paint, paint, paint
Paint the city! *(Blackout)*

SCENE TWO

In his living room, Christian sits in front of a TV with a remote control in his hand, flipping through stations. Thomas enters.

THOMAS. You okay?
CHRISTIAN. Carlos died last night.
THOMAS. Oh God. I'm sorry. *(He seems to be in a hurry)* Look, I've got to go.
CHRISTIAN. I know. Another meeting. See you later.
THOMAS. Are you mad at me?
CHRISTIAN. No. It's just that everyday it's another demonstration, another committee meeting, another spirituality rap group.
THOMAS. I know, I know. I guess I'm obsessed.
CHRISTIAN. I don't want you to be just another statistic. I love you and I, I, it's just that—I can't stand all this dying. I can't stand it.
THOMAS. Maybe you should take a break. Take care of yourself for once.
CHRISTIAN. I'm good at what I do and if I don't do it, it won't be done. A third of the guys I started as a buddy with are dead now. You can't stop yourself and I can't stop myself.
THOMAS. Look—I can cancel on my meeting. Let's have dinner together.
CHRISTIAN. It's really not necessary. I couldn't eat anyway. I'll see you later. We can stay up late and talk.
THOMAS. That'd be nice. *(He exits. Christian looks at the TV set. He's blank. Begins flipping channels again. Doorbell rings)*
CHRISTIAN. It's open!
LUIS. Where's Thomas?
CHRISTIAN. You just missed him.
LUIS. We're late for our appointment with the County Medical people.
CHRISTIAN. Another appointment. Fabulous.
LUIS. And that pisses you off.
CHRISTIAN. Yes, it does. Every single night of the week, Thomas

has a meeting or a late-night, secret God-knows-what. He's
on the edge of a nervous collapse and you don't even
notice.

LUIS. That's not true. When he was sick last week, I was just as
scared as you were. It's going to be months still before he
can get regular care. Activism gives him hope.

CHRISTIAN. If it doesn't kill him first.

LUIS. You know, I have never criticized the work you do.

CHRISTIAN. You called me an angelic vampire.

LUIS. Only after you ridiculed everything I work on. I will never
understand you. You love to complain but you'd never lift a
finger to really change things.

CHRISTIAN. I've been to your AIDS activist stuff. You just didn't
notice me. I can't speak in groups. I really don't understand
politics and I get nauseous when people start fighting with
each other. You scream about people dying but I'm the one
who takes care of them. I'm the one who watches them die.
I never slept around like you. I never did it in a bathroom
or the back room of a bar. The men I slept with meant
something to me.

LUIS. That's what it comes down to, doesn't it? You blame this
whole fucking epidemic on me because I was promiscuous.
You think we'd all be safe if only people like me had been
more repressed. Well I didn't cause AIDS, you prissy little
son of a bitch. It's a virus. So I'm HIV positive. I practice
safe sex and I'll tell you something else. I loved it all. Every
cock, every nipple, every man. I saw more passion and truth
in any ten minutes looking at a cock through a hole in a
bathroom toilet stall than you've seen in your whole life.
(Christian slaps him) Did that make you feel better? You
wanna do it again? *(Christian slaps him again. They begin to
struggle)*

CHRISTIAN. Carlos is dead! My friend is dead! *(Luis forces Christian to the ground and locks his arms around him to subdue him.
Christian stops struggling. After a moment, Luis lets him go, knowing the fight is over)* Hold me, just hold me. *(Luis tentatively
puts his arms around Christian. Christian embraces him tightly.
After a few moments, Christian begins to kiss Luis' neck)*

LUIS. Wait a second. I'm not ready for this.

CHRISTIAN. Please. You've slept with half the members of ACT UP/Los Angeles.

LUIS. If you need some physical contact, I'll take you out. We'll find someone for you.

CHRISTIAN. I have never picked someone up in a bar successfully. I'm not coherent tonight. Everything's broken in me, smashed up.

LUIS. Why me?

CHRISTIAN. Because you're here. *(Singing)*
I'm feeling so numb, it's like nothing is left in my soul
But the touch of your skin brings hope that I need to be whole

I want you just for tonight
I don't care if it's right
I look at your body and darkness gives way to the light

I want to be in your body with you
To see God in your body with you
I want to come in your body with you
And anybody's body would,
Even your body could do.
(As Christian and Luis begin making love, a ghostly Carlos enters)

CARLOS. *(Singing)*
Momma, I need a gun for my birthday
Momma, I'm sure a gun would chase this sorrow far, far away.

CHRISTIAN AND CARLOS.
My life is filled with problems and pain,
I find it harder each day to maintain.
I need your love to help me regain,
The strength I need to help to stay sane.

CARLOS. Momma, I need a gun for my birthday.
Momma, Momma, Momma . . .

SCENE THREE

Thomas' room at Christian's house. Thomas throws his suitcase on the bed, opens it, and begins throwing his things into it.

BOB. *(Appearing)* Going somewhere?

THOMAS. I'm moving in with Lisa.

BOB. And you've conveniently snuck in here when you knew Christian wasn't going to be around.

THOMAS. Oh, I guess you think I should stay here and "work everything out" with him and Luis. Fuck them! They were screwing each other for weeks before I found out.

BOB. Thomas, you know how you are. You want to break both of their little necks and the odds are you'll never mention a word of it to either of them.

THOMAS. Do you have any idea how tired I get listening to you? You taught me to how to masturbate, you discovered comics, you discovered—

BOB. And all those superheroes with those tight little bulges.

THOMAS. You were the one who knew he was gay from the second he was born and I just have to catch up and figure it all out while you watch with that smug smile.

BOB. Yes, get mad. Get it out. Otherwise, you'll actually kill some fag basher next time. And your mother, and your father, and everyone else you can't deal with.

THOMAS. Oh, great. What a profound message. Look where your advice has led me so far. *(Revealing bloodstains on his undershirt)* I just kicked someone's ass because they called me a faggot. I just wish it would all end. All I wanted was a little happiness.

BOB. Happy. I hate that fucking word. Cut out all the bad stuff in your life and everything's gonna be fine! Chin up, face it with dignity, think only good thoughts. There's a new vaccine they're testing! Fuck hope! Hope is for TV movies. The truth is that most of us are going to die ugly, violent deaths. We're going to lose everything and, sure, we're shitting-in-our-pants scared. All of us. But you forget that. Sometimes you think you're the only one who's hurting. *(Thomas goes to Bob and holds him)*

BOB. That feels so nice. How many times did we jack off together in that tree house, how many times did I pray that maybe once, just for a moment, we could hold each other. Sometimes when I was dying, I would look up at you and you glowed, golden and lucid. Other times, all I saw was fear. You're a lot stronger than you realize, Thomas. *(Singing)*

There was something in the dark,
And it was horrible.
There was something in the dark,
And it was mine.
There was something in the dark,
And it was frightening.
There was something in the dark,
It was sublime.

There was something in the dark,
And it was calling me
To a place there in the dark,
To set me free,
All my hope was in the dark,
As clear as lightning,
I found power in the dark
It let me see

It was my hate,
It was my fear,
It was my rage,
It was my dreams,
It was my strength,
It was my love,
It was a vision.

And sometimes I embraced it with all my heart,
And sometimes it pierced me and tore my dreams apart.

There was something in the dark,
And it was beautiful,
There was something in the dark, it was divine

And it was mine
It was divine . . .

SCENE FOUR

*Lisa and Vanessa are backstage at an ACT UP bar benefit,
chugging beers, while Lurleen applies her makeup.*

VANESSA. *(To Lurleen)* You wouldn't believe how much she was flirting with that girl.

LISA. I was not flirting.

VANESSA. If you were standing any closer to her you would have had that pierced tongue down your throat! *(Lisa opens another beer)*

LURLEEN. Well, if you weren't flirting, you will be soon. That's your fourth beer and the show isn't even over yet.

LISA. We have a deal. If I take the time to explore three new clubs with Vanessa this month, she'll come for a visit to the women's commune this summer.

VANESSA. Aren't there animals out there that could eat me up?

LURLEEN. Honey, I've seen you in the streets. If you can face down a line of L.A. cops, you can handle a bear.

LISA. Maybe I should leave you here.

VANESSA. Oh no! Who'd take care of you? If you're going to be eaten by a bear, I want to see.

LISA. Isn't she sweet? She's made me forget all about that rat Penny. Lurleen? Are you nervous?

LURLEEN. Happens every time before I go on. *(Looks in the mirror)* I love myself, I love myself, I am fabulous!

VANESSA. *(To Lisa)* Uh oh, here comes your roommate.

LISA. We'll see you later, doll. Knock 'em dead! *(Vanessa takes Lisa out into the bar. Thomas enters)*

THOMAS. You ready, Lurleen? You're on next.

LURLEEN. Honey, why'd you have to schedule me after all those drag queens? I'm not nearly as flashy as they are.

THOMAS. Don't worry. You'll be a big hit. People have been drinking a lot of booze tonight. We need to take them down a little, get some coffee in 'em before they drive home. You are a perfect show closer. Is Lisa okay?

LURLEEN. I don't like it. That girl has been getting drunk regular lately. And I don't mean to be anti-Semitic but that is weird for a nice Jewish girl.

LUIS. *(Enters)* We've made over five-thousand dollars tonight. You've done an incredible job with this fund-raiser. I can't tell you how much I appreciate this.

THOMAS. Contrary to whatever you may be fantasizing this week, you don't run ACT UP/Los Angeles and I'm not doing this for you. We have a thousand people coming to our vigil at the county hospital in a few days. And dozens of people have been working their butts off making sure we have the news media there. This money'll back them up.

LUIS. I don't see what you're so mad about now. You know, Christian doesn't really mind. We're still seeing each other.

THOMAS. At the same time you're seeing this new boy? You sure scooped him up quick. His first meeting and you're already inviting him to private committee meetings. He doesn't talk much, does he? Oh well, I'm sure he'll find something to say as soon as he turns eighteen.

LUIS. I never lied to you and I never promised I was going to be anything close to monogamous. You don't have to like me, but we have to be able to work together without driving everyone around us crazy.

THOMAS. I was just one more guy helping you forget that you're HIV positive. Sooner or later you are going to die, Luis, just like everybody else.

LUIS. Why don't you just get over it? We could still be together if you weren't so damned possessive.

THOMAS. Excuse me, I've got to introduce Lurleen. *(Thomas and Lurleen go into the bar, leaving Luis behind)*

LURLEEN. Sweetheart, it's been two months now, don't you think it's time you got over Luis? If you want something to worry about, concentrate on your roommate. Something is definitely wrong with Lisa, and I don't think it's just her breakup with Penny.

THOMAS. *(Moving past her to the stage)* And now, for our last number of the evening, ACT UP's own Lurleen Devereaux!

LURLEEN. Now, a little song for anyone who's ever felt betrayed by some dirty snake in the grass. Hit it! *(Singing, while the chorus dances, country-western style)*
Your touch was as soft as the fresh morning dew
The dawn was shining in on us, I was there in bed with you.
You let sunshine into my heart and make it dance,
Making my skin wild with them strange thoughts of romance.

But I've been two-timed, two too many times,
And I would call you back but why waste all them dimes?
Every time you say that you love me
Something snaps and then you shove me.
I've been two-timed, too many times.

THOMAS. *(Thomas jumps up to duet with Lurleen)* Yeah! Here's to all the two-timing jerks in the world.

LURLEEN AND THOMAS. *(Singing)*
Your eyes were as blue as I feel when I'm alone,
Trying to fill the holes in time with a drunken L.A. stone
You lie next to me when you have no place to go.
Your loving isn't constant so you find it hard to show.

But I've been two-timed, two too many times,
And I would call you back but why waste all them dimes?
Every time you say that you love me
Something snaps and then you shove me.
I've been two-timed, too many times. *(Lisa joins Lurleen and Thomas)*

LURLEEN, THOMAS, AND LISA. *(Singing)*
My need was as hot as the fiery pits of Hell,
I knew I had to be with you from the moment that I fell
In love with your lies, with your dreams and with your charms,
Each night I burn alive again when I'm lying in your arms.

But I've been two-timed, two too many times,
And I would call you back but why waste all them dimes?
Every time you say that you love me
Something snaps and then you shove me.
I've been two-timed, too many times.

LURLEEN. Goodnight, everyone! ACT UP/Los Angeles! *(Chorus disperses and exits. Vanessa retrieves Lisa)*

VANESSA. Forgotten all about Penny, huh?

LISA. That wasn't about Penny.

VANESSA. I think I'd better take you home, put you to bed. *(They exit kissing, holding hands. Meanwhile, Thomas is approached by a bar patron. Lurleen eavesdrops)*

BAR PATRON. Hey, you have a great voice. Could I buy you a beer?

THOMAS. No, it's bad for your immune system.

BAR PATRON. Well, excuse me!

LURLEEN. Look, shug', I don't mean to be rude, but isn't the correct answer, "No thank you, but I'd love a mineral water"? Honey, you're so sour tonight you make my private parts pucker just listening to you.

THOMAS. What do you expect? I'm so sick of those chichi West Hollywood boys. People are dying all over this city and they act like you're rude if you even mention the big vigil coming up. Fuck them!

LURLEEN. Honey, there are boys here who haven't even heard you say a word about your latest political position. If you aren't getting laid maybe you should consider your attitude.

THOMAS. What's the use? As soon as they start talking about their stupid lives it takes about a minute to discover they're either hairdressers or growing plants in some fag nursery. All they care about is sex.

LURLEEN. Well listen to you. Somebody better get his cock in you quick before you wither up with nastiness and blow away. I'm gonna tell you this only once. You got AIDS because you were in the wrong place at the wrong time. If you're looking for fairness in the world, forget it. Babies in Bangladesh don't deserve to starve to death. You just may have a limited amount of time left, but you're not morally superior to anyone including a hairdresser. There are thousands of guys out there tonight looking for a little physical release, a little comfort. And some of the guys are spending their last days, or months or years. If we can't allow each other to have a little tenderness, then we're just a bunch of authoritarians lecturing the masses about moral superiority.

THOMAS. Oh, Lurleen, you're right. But I can't handle talking to a bunch of guys telling each other their life stories. I feel like I'm exploding. I'm angry, I'm tired, and I'm running out of time, and my dick still insists on dragging me out tonight.

LURLEEN. Well, honey, why didn't you say so. I know just the place for you. It's a private men's sex club. It has mazes and stalls and back rooms filled with guys who don't need to know your last name to do it tonight.

THOMAS. You mean they do it right there? I thought they closed all those places down!

LURLEEN. Not yet. Our community pioneered safe sex. There are thousands of ways of getting hot safely. All you need is your tight black pants, don't wear underwear, and don't have any extra cash in your pants. You don't want someone emptying your pockets while you experience the joys of fellatio. Just make sure you have plenty of condoms.

THOMAS. Will you come with me? I just can't go alone.

LURLEEN. Honey, they don't let tits in that place.

THOMAS. But you don't have real tits.

LURLEEN. *(Putting her hand in her blouse)* The best money can buy. Shug', it's time you go out and get laid. I'm sending you to the Flesh Pit!

SCENE FIVE

Thomas is inside the Flesh Pit.

THOMAS. The front room was bright and friendly with a bunch of guys sitting on pillows watching Rosalind Russell in *Auntie Mame* on video. But as soon as you open that side door the lights go out. I am walking down a narrow hallway that leads into another dimension. Remember when Superman used to get hit by the ray gun and bam, he's in another space time continuum parallel to our own? Gay men have always known how to open that door into the other world that waits so close to ours. I smell sweat, and sperm, and sour smells I can't quite pinpoint, but which seem as if they were there in my memory from farther back than I can recall. I know this place, even though I've never been here in my life. At first it scares me. I pass stalls with half-naked couples and threesomes doing things. Things I haven't done in a while. I walk through a maze around a corner past barred windows. I look in and see ten or fifteen men in a secret space sucking and licking and humping and stroking. Time is slow at first, and then it speeds up in this dimension, swirling around me as I find myself pulled into the back center room I had glimpsed through the bars. The night explodes. For a while I am kissing and biting and touching and flowing into hairy legs, hard nipples, wet mouths, pulsing cocks. And then I pull back, stagger down a hallway around a corner and out into a dark courtyard. The sky is actually clear tonight and in the moonlight I hear a voice from the side of a huge tree. *(Ben steps out of the shadows)*

BEN. Welcome to the Flesh Pit. *(Thomas just stares)*

BEN. This is your first time, isn't it?

THOMAS. Is it that obvious? What are you, the official greeter?

BEN. No, I only come once a month just before the full moon.

THOMAS. Isn't that a full moon tonight?

BEN. No, that's tomorrow. It feels very different. But you can still feel the power tonight.

THOMAS. Power?

BEN. Power. Tonight I celebrate with my body. Tomorrow I celebrate with friends and my spirit. At the ocean.

THOMAS. You make it sound like church.

BEN. I hate church.

THOMAS. Me too. Let's celebrate. *(Sex Club chorus enters)*

BEN. *(Singing)*

I wiped you with the blood I tore from deep inside my heart.
I smear my cum across this page and then I call it art.
My heart is filled with blinding pain searing till it hurts.
I find release with you in spasms and in spurts.

BEN AND CHORUS.

I suck you, lick you, take your body deep inside,
In a place where there is nothing left that you can hope to hide.
I reach across to touch you deep inside this space, this criminal space (criminal space)

BEN.

Now they say our love is evil and our bodies filled with sin.
And they swear that Jesus hated us for ever loving men.
Now they ask for much more money to arms for wars to come.
Let us die in record numbers 'til our souls are growing numb.

BEN AND CHORUS.

> I suck you, lick you, take your body deep inside,
> In a place where there is nothing left that you can hope to hide.
> I reach across to touch you deep inside this space, this criminal space (criminal space)

BEN.

> I hear the words come calling from two thousand years ago,
> Singing tales of blood and sperm and earth, I feel the power grow.
> Inside this space I find the strength I know I need
> I saw the earth inside your face when you looked back at me.

BEN AND CHORUS.

> I suck you, lick you, take your body deep inside,
> In a place where there is nothing left that you can hope to hide.
> I reach across to touch you deep inside this space, this criminal space (criminal space)

THOMAS. *(Dialogue)* You really mean that, don't you? You, me, all of this, has something to do with something really old, totally primal.

BEN. Can't you feel it too? On nights like this I feel as if we really could save the earth. I feel like some old, old memory is stirring inside of me and making love to you becomes a kind of magic.

THOMAS. It does feel like magic tonight. I wish it would never end.

BEN. It doesn't have to. Come to the beach tomorrow. I want to show you magic. I want to show you a faerie circle.

THOMAS. Faeries! I had a friend who was a faerie. I've been looking for you guys, I just didn't know where to find you. I mean, I couldn't just look you up in the phone book. Yes. I'll be there.

SCENE SIX

At the beach, there is a full moon. Ben, Thomas, and group of Faeries including Jack, Pat, Karen, Faerie 1, 2, and 3 in skirts and beads enter.

ALL. *(Singing)*

> We're here, we're there, and we're everywhere, we're the people you meet all week
>
> But when the earth and the moon and stars, causes the tides to peak.
>
> The goddess calls each one of us, there's a circle forming tonight
>
> What to do and what to wear, forget about wrong and what's right
>
> Everything's gonna be wild, 'cuz we're faeries

JACK.

> My name is Jack, I'm a CPA, crunching from eight to five.
>
> But when I lose this suit and tie, Sister Black Hole's alive.

ALL.

> Grab your skirt and your faerie dust, milagros shiny and bright.
>
> Join the circle energy, offer yourself to the light.
>
> Gather together, we're . . .
>
> Radical, Magical, Mystical, Whimsical, Ultrafantastical
>
> Radical, Magical, Mystical, Whimsical, Ultrafantastical
>
> Fabulous faeries!
>
> We're boys, we're girls, we're androgynous, we're water, we're earth, we're fire.
>
> It's not a church, it's our pagan rite, it's a promise we've had since birth.
>
> Everybody's equal here, together we reach for the stars.
>
> Ride the cosmic tidal wave, shooting past Venus and Mars.
>
> Together forever, we're . . .
>
> Radical, Magical, Mystical, Whimsical, Ultrafantastical
>
> Radical, Magical, Mystical, Whimsical, Ultrafantastical
>
> Radical, Magical, Mystical, Whimsical, Ultrafantastical
>
> Radical, Magical, Mystical, Whimsical, Ultrafantastical
>
> Nothing's impossible, completely unstoppable,
>
> Fabulous faeries! *(Song finishes. One faerie brings out an altar and the group gathers around it. Karen places a photo of Sharon Tate as "Jennifer" in* Valley of the Dolls*)*

KAREN. This is for Jaemy. He was upset this week when we had to cancel his goodbye party. We were supposed to have burritos and chile rellenos and we were all going to get high and say goodbye and he'd take the pills. But the sores in his throat got so bad he couldn't swallow at all and he was afraid he wouldn't be able to take the pills if we waited a day and then they'd get him hooked up to one of those damned machines. I just held him in my arms, and then eventually the pills kicked in and he died. I really didn't mind him dying that much. I was ready for that. I was pissed because he didn't get the party. I guess we've all had a really shitty week. Thank Goddess we have this group. This is the one place I can just let it down. *(Karen turns to Pat. Pat places a picture of Stephen Sondheim on the altar. There's an audible gasp. Faerie 1 says in loud whisper, "Sondheim!")*

PAT. This is for Larry. Larry didn't admit to me he had AIDS until I had to rush him to the hospital. He told everyone he had cancer, made an agreement with the family doctor to list cancer on his death certificate to save his family one last "indignity." I was so mad at him, and I quoted Sondheim to him—and don't even start!—that "no one is alone," that we're all responsible for one another and the animals and the plants and the earth, and that if he lied about dying of AIDS, there'd be undercounting and less funding. Larry told me, "Go to hell!," of course. How could I tell him how to die? And maybe he was right. *(Pat turns to Thomas who places a beaded necklace on the altar. Bob appears in the background)*

THOMAS. This is from Bob. He gave it to me after he died. I mean—

FAERIE 1. Oh, you slipped! Bob's haunting you, isn't he? I always knew he would. I had someone haunting me, too. She appeared poof! right after the funeral. Is that the way it is for you? You were his best friend, right? Thomas.

THOMAS. Yes, but it's not the same thing. I don't really see Bob. He's with me, you know, inside.

BOB. Liar!

THOMAS. Wait, I take that back. We do talk, get into fights, everything. Is that crazy?

BEN. Have you grieved for him?

THOMAS. Of course. I didn't go to his funeral because I was sick, but yes, I grieved in my own way.

BEN. And he still haunts you? As long as he does, you can pretend he's not dead. And he is.

THOMAS. Maybe I am in denial, but I don't care. I'm not ready to give in to death. If I've learned anything, it's that I'm living with AIDS, not dying of it. Is that denial or is it hope?

BEN. How can you have any hope for Bob?

FAERIE 2. You gotta face it. Scream, shout, let it all out! This is the place to do it.

FAERIE 3. I kept my lover's death in for over a year. I never cried. At the last gathering I hesitantly went to this grieving circle and when the person next to me started crying, I started, too. Man, I was gone. I couldn't stop. I didn't realized how much I was holding in. When it was over, I knew I wasn't done, but I was better.

THOMAS. No, no, I couldn't do that.

BEN. It helps a lot, believe me.

THOMAS. I have to deal with it in my own way, okay? Can you respect that?

BEN. Fair enough. Just know that we're here for you.

THOMAS. I'm fine. Really. *(Ben begins to chant "Omm." The rest start to get up and Ben grabs Thomas' hand. Thomas pulls away. He walks toward Bob)*

FAERIES. *(Singing)*
We all come from the Mother and to her we shall return,
Like a drop of rain, flowing to the ocean.
(Repeat till scene end)

BOB. I've come to say goodbye.

THOMAS. Goodbye? How can you leave? You're *my* hallucination.

BOB. Too late. I've got my fake furs and my hats all packed. It's a big universe out there and a girl needs her outfits.

THOMAS. Bob, you're the only one I can talk to.

BOB. Bullshit. You just want to keep me tucked away backstage so that you never have to accept that I'm dead. Until you do that, you can't grieve for yourself and you can't go on. And you have to, because people need you. So kiss me and say goodbye.

THOMAS. No.

BOB. You don't have a choice. My comet's waiting. *(Bob kisses and hugs Thomas and then disappears)*

THOMAS. Bye. I love you, Bob. *(The group forms a circle and link arms around one another. Thomas, however, stands outside the group, not sure whether to join in. Finally, he does and the song ends)*

SCENE SEVEN

Lisa's bedroom, early morning. Lisa is in bed. She looks ill. As she starts to get out of bed, Vanessa stops her.

VANESSA. You're not going anywhere. The vigil's amply over-organized. You can just breeze in, give your speech, and leave.

LISA. What are you? My mother?

VANESSA. Yes, and your sister and your lover and your nurse. And we all say, "Get back in bed or *else*." *(Thomas bounces in, singing, as Lisa gets back in bed)*

THOMAS. Radical, Magical, Mystical, Whimsical, etc.

LISA. Would you shut up with that stupid song!

THOMAS. Oops! Sorry. I had the best time last night. I was at a faerie gathering!

VANESSA. Lisa's had a bad night.

THOMAS. What's wrong?

VANESSA. She's had a really bad vaginal infection for a while now and she's got a typical doctor.

LISA. He never thought to test me for HIV. "Lesbians don't get AIDS." So, I made him test me and guess what? I'm positive. *(Thomas turns towards Vanessa concerned about her)*

VANESSA. I tested negative a few months ago. We've been safe together, but I'm testing again just in case.

LISA. I think I got it from that artist guy I dated years ago when I was in my disgusted-with-women phase.

THOMAS. Are you all right?

LISA. Were you when you found out?

THOMAS. Okay, stupid question. I was expecting to be dead by now with no insurance.

VANESSA. Oh, Thomas, it's here. *(She pulls a letter)*

THOMAS. My medical! I've been accepted into the county system. I've got health care.

VANESSA. Just in time to watch the whole system collapse.

LISA. *(To Thomas)* Tell me one thing. Am I going to have to mope around the way you have? If so, let me die now.

VANESSA. Yeah, you've been a real jerk.

LISA. A selfish cranky jerk.

THOMAS. I know and I'm sorry. I guess I owe you guys an explanation for why I've been so pissy these past two months.

LISA. For a start. We'll think of what else you can do to repay us.

THOMAS. It was Christian and Luis, yes, but it was much more than that. I just wasn't thrilled at the prospect of being sick and dying. And it seemed like no matter what I did, I couldn't save my life or anyone else's. Maybe I didn't handle it so well, but who could have expected me to?

VANESSA. So what's changed?

THOMAS. I met a man! I know I swore off men, I know men are pigs, but he's different. He's a faerie!

LISA. One good fuck and you're all better. Men!

THOMAS. No, it was a lot more than that. I've just learned a lot about myself, even if I didn't want to, and why I want to stick around on this planet.

LISA. I thought if this ever happened to me, I'd be strong. But now I don't know how or what to feel.

THOMAS. There isn't any right way. People say you go through stages like anger and denial before accepting it. I can't accept it. Not while I'm still here. Not while I have friends like you in my hands, living and breathing.

VANESSA. So, what. Are we going to live in denial?

THOMAS. No, we're going to hold onto each other. *(Singing)*
Looking at you . . . here, I want to run so far away
So many times, I've . . . tried to hold on, for one more day

How can I watch . . . while, those who I love just slip away

I've buried one too many,
There's no way I'll say it again,

Say goodbye again

Right by my side, you . . . kept me alive, so selflessly
You held my hand . . . while, all of the rest abandoned me

How could I leave . . . you, all of the love you gave to me

I've buried one too many
There's no way I'll say it again,
Say goodbye again

I was dreaming, we flew high
We were soaring, we knew why
The sea below us called us by our name

We were breathing, the blue sky
We were angels, amused by
All our loves and all our losses in the game

How can I watch . . . while, people I love just slip away

I've buried one too many
There's no way I'll say it again,
Say goodbye again
Say goodbye again
Say goodbye again

SCENE EIGHT

At the vigil outside the County Hospital, the rally is about to begin. Lisa paces back and forth, trying to learn her speech. Protestors picket with signs. A talent scout chases after Lurleen.

TALENT SCOUT. Ms. Devereaux, you have to come on this talk show! America just can't enough of you people. We're featuring a transsexual who kept his dead mother's head by his pillow for two years, a lesbian who murdered a series of unsuspecting heterosexual husbands, and you: a crazed transsexual who leads AIDS protestors to attack normal people. "What Happens When Gays Go Bad?"

LURLEEN. You stupid jackass. I've been camping out here with all these protestors for three nights! We've got a thousand people out there and in just a few minutes speakers from every part of the AIDS community are going to be demanding proper funding for the County AIDS Ward. We don't need your tabloid journalism. *(She shoves him aside)* Asshole! *(Vanessa enters with Christian)*

VANESSA. Lurleen, you've got to do something to calm him down. We can't just have ACT UP speakers. We have to have the spiritual community; we have to show that the AIDS buddies are with us.

CHRISTIAN. I'm not a public speaker. There is no way I'm going to make it through this speech. *(Feeling around his neck)* Oh God, where's my crystal?

LURLEEN. *(Giving Christian a crystal)* Honey, have one of mine. Where's Ben? He's supposed to be speaking for Queer Nation. *(Ben enters with Luis and Thomas)*

BEN. We've got a problem. The police have just revoked our permit. They're scared we're planning to march into the hospital.

VOICE ON LOUDSPEAKER. This is an illegal assembly. If you do not disperse at once you will be subject to arrest.

CHRISTIAN. What are we going to do?

LUIS. Spread out. Make a human chain around the hospital. It'll be harder to arrest us if we're not all in one spot. Pass the word. *(Lurleen grabs Christian and Lisa who grabs Vanessa)*

LURLEEN. Everybody! Join hands! Circle this building!

VOICE. This is your second warning. If you do not disperse you will be arrested.

CHRISTIAN. *(To Lisa)* Are you well enough for this?

LISA. If we get arrested, try and stick with me.

VANESSA. I'll be with you.

THOMAS. Lurleen, start talking to the press. We need to get the message out now.

LURLEEN. Hey, all of you press people! Listen up. This is an official statement. My name is Lurleen Devereaux and I'm here with the AIDS Coalition To Unleash Power, ACT UP/LA. But I represent only one of the many groups here today. This is Lisa Diamond.

LISA. I'm living with AIDS and I'm here because women are dying of AIDS all over this country.

VANESSA. It's the number one killer of women of childbearing age in New York City.

LURLEEN. And they only test AIDS drugs on men. They work

differently on women! This is Christian Martin on my other side.

CHRISTIAN. I work taking care of the dying. But there are too many. Everyday, more people are forced to die alone without someone to help them. The hospice where I work and the AIDS buddies can't take care of it all.

LUIS. We need health care for all people.

THOMAS. I'm here fighting for the release of AIDS drugs.

BEN. I'm here to speak up for gay men. People keep claiming some people are innocent and others are not. All people in this nation deserve decent treatment.

BEN. They're clubbing people at the end of the line!

ALL. No violence! No violence! No violence! *(All lie on the ground for a "die-in." Then, one by one, they stand, calling out names of people they have lost. Lurleen and Thomas have two specific names)*

LURLEEN. I'm here tonight for Larry Day.

THOMAS. I'm here for Bob Summerbell.

LURLEEN. *(Singing)*

Well you're traveling through the dark when you see that face again,
The one you haven't seen around since God-knows-when,
And you want to howl and you want to rage, to prove you're still alive,
And you have to have that friend back or you simply can't survive.

Exploding with need, and the sweetest desire,
Your life is consumed, with passion and fire,
You know you're alive, cause your heart goes on beating,
It's driving you wild, because the moments are fleeting,

I am alive screaming out in the streets,
Alive making love between sheets,
I am alive taking care of sick friends,
This is not where it ends, this is not where it ends

ALL.

We're hurtling through the stars on a cursed and bleeding rock,
And we're looking for the key to open up that final lock,

We remember your face, we recall your voice, we find you
in our dreams,
You're in our lives when we force the world to listen to our
screams.

Exploding with need, and the sweetest desire,
Your life is consumed, with passion and fire,
You know you're alive cause your heart goes on beating,
It's driving you wild, because the moments are fleeting,

I am alive screaming out in the streets,
Alive making love between sheets,
I am alive taking care of sick friends,
This is not where it ends, this is not where it ends
This is not where it . . . *(Blackout. Music for song "Silence
Equals Death" begins and plays while cast comes out for bows)*
ALL. *(Singing)*
Silence Equals Death!
Action Equals Life!
We are alive!

victor bumbalo

what are tuesdays like?

for Robert Chesley

author's note

AIDS compresses everything; strips away the unessential; allows few, if any, self-deceptions. Friends and family are common terms. Those who know they may have a limited time left, who wait for hope and answers, find they must challenge these basic bonds. Every Tuesday, in a waiting room, strangers come together at their most unprotected moment, and begin to travel the way to friendship and, finally, to family.

performances and productions

What Are Tuesdays Like? was produced at Carnegie Mellon's Showcase of New Plays in the summer of 1993. The Showcase of New Plays is produced by Elisabeth Orion and Donald Marinelli. The artistic director is Frank Gagliano. The production was directed by Marc Masterson. The cast was as follows:

HOWARD SALVO: Anthony McKay
JEFF FERRIS: Court Whisman
SCOTT: John Hollywood
GENE: Greg Stuhr
DENISE: Tamilla Woodard
RANDY: Brandon Williams

characters

HOWARD SALVO

JEFF FERRIS

SCOTT

GENE

DENISE

RANDY

SCENE ONE

The outpatient waiting room of a hospital. Tuesday afternoon.

At this time every week only people with AIDS are scheduled for services. Four men are in the room. Two of the men, Scott and Gene, are seated close to each other. The other two, Howard and Jeff, sit apart from the couple and each other.
Howard is gregarious and commands authority. His chatty nature stems from a genuine interest in people. There is an inner calm to this man that people find attractive.
Jeff is obviously frail. Although he tries to hide it, the fear Jeff lives with is evident.
Scott is attractive and intense. He holds on to his individuality by hiding his true nature from most people.
Gene likes to be in control.
At the moment no one is speaking. Gene has his arm around Scott. Howard is watching Jeff who is staring at a page of a magazine.

HOWARD. Excuse me, may I ask, what is it you're reading?
JEFF. What?
HOWARD. I know it's is none of my business, but you've been staring at the same page for over thirty-five minutes. I was just curious what was so fascinating.
JEFF. *(Showing him the magazine)* It's a picture of the Grand Canyon. I was meditating on it. Trying to put myself into the picture. *(Pointing to a specific spot in the picture)* I was standing there.
HOWARD. You weren't planning to jump in?
JEFF. Why? Do I look suicidal?
HOWARD. No. I was kidding.
SCOTT. *(From the other side of the room)* Just what we need in this room—a comic.
HOWARD. Excuse me?
SCOTT. *(From the other side of the room)* Nothing.
JEFF. I don't understand. I was scheduled fifteen minutes ago

for my chemotherapy, and there's no one here to give it to me. I can't be waiting around here all day.

HOWARD. It's usually not like this on Tuesdays.

SCOTT. *(From the other side of the room)* I don't want to do this.

GENE. It won't be as bad as you think.

SCOTT. How do you know?

HOWARD. *(To Jeff)* Does it work?

JEFF. What?

HOWARD. Your meditation.

JEFF. No. Maybe. I don't know. It passes the time. I can't be waiting all day for them. If they don't take me in a few minutes, I'm going to have to go.

HOWARD. You shouldn't do that.

JEFF. I'm going to have to.

HOWARD. Why don't you go back to your picture.

JEFF. I can't concentrate anymore. *(Offering Howard the magazine)* Would you like to try?

HOWARD. No, thank you.

SCOTT. *(To Jeff)* Excuse me, what's it like, the chemotherapy?

JEFF. It probably isn't as bad as you imagine.

GENE. *(To Scott)* See.

SCOTT. But you've lost some hair.

JEFF. Not everyone does.

GENE. *(To Scott)* See.

JEFF. *(To Howard)* What are you here for?

HOWARD. To see Louise. She's a therapist.

JEFF. Is she nice?

HOWARD. Very nondirective. But she could use some help dressing.

JEFF. I used to see Don, the other therapist.

HOWARD. Was he nice?

JEFF. Wonderful. Very humane. Had these sparkling eyes. But he flipped out.

HOWARD. I can understand.

JEFF. One day I arrived here for my appointment and he wasn't here. He disappeared. Never even gave the hospital notice. My lover, Mack, tried to track him down, but he wasn't very successful. The last thing any of his friends heard was that he was getting in his car and just going. I hope he's all right.

HOWARD. He's probably at your Grand Canyon leading those donkey tours.

JEFF. That would be great, wouldn't it?

SCOTT. *(From the other side of the room)* Or maybe he jumped in.

GENE. Scott!

JEFF. I'm going to check to see how much longer I have to wait. This is not right. I told them I had to be taken on time. I called them twice and told them.

HOWARD. Try to relax. Let's find you another picture.

JEFF. I'm going to find out what's going on.

Jeff exits.

HOWARD. He's a nervous little thing, isn't he? *(No one responds)* I'm sorry, I'm disturbing you. I had nothing else to do this afternoon. So I got here early. That's why I'm waiting. That kid made me edgy. Sorry. I'm disturbing you.

GENE. It's all right.

SCOTT. *(To Howard)* Do you get chemo?

HOWARD. No, I'm sorry.

SCOTT. *(Sarcastically)* What do you have to be sorry about?

HOWARD. I'm sorry I can't tell you anything about it. You seem worried. I'm sure the nurse will answer all your questions. *(He picks up Jeff's magazine)*

SCOTT. I bet she will. *(To Gene)* You're going to be late getting back to the office.

GENE. It's okay. I told them what I was doing.

SCOTT. You told them what I was coming here for?

GENE. Of course. What's the secret?

SCOTT. Goddamn it, Gene. I don't want people to know about my treatment.

GENE. Why not?

SCOTT. Because it's my treatment.

GENE. People want to know what's going on with you.

SCOTT. Why? They're not my close friends.

GENE. They're mine. And I need their support.

SCOTT. Your office friends are arrogant bastards.

GENE. You don't like anybody these days.

HOWARD. *(Putting down the magazine)* I wish I had my book with me. I forgot it at home. I'm reading *Middlemarch*. It's fat and glorious. I only read thick books now. I figure nothing bad can happen to you when you're in the middle of a long, long story. It's been working so far.

Jeff enters.

JEFF. They're going to start taking people in a minute. *(Referring to Scott)* They said you're ahead of me.
SCOTT. You can go first if you want.
JEFF. *(Suddenly)* I have to go. I've waited too long. You know, the pay phone is broken. I have to call home or get home. I better go.
HOWARD. Do you think you should?
JEFF. I have to. I told them they had to take me on time today. I told them.
HOWARD. What's the matter?
JEFF. I have to go. Maybe I'll see you next week.

Jeff exits.

GENE. That guy is setting himself up for a coronary.
HOWARD. I wonder how he's going to get home? Should somebody have gone with him?
GENE. Is he a friend?
HOWARD. No. I just met him today.

They are interrupted by a voice coming from the public address system.

VOICE. Mr. Donnelly. Mr. Donnelly, please report to room 4. Room 4.
SCOTT. *(Frightened)* I don't want to go!
GENE. Come on, you have to.
HOWARD. I should have helped him home.
VOICE. Mr. Donnelly . . . room 4. Room 4.
SCOTT. I don't want to go!

Blackout.

SCENE TWO

Another Tuesday. Jeff is alone in the room. He is staring intently at the postcard he is holding. After a few seconds, Howard enters. He has been shopping. He is clutching several packages and his copy of Middlemarch.

HOWARD. Well, hello. What's the picture this week?

JEFF. It's a painting. By Monet. *(Showing Howard the postcard)* Of his gardens at Giverny. Wouldn't you love to live in this painting?

HOWARD. Never. The pollen would kill me.

JEFF. That's too bad.

HOWARD. Did you get home all right last week?

JEFF. Yes, thank you. They promised they would take me exactly on time this week.

HOWARD. That's good.

JEFF. On Tuesdays, I'm on a tight schedule. I have banking to do. I have to go to social services, get shopping done, come here. I can't afford to waste any time.

HOWARD. You sound busy.

JEFF. I don't like being away from my apartment too long. My lover's there. He's sick. Quite sick. I don't like being away from him. These are precious moments, right?

HOWARD. Right.

JEFF. At this point, he only likes me to take care of him. When he's up to it, sometimes we sit together, hold hands, and listen to music. Or maybe watch a movie on the VCR. Our friends chipped in and bought us one. That was good of them, wasn't it?

HOWARD. Yes.

JEFF. We know lovely people. On days when we both have a resurgence of energy, I play for him. He loves that. I used to be a concert pianist.

HOWARD. What a comfort your music must be.

JEFF. I love the very idea of it. Selecting sounds from the universe. Giving them an order. They apologized for last week. Did I tell you they said they might even take me early?

HOWARD. Great.

JEFF. You've been shopping.

HOWARD. I've been depressed. This morning I was paying bills. I used to make a good income, but now even the telephone bill terrifies me.

JEFF. May I ask what you do?

HOWARD. Right now, I'm bartending a few days a week. Off the books. But I used to be a therapist. Both occupations are frighteningly similar. All you have to do is listen, and people will throw money at you.

JEFF. Did you have fun shopping?

HOWARD. I should have done this a few weeks ago. I'm sure those T cells of mine are dropping through economic fear. I've been pinching pennies for too many months now. So this morning I gave myself a good talking to and then went out on a spree. I just handed the cashiers my credit card and never peeked at the bills. I figure I'll take a look while I'm in session with Louise. Let her deal with it.

JEFF. Let anybody else deal with it.

HOWARD. Wouldn't it be fabulous if you could wrap AIDS and all that comes with it in a box and hand it over to a friend? Just for a day. How about a week? A month?

JEFF. That would be mean.

HOWARD. I mean temporarily. It would give us a break. They would learn something. Know what it's really like. It would be fabulous. Maybe for a year.

They are interrupted by a voice coming from the public address system.

VOICE. Mr. Ferris. Mr. Ferris, please report to room 4. Room 4.

JEFF. See, they kept their word. They're taking me early.

HOWARD. So it's Ferris.

JEFF. Yes. Jeff Ferris.

HOWARD. Howard Salvo.

JEFF. Good meeting you. I've got to run. I don't want to keep them waiting.

Jeff begins to leave.

HOWARD. *(Calling after him)* When you gave concerts, did you specialize in anything?

JEFF. Yes. The French. I was known for my French repertoire.

Blackout.

SCENE THREE

*Another Tuesday. When the lights come up, Scott and Gene are
the only men in the room. They are in the middle of an
argument.*

GENE. It was four-thirty. Four-thirty in the morning. An ACT UP
meeting, my ass.

SCOTT. After the meeting, some of the guys took me out for a
beer.

GENE. A beer? You smelled like a brewery. What kind of jerks
do you hang out with? Don't they know you're sick?

SCOTT. They know.

GENE. Then they're fools.

SCOTT. Why don't you leave and go to work.

GENE. You shouldn't be drinking.

SCOTT. Gene, two beers.

GENE. You should be in bed early.

SCOTT. I had fun last night.

GENE. Doing what?

SCOTT. Go! Just leave!

GENE. You don't know how to take care of yourself. That's always
been your problem.

SCOTT. What do you mean by that?

GENE. Just that I want you taking better care of yourself.

Howard enters carrying a package and his copy of
Middlemarch.

HOWARD. Well, how are my sweet ones?

SCOTT. We're not your sweet ones.

HOWARD. Missy is sour today.

SCOTT. God, what a tired queen.

HOWARD. I hope your chemo makes you bald.

SCOTT. Take that back!

HOWARD. Twirl on your own finger!

SCOTT. Take it back!

HOWARD. Bald!

Scott leaps at Howard and grabs Howard by his shirt.

GENE. *(Trying to separate the men)* Stop it!

SCOTT. *(Not letting go)* I'll clean this room with you if you don't take it back.

HOWARD. Little tough boys bore me. Move those hands.

SCOTT. Take it back. *(Beginning to break down)* Please. Please, take it back.

Scott releases Howard.

SCOTT. *(Breaking down)* Please.

HOWARD. *(Trying to calm Scott down)* I'm sorry. Really. I am.

SCOTT. Please.

HOWARD. I take it back.

Scott is sobbing. Howard takes him into his arms.

HOWARD. I take it back.

Blackout.

SCENE FOUR

Another Tuesday. Howard is reading his book. Denise is pacing back and forth. She is an attractive black woman who is trying to conceal her nerves.

DENISE. You can't smoke here, can you?

HOWARD. No.

DENISE. That's too bad.

HOWARD. I don't think so.

DENISE. *(Suddenly)* You have AIDS, don't you?

HOWARD. Why?

DENISE. I want to make sure I'm in the right place.

HOWARD. You're in the right place.

DENISE. Good. What kind of treatment do you get here?

HOWARD. I talk to a therapist.

DENISE. I like therapy. I'm in a group. It's a lot of fun.

HOWARD. Fun?

DENISE. All you do is talk and listen. It's fun. People are usually polite. They make you feel good. But I don't take it too seriously. I mean, we all have to leave and go home. And these days, that definitely is not fun.

HOWARD. Where do you live?

DENISE. Out on Long Island. I had to take that goddamn train to get here. I've been selected to be in some study. Some experimental drug. My family is all excited. But to tell you the truth, if I had to win something, I would have preferred the Lotto or a scholarship to Yale. Experiments make me nervous. My doctor said I should be delighted. But I can't help wondering, why me? Is it because I'm black? When I said that to my doctor, she said I was getting paranoid. Perhaps. Then she told me that a lot of gay men were going on this drug. I asked her to show me one straight white man who would be participating. Then maybe I would show more enthusiasm.

HOWARD. You're too much.

DENISE. Denise.

HOWARD. Howard.

DENISE. I wish we were meeting somewhere else.

Scott and Gene enter.

SCOTT. Not one hair. Not one hair has fallen out.

HOWARD. Terrific. *(Howard and Scott embrace)*

SCOTT. I appreciated your call. It helped.

HOWARD. Don't isolate yourself.

GENE. He's not isolated.

HOWARD. *(Purposely leaving Gene out of the introductions)* Denise. Scott.

DENISE. Hi.

GENE. Gene.

DENISE. Hi. *(To Scott)* You're on the chemotherapy? You look terrific. You don't even look sick. *(To Gene)* What are you here for?

GENE. I'm not sick.

DENISE. Really?

GENE. What do you mean? Do I look sick?

DENISE. I was just wondering what you were doing here?

GENE. *(Indicating Scott)* I come with him.

DENISE. Aren't you kind.

GENE. But I'm not sick. As a matter of fact, I'm not even HIV positive. I test negative. Every time.

Scott starts applauding.

GENE. Stop that!

SCOTT. I'm proud of you. You refrained from mentioning that here for over a month. *(To Denise and Howard)* Usually it's within an hour of meeting someone new that he makes his announcement.

GENE. That's unfair.

SCOTT. You practically carry a banner.

GENE. I'm leaving.

SCOTT. Fine.

GENE. To treat me like this in front of your friends.

DENISE. I just met him.

GENE. *(Referring to Howard)* I meant him.

SCOTT. Gene, go to work.

GENE. Aren't you relieved I'm negative?

SCOTT. Of course. But you advertise it the same way you advertise your condos. You're relentless.

HOWARD. You own condos?

SCOTT. He sells them.

DENISE. So does my sister-in-law. She loves it. Says it's a real cushy job.

GENE. I work hard.

DENISE. I'm sure you do. But she used to teach in a city school.

GENE. May I say something?

HOWARD. No.

GENE. Why not?

HOWARD. Because whenever someone starts a statement like that, they are about to tell you something you don't want to hear.

GENE. I'm going to say it anyway.

HOWARD. I knew you would.

GENE. You people can be pompous and self-righteous. There. I said it.

DENISE. What people does he mean?

HOWARD. Sick people.

GENE. I'm sorry, but I had to say it.

HOWARD. Bravo.

Gene walks over to Scott and awkwardly gives him a kiss.

GENE. I'll see you at home. *(He waits for Scott to respond)* I said . . .

SCOTT. I heard you.

Gene leaves.

SCOTT. He didn't used to be like that.

HOWARD. It's the pressure.

DENISE. It's men. God, I'm glad I'm taking a break from them. *(To Howard)* You live with somebody?

HOWARD. I used to.

DENISE. *(To Scott)* What you need, honey, is a vacation from him.

SCOTT. Impossible. At the moment he's supporting me.

DENISE. That's a bitch.

HOWARD. *(To Scott)* Aren't you still working?

SCOTT. My employers forced an early retirement on me. I worked at Fairyland.

DENISE. Is that a dance club?

SCOTT. No, it's a preschool. They told me they didn't want me deteriorating in front of the children's eyes. Forcing concepts on them that they weren't ready for. They said at my kids' ages only bunny rabbits should get sick and die. So I let them buy me off. They told the kids I was going on a trip. They gave me a bon voyage party and kept me on the payroll for six months. Maybe I should have fought them. I miss the kids.

DENISE. Anytime you want, you can take my two.

They are interrupted by a voice from the public address system.

VOICE. Mrs. McMillan, report to room 3. Mrs. McMillan to room 3.

DENISE. They better answer all my questions.

HOWARD. They'll try to rush you, but see to it that they don't.

DENISE. See you later.

HOWARD. Good luck.

Denise exits.

SCOTT. *(After a moment)* How do you keep it together?
HOWARD. Linguini and clam sauce. Anytime I want it.

Blackout.

SCENE FIVE

Gene is standing away from Scott thumbing through a magazine. Scott is seated staring at the door that leads to the treatment center.

GENE. Maybe we should think about Europe next year.

Scott starts to cry.

GENE. Oh babe, please don't.
SCOTT. *(Trying to control himself)* I'm okay. I'll be okay.

Gene goes over to Scott.

Blackout.

SCENE SIX

Another Tuesday. Howard, Scott, and Gene are seated.

HOWARD. I'm worried about that guy. The pianist.
SCOTT. Jeff?
HOWARD. I haven't seen him in weeks. I tried calling him, but he's not listed. And they won't give me any information here.
GENE. Confidentiality. You should be glad.
HOWARD. His lover is sick.
SCOTT. I don't think I want to know.
HOWARD. I hope he's all right.
GENE. He said he doesn't want to know.
HOWARD. Maybe they're listening to music.
GENE. Did you hear him?
SCOTT. Gene, chill out.
HOWARD. Sorry. *(To Scott)* How are you doing?
SCOTT. *(Cheerfully)* Pretty good.
HOWARD. Great.

SCOTT. How about you?

HOWARD. Getting along.

Pause.

SCOTT. It's a fine day out there, isn't it? So clear.

Pause.

HOWARD. Do you think he's got somebody to take care of him?

Blackout.

SCENE SEVEN

Another Tuesday. Howard, Denise, Gene, and Scott are sitting almost totally still listening to Jeff. Jeff is in a state of near hysteria.

JEFF. . . . I kept repeating, over five thousand times a day, "This isn't happening to me. This isn't happening." In one month my entire life . . . gone. It disappeared. Everything. And where to? Mack's death wasn't what I expected. And what happened afterwards I just wasn't prepared for. "This isn't happening to me." He was home. He slipped . . . that's the expression people used . . . slipped into a coma as if by means of a slate of ice. He slipped. I was afraid to be alone. Afraid I was going to do something wrong. Hurt him in some way. Friends stayed with me around the clock. Took shifts. I could tell they were praying for him to die. Some of them had done this before. They knew what to do. They were sad. I know that. It just wasn't that special to them. Not anymore. "It's time," they said. I knew they had said that in some other room. In someone else's home. "This isn't happening to me." Still, I was holding on to him. Didn't want him to die. I couldn't imagine living in a world where Mack wasn't breathing. "This isn't happening to me." I was exhausted when he died. Had been up for three days. Harry was with me. He made a mistake. Instantly he called 911. The police came. Since the apartment wasn't in my name, they told me they would have to seal it up until the official cause of death was documented and Mack's next of kin arrived. Mack's brother—Mack never liked him—would be handing me back our things, my things. "This isn't happening to me." As they were taking Mack away—they put him in a bag— Harry was putting some things together for me in my overnight bag. Everyone was rushing around as if we were running to catch a plane. "Mack, we're not taking a plane anywhere. We're not going on a vacation. This isn't happening to me." The police were not mean. Just chilly people. Our friends were in a fury at my being locked out of my home. That's what they kept talking about all evening. Not the obvious. Mack was dead. I would never see him again. "This isn't happening to me." A quick cremation. I scattered his ashes near the boat pond in Central Park. A little place where we picnicked. His brother and mother were furious. They wanted a body. Lots of ceremonies. But I did what Mack wanted. They were as much a part of his death and illness as they were a part of his life. They were no part. They wanted things. In the apartment, once I was allowed back in, they kept asking me, "Is this yours?" How does "ours" get split into "yours," or "his," or "mine?" What right did they have to ask me? "This isn't happening to me." I didn't want to fight them. I let them have so many of our things. The truth was—what was I going to do with a complete household and no home? The landlady thought she was being so loving by letting me stay one more month. Nine years in that apartment. I made it a home. Our home. My home. "This isn't happening to me." My lover's dead. I'm sick. I don't have much money. I have to find a place to live. I'm living out of a suitcase in a friend's living room. Did I tell you, I had to sell my piano?

Blackout.

SCENE EIGHT

Howard and Gene are seated on opposite sides of the room.

GENE. *(After a moment)* I've joined a support group for guys who have lovers with HIV.

HOWARD. *(Barely paying attention)* Good.

GENE. We've started a bowling league.

HOWARD. *(Sarcastically)* You guys really know how to get down and dirty.

GENE. You can't stand me.

HOWARD. *(Friendly)* You're right. And it's so upsetting to me. You can be rude, but God, I live in New York. I should be used to it. I spent my entire last session with my therapist only talking about you.

GENE. I wish you hadn't.

HOWARD. Oh, I had to. I have to get to the bottom of this. I must say I was disappointed in Louise's first analysis. She jumped to the obvious. That I was attracted to you. Who does she think she's talking to? Of course, I had already thought of that. In fact the other night I even tried getting up a fantasy about you. I tried to picture you undressed . . . My sitting next to you . . . But I swear, nothing, nothing happened. But don't worry, I'll figure it out.

GENE. I don't care. This is not my problem.

HOWARD. You're absolutely right. I was talking to my friend Willy about you . . .

GENE. Next you'll be on Oprah . . .

HOWARD. Relax. Willy is such a hoot. You'd love him. But maybe you wouldn't. He said it was our past lives. That you must have been a real prick to me in one of them. And that it's sort of spilled over into this lifetime. Who were you, Gene? Attila the Hun, the Marquis de Sade, Medea . . .

GENE. She wasn't real.

HOWARD. You're right. Very good. Oh, don't look so worried. Maybe I was the prick.

Scott enters from the treatment center.

GENE. That was quick.

HOWARD. They think they're working on an assembly line in there.

SCOTT. I didn't take my treatment today.

GENE. Why?

SCOTT. I want to go for a bike ride.

GENE. I know what this is about. A few hairs. You lost just a few hairs.

SCOTT. They were mine.

Scott exits.

GENE. *(After a moment)* He'll be back.

Blackout.

SCENE NINE

Another Tuesday. Howard is seated. Denise is pacing.

DENISE. I want it just like the old days. I want a good old-fashioned public hanging. You know the kind where people would bring their sewing. I don't sew, but maybe I'd file my nails. I'd get there early. Sit right in the front row. He would scream and cry. I know it. I'd be humming while I was filing my fucking nails. I'd even give the bastard a smile when he climbed the platform.

HOWARD. And I'd be sitting right next to you.

DENISE. What would you be doing?

HOWARD. Reading my book. I'd glance up a couple of times. I'd pretend I was bored. That his execution didn't matter that much.

DENISE. We'd act just like he did. Social services, my ass. Social abuse, that's what they should call his department. He was filling out his appointment book while he was talking to me. *(Imitating a man's voice)* "I'm going to have to bring up something that you're avoiding. Have you thought of your children, Mrs. McMillan? Where will they go when you're not here? It's best not to wait until the last minute for these kinds of things. We better start making plans." We? That scumbag doesn't think I have a brain in my head. What does he think I think about day after day after day? My mother is old. She may go first. What's he think I am? Some dog? Some bitch that has a litter that has to be disposed of? *(In a fury)* He wasn't even looking at me. He was writing things down in his appointment book.

HOWARD. He'd hear us. Talking about a new restaurant we'd be going to as soon as the show was over.

DENISE. *(Breaking down)* He glanced up at me, maybe twice. Like over his glasses. Checking me out. Seeing if the animal had a reaction.

HOWARD. I'd tell you a joke.

DENISE. *(After a moment)* And I'd laugh as I looked at him.

Blackout.

SCENE TEN

Another Tuesday. Howard is staring at Scott who is beaming.

HOWARD. Give me some.

SCOTT. What?

HOWARD. Whatever it is you are on. You look euphoric.

SCOTT. Not quite. Almost. Where's our little friend?

HOWARD. Jeff? He's moved away. Down to Florida. His mother has taken him in. He said he would write. I hope he does.

SCOTT. I hope she's good to him.

HOWARD. I'm sure she will be. She's a piano teacher.

SCOTT. Good. They'll have something to talk about. What time is your appointment?

HOWARD. In a few minutes.

SCOTT. Do you want me to wait around for you? And then maybe we could do dinner—cheap, of course.

HOWARD. Of course.

SCOTT. . . . and maybe a movie or something.

HOWARD. That would be lovely.

SCOTT. Great.

HOWARD. I don't believe it. This is fabulous. I have a date.

SCOTT. *(Suddenly worried)* It's not a date. We're just going to be like buddies—hanging out.

HOWARD. *(Nervously)* I know, I know.

SCOTT. No date.

HOWARD. Right. We're just friends. Spending some time together.

SCOTT. I just didn't want you to expect something that's not going to happen.

HOWARD. You *are* feeling good.

SCOTT. What do you mean?

HOWARD. You instantly jumped to the conclusion I was after your ass.

SCOTT. But you said "date" . . .

HOWARD. Don't worry. You'll be safe with me.

SCOTT. Let's just forget it.

HOWARD. No, please. I'd love to go out with you. But not on a date. Be assured, I'm not going to think of it as a date.

SCOTT. Am I acting like a slime ball?

HOWARD. *(After a moment)* No.

SCOTT. It's just that I never imagined I'd be feeling like this again. Alive. Almost—do I dare say it—hot.

HOWARD. Somebody must have had an awfully good time last night.

SCOTT. No. It's just that I'm going to be free from all this. Free, Howard. Forevermore free.

HOWARD. Then what are you doing here? I thought you had come back.

SCOTT. I'm getting my records.

HOWARD. Please, please don't do this.

SCOTT. My Tuesdays are going to be spent in a more pleasant place. Screw their charts. Screw the number they've turned me into. Screw their claim over this body. It's mine again.

HOWARD. *(Worried)* Scott, this is the only help there is for us.

SCOTT. I don't believe their medicines are going to make me any better. I don't believe their drugs will retard my virus.

HOWARD. But they do.

SCOTT. In my soul I don't believe it.

HOWARD. What the hell are you going to do? Get a crystal and start chanting?

SCOTT. Maybe that, too. I'm going on a totally holistic trip. Under a doctor's supervision. I'm blowing this joint.

HOWARD. You're playing with your life.

SCOTT. And you're not? You've been brainwashed. I'm going a different way, that's all.

HOWARD. Oh Jesus, I'm scared for you.

SCOTT. For the first time in ages, I'm not.

Blackout.

SCENE ELEVEN

*Another Tuesday. Howard and Denise are seated. Both are
eating a piece of cake and seem to be enjoying it.*

DENISE. God, it's good. Are you sure you didn't buy this?

HOWARD. Made it from scratch. I'm totally talented.

DENISE. Will you marry me?

HOWARD. Are you neat?

DENISE. Forget it. Listen darling, can I ask you a question?

HOWARD. Shoot.

DENISE. Have you had any intimacy lately?

HOWARD. A friend came over to dinner the other night, and I
couldn't believe how close we got. We talked and talked . . .

DENISE. And then?

HOWARD. That's all. We just talked.

DENISE. I'm talking about the old push-push.

HOWARD. Oh.

DENISE. Yes, oh. Well?

HOWARD. No.

DENISE. Don't you want to?

HOWARD. Sometimes. I guess so.

DENISE. Then why aren't you getting anything?

HOWARD. You sound like my shrink.

DENISE. I'm making you nervous. I'm sorry. I just thought you
were all liberated . . .

HOWARD. I am.

DENISE. . . . and being a shrink yourself you were able to talk
easily about all sorts of things.

HOWARD. I can.

DENISE. You are lying. You are as uptight as any of us.

HOWARD. I am not. It's just that I'm ambivalent right now.

DENISE. Same as being uptight. Do you feel unclean?

HOWARD. Sometimes . . . yes.

DENISE. That's how I usually feel. That was until the other night. Two of my girlfriends took me out. They're in the drug program with me. I usually say no to them, but this time I felt—why not? They act superior sometimes. They don't have AIDS. But generally they're nice. What a party crowd we make. We don't do drugs or drink. But we chain-smoked our cigarettes and tried to act "with it." The music was loud. I was about to get a headache when this guy asked me to dance. It was the first time in over two years that a man had his arms around me. That dance depressed the hell out of me.

HOWARD. Why? Didn't you like the song?

DENISE. I felt like an old lady. There could be no follow-up to the dance. Not even a dream of one.

HOWARD. Of course there could be.

DENISE. Get real, girl. What was I supposed to say? "Let's get to know each other? Should we go to a movie next week? How about dinner?"

HOWARD. *(Interrupting her)* Yes.

DENISE. ". . . But don't get too interested in me, because I have . . . Should I give you three guesses? Let's just say it begins with an A, and it's not asthma."

HOWARD. What happened?

DENISE. Nothing. I pretended I was from out of town. I feel like I'm from the moon.

HOWARD. We know how to be safe. We can't stop living.

DENISE. It's fucked.

HOWARD. *(After a moment)* We have to do something.

DENISE. Well, Einstein, think on it. When you get a vision, give me a call. You wouldn't consider going straight, would you?

HOWARD. That's your second proposition tonight.

DENISE. I'm getting desperate.

HOWARD. Thanks a lot. Maybe you should take out an ad.

DENISE. Where? In some porno rag?

HOWARD. No. In a classier publication. Something like *The New York Review of Books*.

DENISE. You need a CAT scan. The virus has hit your brain.

HOWARD. You have a pen?

DENISE. Yes.

HOWARD. Okay. As fast as you can, write an ad for yourself. I'll write one for you. We'll see what we come up with.

DENISE. I wonder how long you have after the virus enters your brain.

HOWARD. Come on.

Howard starts writing on the back cover of his book. Denise picks up a magazine to write on.

HOWARD. And make sure you give it a bit of spark.

DENISE. Of course. "Poor Black Diseased Woman with two children . . ." Won't that send them beating down my door?

HOWARD. That's not all you are. You're also attractive, witty . . .

DENISE. Okay. "Poor Witty Diseased Black . . ."

HOWARD. You are not diseased . . . so to speak.

DENISE. So to speak.

Gene enters.

GENE. Hi, guys.

HOWARD. Is Scott coming back?

GENE. Howard, you have to talk to him.

Although Howard and Denise seem to be giving Gene their attention, they still continue, at various moments, working on their ads.

HOWARD. How is he?

GENE. Fine. For the time being.

DENISE. Good.

GENE. No, not good. With all this seaweed nonsense, he's endangering his life. He won't listen to me. But he respects you Howard. Why don't you give it a try?

HOWARD. This is not my business.

GENE. But you've become his friend.

HOWARD. And I'd like to stay that way.

GENE. Your friend is standing on a train track and a train is speeding towards him. You're not going to suggest that he might get the hell out of its way?

HOWARD. This is different.

GENE. Do you believe in what he's doing?

HOWARD. No. But he does.

GENE. Don't give me that New Age nonsense.

HOWARD. *(To Denise)* Do you like books?

DENISE. Who's got time to read?

HOWARD. Do you like them?

DENISE. I guess so.

GENE. What are you people doing?

DENISE. We're writing an advertisement for me so I can get a boyfriend. You got any ideas?

GENE. You people are no longer playing with a full deck.

DENISE. This is a hell of a lot more fun than thinking about the new drug they're going to shoot me up with today. I think I'm going to say I'm sophisticated. It sounds more high-toned.

GENE. My lover is killing himself . . .

HOWARD. That's not necessarily true.

GENE. And you guys are in lulu land.

HOWARD. Let go, Gene.

GENE. These goddamned cliché phrases. "Let go." I'm not talking about an idea here. I'm talking about a man. My lover. Because of all this wheat-grass shit, he no longer trusts me. Doesn't think I have his best interest at heart. Lumps me in with the government, the medical profession. We can't even sit in front of the television without there being some kind of tension. My home is no longer a pleasant place to be.

HOWARD. *(Not paying attention)* I'm sorry.

GENE. My kitchen now looks like a laboratory. He can't take on a part-time job because of his health. But he spends five hours a day cooking up this slop. Did you know, he has to bleach his vegetables with Clorox?

HOWARD. *(Not paying attention)* I'm sorry.

GENE. We can't even go to a restaurant together anymore. We used to love going to restaurants.

HOWARD. *(Not paying attention)* I'm sorry.

GENE. *(Furiously)* Listen to me, goddamn it!

Gene grabs the book out of Howard's hand and rips the page Howard has been writing on.

GENE. *(Trying not to break down)* My whole life I dreamed of having a lover. A partner. A sane, whole one. I wanted a lover with a future. I wanted us to have a future.

HOWARD. *(Meaning it)* I'm sorry. I am.

GENE. Like hell you are.

Gene exits. Howard and Denise watch him leave.

DENISE. *(After a moment, looking at the crumbled page from Howard's book)* What did your ad say?

Blackout.

SCENE TWELVE

Another Tuesday. Jeff appears excited. On the other side of the room a young man sits filling out forms. After a moment, Howard enters. When he does, Jeff jumps up, pulls out a toy horn, blows it and shouts.

JEFF. Surprise!

The man appears shocked by this behavior.

HOWARD. I don't believe my eyes.

JEFF. I'm back.

HOWARD. For how long?

JEFF. Forever. Two more weeks in Florida and I would have been up for matricide.

HOWARD. Your mother and you got along that well?

JEFF. Don't get me wrong, I love my mother. She's a decent human being. Brimming with humanity. But my AIDS made her hyperactive. It was like she was on speed. She talked constantly. I fell asleep and woke up to the sound of her voice. She became obsessed with becoming the greatest mother who ever lived. She was out to prove that Jesus got gypped with that lightweight mother of his. By the time I arrived she was an expert on AIDS. N.Y.U. Medical Center could use her. She cooked all the time. Special foods for the immune system. My mother can't cook. Never could. Have you ever tried to digest charcoal-broiled, burnt, bean curd? Did I ever tell you when we were children, my sister and I had ulcers? Little baby ulcers? They're back. Only this time they're great big ones. She developed a routine. She became kind of a positive-thinking Miami Beach Cassandra. Always talking about how fabulously I was doing. Peppering all talk with a kind of Walt Disney spirituality. Introducing me to everyone—"This is my brave, wonderful son. He has AIDS, you know." By the end of two weeks we were more famous than Regis and Kathie Lee. I was beginning to forget my own name. I was just the son with AIDS. I knew I had had it the night I dreamt my mother was pureed to death in a juicer. The next morning she was doing her act in K-Mart. *(Imitating his mother)* "What's your name, honey? Fay Ann. Fay Ann, this is my son. Do you see the light in his eyes? That's because he's special. He's been given a special burden, and he's conquering it. He has AIDS." I lost it. I turned to her and said, "Mother, you have to stop telling that story up and down the beach. You have to accept that you're the one with AIDS." The poor woman just started screaming. It was the first real feeling she had since I arrived. She screamed all the way home. Even up the elevator. I told the ladies who were riding with us that she had just heard Lucille Ball was dead. She so wanted me out of Miami that she believed the most stupid lie. I told her that the Academy of Music—whatever that may be—was giving me a rent free apartment in New York. She said she would visit. In a few months.

HOWARD. Where are you staying?

JEFF. With a friend. I told him it's only for a week. He thinks I'm just visiting from Miami. I don't want to freak him out.

HOWARD. Jeff, you have no money. What are you going to do?

JEFF. I don't know. I'm just happy to be out of Miami. I never thought I would do anything like that. Just pack up and leave. I'm getting daring.

MAN. *(Under his breath)* Fool.

JEFF. What?

MAN. Go home.

JEFF. This is my home.

HOWARD. Honey, now this might not happen, but suppose you get sick?

JEFF. There's no reason for anyone to worry, because I have

health insurance. I have no money. But I do have health insurance.

MAN. *(Nervously)* I'm trying to fill out these forms. Will you please keep it down?

JEFF. Sorry.

HOWARD. *(To the man)* This is a public space. People can talk.

MAN. Well, I just don't feel like listening to other people's problems at the moment. Okay?

HOWARD. Then go somewhere else. Try another planet.

MAN. But I may need their help.

HOWARD. Then you're just going to have to concentrate harder.

JEFF. Maybe we should continue this conversation over coffee.

HOWARD. No, we'll have it now.

JEFF. Later. After you're finished with Louise.

HOWARD. I'm not seeing her today.

JEFF. Then why are you here? Who are you seeing?

HOWARD. Doctor Willis.

JEFF. But he's the cancer doctor.

HOWARD. A couple of spots. That's all.

JEFF. Not K.S., too?

HOWARD. Please don't get upset.

JEFF. *(Obviously shaken)* Can I hold you?

HOWARD. I'm all right.

MAN. They expect me to fill out their damn forms with the two of you in the room. Well, the hell with them. I shouldn't be here. I'm not like you guys. I'm not going to make a career out of this disease.

HOWARD. *(To the man)* Good for you.

JEFF. *(To Howard)* How long have you had K.S.?

MAN. I'm getting out of here.

HOWARD. *(To the man)* Do you need help with the forms?

MAN. Why do they need to know some of these things?

JEFF. Howard, I just asked you a question.

HOWARD. *(To the man)* What things?

MAN. *(Ripping the forms up and giving them to Howard)* If they come looking for me, tell them here are their forms.

HOWARD. *(To the man)* Oh, sit down.

MAN. And tell them they can shove every one of their questions.

The man exits.

HOWARD. Denial.

JEFF. What about yours?

HOWARD. And yours?

JEFF. That you can't lay on me.

HOWARD. You have no place to live.

JEFF. How long have you had K.S.?

HOWARD. Over a month. *(Strongly)* I don't want to talk about that right now.

JEFF. Fine. *(After a moment)* And we're not going to talk about my living situation.

HOWARD. Fine.

JEFF. So what are we going to talk about?

HOWARD. *(After a moment)* What are you doing tonight?

JEFF. Nothing.

HOWARD. How about a movie?

JEFF. I'm watching money.

HOWARD. My treat.

JEFF. Are you sure?

HOWARD. *(Jokingly)* But no popcorn.

JEFF. Cheap.

HOWARD. What should we see?

JEFF. Oh . . . something new . . .

HOWARD. And terrible . . .

JEFF. And funny . . .

HOWARD. With young people.

JEFF. Something where the people look forward to the future.

HOWARD. Something that has nothing to do with life.

Blackout.

SCENE THIRTEEN

Another Tuesday. Jeff is seated. He has a suitcase near him. Howard seems agitated.

HOWARD. You can't keep living like this, Jeff. Permanent plans have to be made.

JEFF. That seems to be impossible.

HOWARD. You're much too passive.

JEFF. No, I'm not. I left Miami.

HOWARD. For what? To be out on the streets?

JEFF. Things have a way of turning up.

HOWARD. Oh, for Chrissake.

JEFF. Look, Scott said he had a place for me. For a whole month.

HOWARD. Where is this place?

JEFF. I don't know.

HOWARD. Are you going to be living with somebody?

JEFF. I don't know.

HOWARD. I don't believe you.

JEFF. *(On the verge of tears)* What am I supposed to do? Please stop this.

HOWARD. I want you to wake up.

JEFF. I'm awake, Howard. I'm handling all that I can. I got through the last hour. I'm getting through this one.

HOWARD. There's something wrong with you.

JEFF. They tell me I have AIDS. *(He laughs)*

HOWARD. How many social service agencies do you have working on your case?

JEFF. *(Yelling)* Shut up!

HOWARD. I'm glad to see you yelling.

JEFF. But I'm not.

HOWARD. However, I shouldn't be the object of your rage.

JEFF. *(Imitating Bette Davis)* "But you are, Howard. You are." Let's change the subject.

HOWARD. To what?

JEFF. *(After a moment)* Who do you think Cher's next husband or steady will be?

HOWARD. You're impossible.

JEFF. Or do you think she'll play the field and keep people guessing?

HOWARD. We're talking about your life.

JEFF. And I'm trying to get through the next hour.

HOWARD. And I'm trying to be a friend.

Scott enters.

JEFF. Then leave me alone.

SCOTT. What's going on, guys? *(Jokingly)* Did Howard make a pass?

HOWARD. We were having a dispute.

JEFF. About Cher's next beau.

SCOTT. Really?

JEFF. Really.

SCOTT. Whatever gets you off. Jeffrey, wait till you see the place I've got for you.

JEFF. Yes.

SCOTT. With a room of your own. Rent free. For six, count them, six weeks.

JEFF. Amazing.

SCOTT. It's a small two bedroom, but real cozy.

JEFF. Is anybody else going to be living there?

SCOTT. Yes.

JEFF. Who?

SCOTT. Me.

HOWARD. Oh, for Chrissake.

JEFF. What happened?

SCOTT. He won't let me live the way I want to live. He criticizes everything I'm doing. *(Imitating Gene)* "Do you want to die? Is that why you're not going to your doctor? Do you want to die?" I can't take it anymore.

HOWARD. You've got to talk to him. Reach some sort of compromise.

SCOTT. It's impossible. It has nothing to do with the holistic stuff I'm doing. When that man looks at me, all he sees is a corpse. I'm not that.

HOWARD. So what are you going to do?

SCOTT. This friend of mine is going to be out of town for six weeks, and he's giving me his place.

HOWARD. After that?

SCOTT. I don't know.

HOWARD. You two can't afford "I don't knows" anymore.

SCOTT. Listen, Howard, I'm alive, and while I am I want as much
- freedom as I can handle. I can't kiss ass and turn over my treatment to somebody for a roof over my head.

HOWARD. That roof is worth a lot.

SCOTT. Not my life.

JEFF. Where's the apartment?

SCOTT. In Chelsea. It faces a courtyard. Gets tons of sun.

JEFF. Does my room have a window?

SCOTT. Yes. A large one.

JEFF. That's good.

HOWARD. It's terrific. In six weeks you can open it and jump out.

Jeff laughs.

SCOTT. Lighten up, Howard.

Blackout.

SCENE FOURTEEN

Jeff is thumbing through a magazine. Howard, appearing nervous, is writing a letter.

HOWARD. Damn! It's just not coming out right.

JEFF. What?

HOWARD. My letter.

JEFF. Not another one to the president.

HOWARD. No, to my sister.

JEFF. You have a sister?

HOWARD. Is there anything wrong with that?

JEFF. You never mentioned her.

HOWARD. Didn't I?

JEFF. Therapists are so secretive. They just love dragging stories out of everybody, but they act like it's a major intrusion if you ask them what they had for lunch.

HOWARD. A stuffed pepper.

JEFF. Are you and your sister close?

HOWARD. Used to be. It's our family reunion next weekend. There's going to be party.

JEFF. Will it be fun?

HOWARD. I can't go.

JEFF. Why not?

HOWARD. Because I don't want to. And this letter's all wrong. Would you listen?

JEFF. Of course.

HOWARD. "Dear Janet, So sorry this note has taken so long . . ." I wrote that "so sorry" part because that's how our mom starts all her correspondence. Even her Visa bills. Anyway . . . "So sorry this note has taken so long. I will not be coming to the family reunion. You see, I'm redecorating my bathroom this weekend, and I'm in a conflict as to what color the shower curtain should be."

JEFF. Howard, what the hell is going on?

HOWARD. "I know you understand why I can't make it to this place you call home. Because wasn't that your same predicament the week that my Greg died? 'Oh Howie,' you wrote . . . 'So sorry'—you actually used Mom's expression—'But they just started the construction on our kitchen . . . Now, after the funeral, come home and I'll take care of you.'" *(To Jeff)* I haven't been able to talk to her for a year. And now, all I can do is quote her own letter. *(Tearing up the letter)* I can't send this. It's humiliating. Too fucking needy. *(Breaking down)* But not one cousin showed up.

JEFF. *(Going to Howard)* It's all right, Howard.

HOWARD. *(Furiously)* What the hell is all right?

Blackout.

SCENE FIFTEEN

Another Tuesday. Denise is pacing. Jeff is reading a magazine.

JEFF. *(After a moment)* Is anything wrong?

DENISE. I don't want to be here today.

JEFF. I don't either.

DENISE. Is it interesting?

JEFF. What?

DENISE. What you're reading.

JEFF. It's about the renovation of castles. It's the latest thing the European yuppies are buying.

DENISE. So . . . how's it going?

JEFF. I don't think I'd buy one. Too damp.

DENISE. I mean with you.

JEFF. Great. I just wish it would stop raining.

Howard, who is walking slowly, enters.

HOWARD. So that's what's bothering you these days.

JEFF. Say "hello" before you start in on me.

HOWARD. Hello. *(To Denise)* And hello stranger. Where'd you disappear to?

DENISE. Scranton.

HOWARD. The one in Pennsylvania?

DENISE. I pray to God there isn't another one.

HOWARD. Were you there on vacation?

DENISE. I'm not tasteless.

HOWARD. You look great.

DENISE. I'm okay. Yes. I think I'm doing okay. I took my kids there.

HOWARD. Why?

DENISE. *(After a moment)* They've moved in with my sister and her husband.

HOWARD. Oh God, no.

DENISE. Yes. But I'm okay. I should be grateful. Now I know where my kids are going to be. My sister—Colleen—is very loving. So is her husband. They have a baby of their own. Now, they'll be a family of five.

Howard starts to cry.

DENISE. Howard, don't cry, please. I'm okay. We decided it was best for my children to do this now, while I'm doing well. This way, I can go down there—once a month if I want—to see how they're adjusting. I can still be a part of their lives. Howard, don't cry. It doesn't help. Look I've brought you a coffee mug. It says, "Scranton, PA." Classy, isn't it? I took a bus back. That's how you get back from Scranton. You take a bus. The man next to me wanted to chat. Wanted to get to know me. "You're not very friendly, are you?" That's what he said. He said it twice. I just stared out the window. Listening to him furiously turning the pages of his magazine. Thousands of people have taken bus rides like mine. Coming from their doctors after they find out. Coming from their families after they've told them. Staring out of windows wanting it to be yesterday. My little one—my boy—when I kissed him good-bye, he immediately left my arms and went and sat in front of the TV. What do you think that poor boy was thinking? My daughter—she acts all grown-up—gave me a big hug and said, "Everything is going to be fine." Sure, darling. Sure. They've seen too much already in their baby lives. I hope someday they're happy. Don't cry, Howard. It doesn't help.

HOWARD. Again and again. It happens again and again.

JEFF. *(Jumping up)* Howard!

HOWARD. *(Yelling)* When will this stop?!?

JEFF. *(Opening the door to the treatment center)* Get somebody!

DENISE. *(In her own world)* Will they ever be happy?

HOWARD. *(Yelling)* How much more can we take?!? How much more?!?

Howard lets out a scream. Denise remains seated. Jeff remains frozen.

Blackout.

SCENE SIXTEEN

Howard is asleep on the floor. Jeff is watching him.

JEFF. *(After a moment)* Howard . . . they called you.

HOWARD. *(Waking up. After a moment)* I was dreaming.

Howard struggles to get up.

Blackout.

SCENE SEVENTEEN

Another Tuesday. Howard appears to be engrossed in his book. Jeff is watching him.

JEFF. Is it good?

HOWARD. *War and Peace.*

JEFF. That should keep you going for a year.

HOWARD. These days I can lick a book like this in a week.

JEFF. You've been that social?

HOWARD. How's Scott?

JEFF. Good. He's fun to live with. He sings. Like around the house. It puts you in a good mood.

HOWARD. When you have to move, do you know where you're going yet?

JEFF. I'm working on it.

HOWARD. What about Scott?

JEFF. He's working on it.

HOWARD. I guess that's good.

JEFF. I wish you'd drop by and visit us.

HOWARD. I don't think so.

JEFF. Why not?

Gene enters.

GENE. *(Tentatively)* Hi guys.

JEFF. Hello. What brings you here?

GENE. Howard left a message. Said he had to see me. That it was urgent.

HOWARD. I'd like to talk.

GENE. Yes.

HOWARD. Over dinner. Soon.

GENE. *(Awkwardly)* Oh. Well, I'm taking off for a while. A vacation.

HOWARD. Okay. When you get back.

GENE. I'm not sure when that will be. I'll give you a call. I guess I'll be seeing you guys.

HOWARD. Wait! Gene . . . do . . . do you miss Scott?

GENE. *(Embarrassed)* That's not your business.

HOWARD. I'm worried about him.

GENE. I try not to.

HOWARD. You care for him, don't you?

GENE. You're embarrassing me.

HOWARD. I know you do. So you've got to take him back.

JEFF. Howard!

GENE. It's over.

HOWARD. Then be a friend. Love him as a friend.

JEFF. *(To Howard)* Stop it! Have some pride.

HOWARD. Screw it!

GENE. I've got to get back to the office.

HOWARD. *(Grabbing Gene's arm)* The office? What the fuck are you talking about?

JEFF. Howard, don't do this.

GENE. *(To Howard)* Let go.

HOWARD. *(Holding tight)* Someone you once loved is sick. Has no money. And in a few weeks will have no place to live.

GENE. *(Shoving Howard away from him)* I can't think about it anymore.

HOWARD. You have to.

GENE. No! No, I don't. Right now, I can't. I've had enough.

HOWARD. *(Begging)* What about Scott?

GENE. I'm not Scott, and I'm not you. The last two years have been a nightmare. But there's a way out for me, and I'm taking it.

HOWARD. *(Pleading)* What about us? People have to help, don't they? You have to help.

JEFF. Shut up, Howard!

GENE. All I have is one life. I want some pleasure.

HOWARD. *(Desperately)* But what about us?

GENE. I pray for you.

Howard hauls off and slaps Gene across the face. Gene just stands there.

JEFF. *(To Gene)* Get out of here.

GENE. I'll still pray.

JEFF. Go!

Gene backs out of the room.

HOWARD. Look at me. I'm going crazy. I am. We all are. Every single damn one of us.

Blackout.

SCENE EIGHTEEN

Two weeks later. Jeff is seated next to Howard. Howard appears dazed. He has a book in his lap.

JEFF. You were home. I know you were there.

HOWARD. I probably went out for milk.

JEFF. You were in there. You don't even answer your phone.

HOWARD. I'm just going through a hermit phase. That's all.

JEFF. Why don't you want to be with your friends?

HOWARD. Jeff, lay off, please. Let me get back to my book.

JEFF. Look at me, Howard.

HOWARD. No, I can't. I love you, Jeff. I love Denise. But I don't want to be with you now. I don't want to think about Denise and her children. I'm like Gene. I don't want to think about you. Your lover. All my dead friends. I just want to read my book.

JEFF. What about you? What kind of thought are you giving yourself? Aren't you sad at what's happening to you? I am. Don't you want to tell me?

HOWARD. Tell you what?

JEFF. That you're getting weaker. That you're losing weight. That you're sleeping all the time. That you're having trouble walking.

HOWARD. Please let me read my book.

JEFF. Talk to me.

HOWARD. Why don't we just forget it.

JEFF. Because we can't. Come on . . . please . . . talk to me.

HOWARD. *(After a moment)* Last night . . .

JEFF. Yes . . .

HOWARD. . . . when I came out of the bathroom, I didn't know where I was. I stood there in my apartment, among my things, and I didn't know where I was.

JEFF. *(Lovingly)* Now, say it. Please.

HOWARD. What?

JEFF. You know.

HOWARD. I'm . . .

JEFF. Yes.

HOWARD. . . . afraid. I'm so afraid. *(He begins to cry)*

JEFF. Don't do this alone.

HOWARD. I don't know how long I stood there. Shaking and wondering where I was.

JEFF. You don't need to do this alone. I'm a terrific nurse.

HOWARD. I can't ask you. You've done it already. I can't ask you to do it again.

JEFF. I'd do it again and again and again if it would help.

HOWARD. You'd come live with me?

JEFF. I'm practically homeless.

HOWARD. Are you neat?

JEFF. I have no idea what a dust ball looks like.

HOWARD. You've got yourself a roommate.

Jeff takes Howard in his arms.

Blackout.

SCENE NINETEEN

Two weeks later. Scott and Jeff are listening to Denise.

DENISE. The kids are doing okay. Teddy has made a good friend so he's busy and happy. Jeff—you'll appreciate this—Michelle is taking piano lessons and loving it. It was a crazy weekend. My sister and I cooked and drank gallons of coffee. The only problem is Bill, my brother-in-law. He's a beautiful human being—don't get me wrong. This is awful, but I've got to say it. He's the most boring person I've ever met. After dinner one night he was talking a blue streak. I sat there trying to listen, but I fell right to sleep. Had a good doze. The poor guy was embarrassed. I said—this is the worst—that people with AIDS fall asleep constantly. He believed me, thank God. Colleen is so vibrant. What could she see in him?

SCOTT. Maybe he's great sex.

DENISE. I doubt it. If I have insomnia now, I picture him talking to me and within minutes I'm in never-never land. I hope his personality doesn't rub off on my children.

JEFF. He can't be that bad.

DENISE. He's a beautiful person. I'm grateful to him. I should keep my mouth shut. He's in hardware. Maybe he's the Michelangelo of light fixtures.

SCOTT. Maybe at night, in his basement, he's working on the great American poem.

JEFF. Or the cure for AIDS.

DENISE. You've got it. You guys are so perceptive. Bill doesn't want to see me get too excited. His boring nature is all a disguise. He's going to come up with a cure for AIDS.

Howard, who is now using a cane, walks in slowly and looks in pain.

HOWARD. Somebody better. And soon.

JEFF. You finished?

HOWARD. Yes. Thank you for coming here, Scott. I need you people today.

SCOTT. Are they going to put you in the hospital, buddy?

HOWARD. Not yet.

JEFF. Great. Then let's get out of here.

HOWARD. I have to sit for a minute. What a day. I got stuck with blind Belinda.

JEFF. I'm sorry. How many times did she stick you before she found a vein?

HOWARD. My arm can now be used as a colander.

JEFF. What did Dr. Willis say?

HOWARD. The news is not good. I may refuse to believe him. I'm wasting away. Disintegrating. I'd rather think of it as a process of evaporation. Do you think I'll be in the air like H_2O?

Denise embraces Howard. Jeff and Scott lovingly watch them.

HOWARD. You smell good.

DENISE. Thank you.

HOWARD. Don't let go yet. I have blossomed into a sentimental sponge.

JEFF. He's even taken to watching the reruns of *The Waltons.*

HOWARD. *(Leaving Denise's embrace)* And you promised you'd never tell.

JEFF. I lied.

HOWARD. Denise, do you believe in God?

DENISE. No.

HOWARD. Shit.

DENISE. Did I give the wrong answer?

HOWARD. I was hoping you did. It would have thrown a nice monkey wrench into my atheism.

SCOTT. I believe in God.

HOWARD. You do?

SCOTT. Why are you surprised?

DENISE. What God do you believe in?

SCOTT. There's only one God.

DENISE. He's a Catholic.

SCOTT. Not anymore. But I am a Christian.

JEFF. No!

SCOTT. Yes.

JEFF. I'll be damned.

SCOTT. I can't believe how shocked you people look.

JEFF. It doesn't seem to fit.

SCOTT. With what?

JEFF. With your politics.

SCOTT. That's narrow-minded.

JEFF. Sorry. Maybe if you told us you were into some New Age philosophy where they read auras and build pyramids we wouldn't be so surprised.

SCOTT. Well, get ready for this one. I go to church.

JEFF. No.

SCOTT. I take communion. I always have, and I always will.

HOWARD. Even before you got sick?

SCOTT. Yes, Howard.

DENISE. Well, I'll be damned.

JEFF. I lived with you. How come I never knew? Why would you keep it a secret?

SCOTT. What secret? On Sundays I told you I'd bring home bagels after church.

JEFF. I thought it was a poor joke.

DENISE. *(To Scott)* You believe in heaven?

SCOTT. Yes.

DENISE. Well, I'll be damned.

SCOTT. If I told you people I was a serial killer, you would be less shocked. Come on, Jeff, come out of the closet and admit you're religious too.

HOWARD. You?

JEFF. Not religious. Spiritual. There were rare moments, when I was on stage playing, I would enter another world. There has to be something beyond this. Many other worlds.

DENISE. Well, I'll be damned.

HOWARD. I envy you guys.

DENISE. I don't.

HOWARD. *(To Denise)* Not even a bit.

DENISE. No. I think some of the stories are nice, but if I believed that there was someone in charge and this is what that person had come up with—I'd walk around pissed all the time.

SCOTT. That's not how it works.

DENISE. I have no interest in any of it. It's better for me to focus on this life and get through it as best I can.

HOWARD. I want to evaporate.

DENISE. Oh, baby.

JEFF. *(Jokingly)* It's humid enough already. We don't need you adding yourself to the moisture.

HOWARD. Jeff, I don't think I know how to do this.

JEFF. Do what?

HOWARD. Die.

JEFF. *(After a moment, lovingly)* You're not dying yet. When the time comes, I'm sure it's real easy. Let's go home.

HOWARD. I don't want another night falling asleep in front of the TV.

JEFF. Then we won't turn it on.

HOWARD. I'm sounding like a pain in the ass.

DENISE. You sound drugged.

HOWARD. *(Smiling)* Well, I am . . . a little. I'd love to be sitting on a porch—looking at something green.

JEFF. Now, you're sounding trite. But if you want, I'll read you an Andy Hardy story.

HOWARD. *(Referring to Jeff)* Do you believe the mouth I live with?

SCOTT. I know of a place.

HOWARD. What place?

SCOTT. A place where you can sit on a porch and look out on beautiful farmlands.

HOWARD. Scott, you're not going to take my hand, and we're not going to start a meditation.

SCOTT. But I know of a place. Upstate. We can all go for a few days. It's owned by two guys I know. Doctors. They only use it on weekends. They're real generous. I know they'll give me the keys. Let's all go.

DENISE. All of us.

SCOTT. Why not?

DENISE. How do we get there?

HOWARD. We rent a car with my credit card. *(Handing his wallet to Jeff)* Here. Jeff, you arrange it.

SCOTT. I'll call my friends.

DENISE. Do I have time to go home and pack?

SCOTT. *(Exiting)* No.

JEFF. Howard, are you sure you want to do this?

HOWARD. Why not? If I croak while you're getting the car, take me to the country anyway.

JEFF. We'll stuff you in the trunk. That way I'll be able to stretch out in the backseat.

Jeff kisses Howard and exits with Scott.

DENISE. Aren't we something.

The young man who appeared in Scene Eleven walks in and sits down nervously.

MAN. Hi.

HOWARD. Hello.

MAN. Randy.

HOWARD. Howard.

DENISE. Denise.

RANDY. *(To Howard)* Do you remember me?

HOWARD. Yes.

RANDY. I'm back.

HOWARD. I'm sorry.

DENISE. I'd better call my mother and tell her we're going on a trip.

Denise exits.

RANDY. A vacation?

HOWARD. Sort of.

RANDY. I'm handling things better.

HOWARD. That's good.

RANDY. How have you been doing?

HOWARD. Not well today.

RANDY. I'm sorry.

HOWARD. You look good.

RANDY. I'm handling things better.

HOWARD. Attitude is important.

RANDY. That's what they say. *(Nervously)* What's it like coming here every week?

HOWARD. I've made some wonderful friends.

RANDY. But what's it like?

HOWARD. Different for everyone.

RANDY. That's evasive.

HOWARD. What do you want me to tell you?

RANDY. The truth.

HOWARD. No. You want me to lie and tell you that you'll never get like me.

RANDY. No. I want to know. What's it like? Please.

HOWARD. I can't answer that. Maybe you'll never get as weak as I am. Things are changing.

RANDY. Not fast enough. Tell me something. Anything.

HOWARD. Try to stay in charge.

RANDY. I feel lonely. So separate from everyone I know.

HOWARD. You've moved. You now live on the other side of the street. People on our side are forced to think about and look at things most people are blind to. I know you're thinking about death. Well, look at it. And then go about the business of living.

RANDY. You're a kind man.

They are interrupted by a voice coming from the public address system.

VOICE. Mr. Tompkins, please report to room 4. Mr. Tompkins to room 4.

RANDY. *(Not moving)* That's me. I'm so scared.

HOWARD. Of course you are. Why don't I stay here until you're finished with your treatment.

RANDY. Would you come in with me?

HOWARD. Of course.

VOICE. Mr. Tompkins, room 4. Room 4.

RANDY. I haven't told anybody yet.

HOWARD. *(Getting up)* You'll feel better after you do.

RANDY. *(Getting up)* You're probably right.

HOWARD. Are you going to be coming on Tuesdays?

RANDY. Yes. Is it a good day?

HOWARD. The best.

RANDY. Will you be here?

HOWARD. Maybe.

Blackout.

tim miller

my queer body

a performance work

author's note

Hi everybody! I began work on this piece about a year and a half ago when I began to tell a story to my dick. This launched me on a journey to discover the stories my body has to tell me and what I can tell my body. If you listen carefully, your lips remember your first kiss . . . and your first loss. Queer places have their history in flesh and blood and breath and spirit.

The houselights dim along with the preshow music by The Smiths. Onstage is only a bowl of water, a piece of lava, and a surprise wrapped in a red cloth. We pause in the dark for a moment to acknowledge the miracle that these humans have gathered together in this theatre. Tim enters through the audience in blackout.

Hello. Hi everybody. This is my entrance. It's sort of a rear entry tonight. It's the mood I'm in. Actually, I'm here because I need a few things from the audience. Think of this as sort of a psychosexual scavenger hunt. I know you've been on a lot of those. I need to gather a few things. *(He grabs an unsuspecting audience member's fingers. And whatever else strikes his fancy during this section)* I need your fingers! Oh those dancing fingers. They do a rhumba! A bolero later perhaps. We summon the fingers to this place. The fingers are here. I need this person's foot! Oh foot. There are entire clubs in this city devoted to your worship? We summon the foot. We need some pulsating brains. There's a bunch of them over here. Have you noticed the brains always want to sit house right? Many open hearts here tonight. I see them shining. These open hearts will be much needed tonight. Bring 'em onstage. Now, this is the first of several audience participation moments in tonight's program. (OH NO!) I know how you love them. This first one is very easy. I need you to call out some favorite places on your body, or someone near your body, and while you do this I will spontaneously improvise a dynamic postmodern dance. Let's begin. *(Audience begins to say body parts. Thighs!!! Breasts!!! Lips!!! Other lips!!!)* I think we're leaving a few things out. Don't censor yourselves. Let's work below the belt for a bit. *(Dicks!!! Pussies!!! Butthole!!!)* Good! We have summoned the body! The body is here. *(He steps onstage)* Let's start at the beginning. The very beginning. My dad is fucking my mom. In a bed. Where else would they be? This is suburban Whittier, California.

They're young and hot for each other. I'm trying to visualize this. Half of me is inside my father's dick. The other half is inside my mom. My biology gets a little vague here. They breathe fast. My dad is going to cum any minute. He's thrusting madly. AH AH AH! Suddenly I am thrown out of my father's dick into my mom's body. I am surrounded by thousands of squirming creatures. I am swimming upstream. Oh humble dog paddle! Oh efficient crawl! Oh stylish backstroke!

I am swimming upstream. As I would swim upstream throughout this life. One queer little spermlet . . . Fighting the odds. A hideous sperm that looks like Jesse Helms tries to catch me in a net. I elude him! A herd of sperm who look like the military Joint Chiefs of Staff try to kick me out of this fallopian tube! I elude them, as well. Then a bunch of hulking macho slimebag straight-pig sperm shove and try to elbow me out of the way. Call me "Sissy! Pansy! Fag! You'll never find an egg! HA HA HA!" Clearly this is homophobia. My very first experience. But! I use my superior agility, fleetness, and sense of style and calmly jeté from plodding straight sperm forehead to straight sperm forehead. I quickly find a willing dyke ovum, we agree to power share. We reach consensus immediately (this is a fantasy sequence, OK) and we . . . FERTILIZE!!!!

There is an explosion of creative electricity. A shifting of queer tectonic plates. Skittering across the well of loneliness to the two boys together clinging on the sea beach dancing! I see Gertrude Stein is in a tutu. She dances with Vaslav Nijinsky in a butt plug. They do a pas de deux on the wings of a fabulous flying machine created by Leonardo and piloted by James Baldwin and Amelia Earhart. They fly over the island of Lesbos where Sappho is starting to put the moves on the cute woman carpenter who had arrived to build her a breakfast nook. There is a puff of feathers . . . an angry fist . . . a surface to air witticism . . . the off-the-shoulder amazon look! Embodying the bridge between woman and man and back again. The sperm is a fish. The egg is a rocket. 5, 4, 3, 2, 1!!! And . . . ECCE HOMO!!! Behold the fag. And the big cry to the universe. Time to be born. WAAAAHHH!

The doctor spanks my butt. WAAAHH! He spanks it again. I look back and I say "Doctor, I won't be into spanking till I'm twenty-four!" With that first preerotic and nonconsensual spank a wave of shame and body fear washes over me. I fight back. I kick the doctor in the balls. Rejecting his authority over my body. I slip on my "Action=Life" Huggies. Slither into my "We're-Here-We're-Queer-Get-Used-To-It" jumper. I see all the other queer babies in the nursery start to shimmer and grow and explode from their diapers. We all grow to adulthood. Some of them find their way to this theatre tonight. Until I stand before you now. *(He takes a huge breath and holds it)*

First! *(Rubbing heart)* It hit me right here. In the heart. Right here. Only later it hit me in the head. *(He walks into the audience and approaches someone)* Could you rub me here please? *(Audience member rubs his heart. They get fresh sometimes)* Well, a lot of things have done that. The election of Ronald Reagan . . . AIDS . . . the first time I got butt-fucked. Oh, and the only date I went on with a boy in high school. *(To person rubbing)* Keep going. A little faster and harder please. If your arm gets tired just switch. I'm going to set the stage now. Everyone pay attention. There is a bed there. Right there up on stage. It has a big old pine headboard painted Pin-N-Save antique green. The Vitalis on my father's head has burnt a hole right through seven layers of paint to the maple wood underneath. My mom's sacred jar of Noxema is on the bed stand. I always tried to use that Noxema to beat off with it but you can never get up a good slide with Noxema. Plus it stings! See, people have tried. This is the bed. The bed I was conceived on. The bed on which I would be born once again. Thank you, person, for rubbing me. *(He walks onstage)*

I offer this now in tribute to the first time this meat and bones got close to other flesh and blood. It's the story of the only date I went on with a boy in high school.

I met him. Robert. The guy I would go on the date with. I was seventeen years old. He was seventeen. So that means I am now old enough to be my own father in this story. It's a stretch, I know, but it's possible. I think maybe I am my own father in this story. Trying to give birth to myself? But I don't want to do that. I really support guys who do. You know, the straight men with the drums and stuff in the woods. I want to do something else. I want to remember and claim and conjure my queer body at seventeen when my entire body was a hard-on. Oh, I had a hard-on for Dostoyevsky. I had a hard-on for Patti Smith. I had a hard-on for many of the boys in my gym class.

Robert went to a different high school in Anaheim near Disneyland. He grew to his seventeen years in the forbidding shadow of the Matterhorn Bobsled Ride. He was slight and fair, cute, and wore glasses, always a plus. He was the lead singer in a protopunk rock band based in Anaheim. They mostly did songs taken from obscure texts of the Marquis de Sade. My friend Lori introduced us. She had met him at one of those bohemian hangs in Fullerton, the left bank of hyperconservative republican Orange County. She loved him. But quickly realized he was a big fag and passed him on to her friend Tim. I called him up. "Hi, Robert. This is Tim. I met you with Lori. Hey you wanna go to the beach with me and then we'll go into L.A. to the 'Shakespeare on Film' retrospective at the County Museum of Art? Huh?" He said he would. I picked him up in Anaheim with my '65 VW blue Bug. This beat-up car was my initiation. My symbol of freedom. I drove the streets of L.A. feeling the future inside my body and listening to Bryan Ferry and Roxy Music on the transistor radio pressed to my ear. Robert and I went to Diver's Cove at Laguna Beach. I had been to this beach many times before . . . mostly with my Congregational Church youth group. But now everything was different. The sand was epic. Like in *Lawrence of Arabia*. Bigger than 70mm. Each word we said hung perfect and crystalline in the cool fall air before it was blown by a wind towards Japan. We found a secluded nook and sat down and talked. While we spoke, I noticed that he was doodling with his fingers and building a wall of sand between us. While he was doing this, he was saying that he always put up barriers between himself and other people. That he kept emotional distance. The wall was shoulder height now. I said, "Robert, this is so intense.

It's such a coincidence. I know exactly what you mean. I feel like I do that too. I put up those emotional walls. But, Robert. Robert, we have to find the way to break through those walls." And our hands moved through the base of that sand wall and our fingertips touched. Our eyes connected in a Star Trek laser beam of awareness and perfect feeling. Our lips projected beyond our bodies' boundaries. We kissed! The Big Bang. YES!!! The triumph over all the times I was chosen last for football. YES!!! The victory over the tears that ran down my face when my fucked up cousin would knock me down, punching me in the face calling me, "Half Man! Half Man! Half Man!" The times my sister dressed me as a girl—I looked like Jackie Kennedy in my wig, pillbox hat and pink dress—and introduced me to our neighbors as her distant cousin Melinda from Kansas. That confusing ping-pong of feelings I would feel when I watched David Cassidy in the *Partridge Family*. I think I love you. But what am I so afraid of? Our lips parted and we put our tongues in each other's mouths. Just like you're supposed to. I tasted his mouth. It tasted like . . . *(He moves his tongue around his mouth tasting it)* The roof of his mouth tasted like cigarettes. His gums tasted like a child's. His tongue tasted a lot like my own. We kissed for a long time. He pulled his high school ring off his finger and slipped it on mine. I have this ring with me. I wear it always. The Valencia High Panthers. I treasure this ring as a symbol of perfect love, of course, but also because I really suspect this will be the only high school ring that any seventeen-year-old boy is gonna give me in this lifetime. We kissed and kissed and kissed again. The wave crashes on a California beach and the page has turned.

We drove blissfully back through traffic on the Santa Ana freeway past the theme parks. Past Disneyland. Past the Movieland Wax Museum. A cloud hovered over my Bug when we drove by Knotts Berry Farm. Robert began telling me about this affair he had been having with Ricky Nelson. Ricky Nelson had fallen from his Ozzie and Harriet glory and was reduced to playing gigs at the Knotts Berry Farm Amphitheater. They had had a very bad sex scene backstage.

This scene seemed to include a large amount of LSD and several enormous summer squash. Should I believe him? I'm not sure. Ricky Nelson? Not a big homo, according to my sources, which are impeccable. What is he telling me? That he's scared of sex? Scared of me? I can relate. I'm scared of everything too!! WE WERE YOUNG QUEERS IN LOVE AND WE WERE SCARED SHITLESS!!! Some things don't change.

We got back to Whittier and picked up my friend Lori to go to the movies with us. Now, this might seem strange to you that we all would go on a romantic date with my friend Lori. But, Lori, though she was not a dyke, was—believe me—the queerest of the queer kids at my high school. And throughout this life the queer kids—whether they're straight or gay—better fucking stick together. OK?

We were going to see the Zefferelli film of *Romeo and Juliet* at the County Museum. SHAKESPEARE ON FILM! I had seen it as a little little boy when it first came out with my sister and her best girlfriend who had the unfortunate name of Kay Hickey. Me and Betsy and Kay Hickey went to the Whittier cinema to see it. It was all a little bit much for me with the cleavage and the heavy breathing so I mostly kept my eyes covered. But, there is one shot in this movie where I had to look. We see the beautiful Leonard Whitting as Romeo face down and naked on a bed. His butt hovering there lunarlike in the soft Verona light. My fingers intuitively opened over my eyes. I rose from my seat and began to walk down the aisle. My fingers reached towards the screen casting ten-foot-tall Panavision shadows onto that perfect butt. I touched the screen and his Romeo's ass undulated and danced above me. And at that precise instant. At that moment . . . I enlisted. I signed up. I am now a career homo officer. Because I knew someday I would get to see that butt again except the next time I would be seventeen, would now have pubic hair, and would be holding the hand of my new boyfriend from Anaheim.

We get to the County Museum of Art and had a romantic walk, just the three of us, past the La Brea tar pits. Now, for those of you that don't know, the La Brea tar pits are primordial pits of petroleum sludge that are next to the County Museum of Art. They've been there since the dawn of time . . . or at least since that field trip in first grade. Anyway, for tens of thousands of years, prehistoric animals, people, tennis balls and coffee cans have fallen into these pits and been sucked to the center of the earth. Well, it hit me right here. Then right here. The feeling of eternity that was there in my heart and in my head was so strong. All of those beasts and those people, they were like me. Feeding and fucking. And then they got sucked to a tarry death. This put us in the proper mood for the movie.

We walked down Wilshire and into the movie theatre. We sat in the front row. The lights dim slowly . . . slowly.

The movie began.

(Yes, dear reader, we now hear the haunting melancholy music from the film, Romeo and Juliet*)* I slowly reached over and grabbed Robert's hand. I had never watched a movie while holding someone's hand before. It's nice! I see why people like it so much. You might wanna try it right now. Just grab the hand of somebody you don't know! Thanks for doing that. That feeling of connection. A lifeline back into the world as the movie rolls and rolls.

And what a movie to watch on your first date with a boyfriend. It had everything. Poetic language. Fabulous swordplay. Doomed love. MICHAEL YORK!!!

Now, what is going on when a coupla fag teenage boys hold hands and watch *Romeo and Juliet* at the L.A. County Museum of Art? There is a survival technique about how we manage to see who we are. Sure, we enjoy all the cute Italian boys stuffed in their tights and bulging codpieces. But, we also project ourselves into the film. Take in the images. Become them. Use them. I was always really good at this. Sometimes I was Romeo/Tim hanging with his friends. And then I would be Juliet/Tim throwing herself on Romeo/Robert's chest. And then I would be Mercutio/Tim, so obviously in love with Romeo/Robert, if you do a careful textual reading. Then, this was my favorite one, once again I was Romeo/Tim and I was gonna run away with Mercutio/Robert. I was gonna heal him of his pain, so haunted by Queen Mab. We'd go someplace safe and good . . . like the Renaissance Faire in the San Fernando Valley or something! We'd build a life together there at that pleasure fair. We'd get a little duplex over a tallowmaker's souvenir shop. There'd be a big fluffy bed with feather comforters. We would take our clothes off, rub our bodies together. Loving the touch of skin. Just like I would when I was a little boy. I would come home from church and take off all my clothes. The suit, the tie, and the tight shoes, and put my naked little boy's body between the polyester sheets. Loving the feelings. Making them mine. Reclaiming my body from church and state. I remember. I remember.

But, then, the sword is pulled. The shit happens. Everyone is torn from everyone they love. And there is a plague on all our houses.

The movie ends and all are punished. The lights come up slowly.

It's very quiet as we leave the movie theatre. We walk silently out past the tar pits. I wander off by myself through the trees down to the chain link fence surrounding the pits.

I look at the moonlight sheen of water hovering over this eternal life filled goo. I stare across the tar pit lake towards the giant plastic sculpture of the woolly mammoth in his death throes. It's been there as long as I can remember. Then, I see something. The woolly mammoth opens his eyes. His trunk snakes out into the night. He lifts one massive leg. Tar dripping from each woolly mammoth toenail. A rapier pierces through the tar. We see Tybalt and Mercutio and Romeo and Juliet rise out of the heavy sticky stuff, hover a bit and whisper to me . . . "Live these days. Love well. Value every kiss. And savour your body's blink between being born and dying."

They wave at me and sink slowly back into the unforgiving tar pit. Only the woolly mammoth is left. I see him wink at me and then he throws his trunk and tusks back in a permanent plastic death trumpet. I shake my head and the vision is gone.

My friends call to me. I run to join them. I want to explain to them what I have seen. I dance in front of them leading them down the path past the bone museum. I leapfrog over the bronze saber-toothed tiger. Climb up on the back of a mastodon . . . and crow to the night.

"And yet I wish but for the thing I have: My bounty is as boundless as the sea,"—I know these lines because I had the soundtrack LP to the movie—"My love as deep; the more I give to thee, The more I have, for both are infinite."

We fall on each other and run galumphing towards my VW. I open the passenger door and Robert gets in the back and Lori in the front. We laugh and scream and joke about stuff. We are just so glad to be together in a car in Los Angeles in 1976 and not in Verona in 1303. I drive a little bit too fast down Sixth Street toward La Brea. I keep trying to catch Robert's eye there in the backseat. I wanna kiss him right then. I want to keep the connection. Stay the link.

Then it happens. It's a wild panic-filled slow-mo. The crunch of metal. The breaking of glass. I'm thrown forward. It hits me in the heart . . . the steering wheel takes my breath. And then it hits me in the head and my face becomes stars as I hit the windshield . . . just in time to see Lori break the glass with her forehead as Robert is thrown between the front seats cutting his face on the rearview mirror. The horn is stuck blowing. The woolly mammoth in the tar pit hears it and tries to come save us but he just sinks deeper towards death. Gas is leaking. Tires are spinning. Why, God? Why. On my only date with a boy in high school did I have to rear-end a hopped-up maroon El Camino at 45 MPH thus totalling my beloved Bug, ruining my date and my entire life? WHY? Questions careen. Can I get the car home somehow? Is anybody hurt bad? How will I explain this? Do I look like I have been kissing a boy all night long??? We get out of the car. We're all basically OK. But, my beloved Bug is dead. The woolly mammoth can't help me now. Who will save us? I'll call my father.

I walk about two inches tall to a phone booth on Fairfax and call my dad. He arrives shortly after, followed by a tow truck. I don't think he does a big shame thing on me . . . but I definitely could be repressing that. Tow truck takes my Bug away and we pile in my dad's Datsun to drive home. My mind races. I plot to myself. How to salvage this evening. I look at Robert. All I want to do is lay down with him and kiss him. I start to improvise plans and strategies. Finally I have it. I say, "Dad, it's very late, isn't it? You know, I was thinking, Anaheim is twenty minutes past Whittier. It would really make more sense for Robert to stay at our house tonight and then you and I can drive him home in the morning." Pretty creative, really, under the circumstances. My dad raises his eyebrow. Seventeen-year-old boys do not do sleep overs. All he said was, "AAAARGHHHHHH!!!!!!" English subtitle, "OK." We get to Whittier and drop off Lori. We get to my house. As my dad tries to open the front door with his keys, my mom keeps locking it on the other side. I decide to use this Freudian moment for the second part of my plan. I say, "Gee, Dad, we're both pretty upset from what has happened. Traumatized, really. I think it would be best if Robert and I sleep in the same room tonight." My dad raised both eyebrows, but all he said was "AAARGHHH!!!!!" Translation, "Whatever." Which was as close as we were going to get to a blessing that night. Now, I know I said "same room," but what I should have said was "same bed," because there was definitely only one bed in my room. Yes, that's right. This was THE bed. The bed I had been conceived on. My parents had recently gotten a new giant double king and I, ever the drama queen, thought I would like to sleep on "The Bed I Was Conceived On."

Robert and I shut the door to my room and I locked it with a chair under the doorknob. We stood there real nervous. Then it happened. The miracle of life. We opened our bodies, walked toward each other, hugged, and we kissed. This is it. This is it! The best thing we get while we're in our bodies on the planet Earth.

I felt it in my heart, where the steering wheel had taken my breath. I felt it in my head, where my face had smashed the glass. And now I felt my love and desire for this boy rise up from those two places on my body.

We took off our clothes but kept our underwear on and got into the cold bed. I think that at that moment, as my skin hit those sheets and I naturally moved to hold my friend's body, that at that moment maybe I became a man. This might have been the moment. Maybe, I am a man now with a man's ways. I comfort my boyfriend as we lay down at the end of a hard day. I will soothe Mercutio who in this story, for tonight at least, does not die from his wide and deep wound. I will honor the little boy I once was who had the good sense to wiggle his body naked between the sheets after church. I will hold that boy and that man close to me throughout this life.

We kissed for a long time. Our hands owning each other's body. But, then, Robert pulled away and looked at me and said, "You know, Tim, I'm still pretty fucked up from that bad sex scene with Ricky Nelson at Knotts Berry Farm. Is it OK if we just hold each other and kiss and don't do a big sex thing?" Well, I didn't care. This was enough of a miracle for one night. The woolly mammoth had taught me that. I am happy to smooth that other rough touch with my gentle kiss. That out of the crash. The explosion of metal on metal. The face breaking the glass. That the end of day has brought me to this bed with a scared and—except for his J.C. Penney white underwear—naked punk rock boy filled me with such feeling. He looked me in the eye. We kissed. And kissed. And kissed again. His senior ring on my finger.

His hand on my heart. His body next to mine. We slept together on THE bed. And I was conceived once again. *(He rubs his heart as lights fade. Breathes loudly)* My skin is a map. A map of my world. My secret world. It tells you where I've been. And how to get to where I come from. It charts my seas . . . my peninsulas . . . my caves . . . and my mountains. I travel with this map over my skin. I go on journeys. Find new coastlines. Hidden borders. I follow my nose along the touch that has pulled me through life. I lead with my tongue. I go by foot . . . by dick . . . by brain sometimes. I know the path by heart. The pleasures I sailed across. The pain I pointed towards. The knowing my bends and hollows. The bodies . . . many bodies . . . I have touched and been taught by. The secret places soothed and stroked. But, then . . . "X" marks the spot.

There is a plague and hatred on the land. An earthquake

within. Whole continents have been lost to us . . . The island, that no man is . . . A hemisphere carved out of my
fucking heart . . . Then the burning began. Burned up those
carefully drawn and protected maps. This fire spread over
our skin. Boiled our seas. Burned up my city of angels. The
flames spread to the tar pits. Smoke to the sky. And burned.
And burned. And burned.

And a COP threw me against that same chain link fence.
Where the woolly mammoth had winked at me. And a COP
threw me against that same chain link fence. Where I had
pressed my seventeen-year-old cheek, trying to see love for
another boy. And a COP threw me against that same chain
link fence when thousands of us queers marched to the
County Museum of Art after our slimebag governor had
vetoed the state lesbian and gay rights bill. We marched
there pissed off and strong because we felt like it. Shut down
our city. Trapped the governor inside that museum while he
giggled nervously, sipping champagne in front of a Rem-
brandt. *(He goes into audience)* A lot of things happened in
those days. Some good. Some scary. When we started tonight
we called up some places on our bodies. Some things happened to those places too. Somebody said fingers. *(Touches
people with each body place)* Your fingers were smashed by a
horse's hoof. When hundreds of L.A.P.D. on horseback
trampled through us, hurting a lot of people. Your beautiful
arm struck with a cop's nightstick. Your wrists swelled real
bad from the tightness of the handcuffs after you were arrested and were kept in the basement of the parking structure at the Century Plaza Hotel. Your beautiful ass got
dragged along the pavement. All our spirits battered by the
fuckheads in charge. My face up against the wall of art.

I watched this happen here at my tar pit. As they surrounded us, hundreds of L.A. cops on horses. Hurt. Hit my
friends. Bully with horses.

Everything rushed in. So many friends and lovers dead
from AIDS. City of plague. Government of hate.

Vain and crazy men in power. The war they make on our
bodies. My body's in a state. The state of California? I saw
the flag of my state burn many times that night. The last

time it burned . . . at the last possible moment the California bear that is on that flag jumped off, walked over to me, and said, "Tim, let's get outta here."

Now I firmly believe that if a bear jumps off of your burning state flag, you should do whatever it tells you to. I took a drink. *(He drinks from bowl and picks up big piece of lava)* Gathered my personal effects and followed the bear down Wilshire Boulevard. Everyone was frozen where they stood, the activists and the cops, just like in a bad mid-70s science fiction film starring Charlton Heston. I followed the bear for a long time down Wilshire Boulevard. For about two years. I grew tired and couldn't stand. I crawled on my knees. I eventually collapsed in the parking lot of a Denny's restaurant in Barstow. I lay there with my face on the broken glass. But then a graceful Denny's waitress with big hair came to me. She cradled my head on her mustard blouse and spooned weak spoonfuls of coffee with nondairy creamer into my parched lips. And then she sent me into the desert.

I crawled through sand along a wash. The sand went into my skin. Into my bones. Into my blood. Into my breath. Until I became just a speck of sand. And was blown by a hot wind far east into the Mojave desert until I came to the Amboy volcano. AM BOY—it's a real place. I'm not making it up. A scar on the horizon. A wound open to the sky. Is this the mouth or asshole of California? Great chunks of lava. Black and grimacing. Looking like angry clenched faces.

This is the volcano of my family. I came here with my dad when I was a little boy. The only time we went on a journey by ourselves. Left the City of Angels. Had breakfast in Barstow. Passed through the wreckage of Baghdad on old Route 66. Walked the lava fields of Amboy. Went through Needles. Crossed the river to King Man. King Man, Arizona . . . where my grandfather homesteaded a ranch.

This is the volcano of my family. A frayed snapshot in 1919 of my grandparents passing the volcano on their way from the farm in Kansas to a new life in California. My dad and I wandering in the lava fields of Amboy. My brother knowing

I would come to this volcano once again. *(He dangles the big lava rock over his head)*

This is the volcano of my life. It has a sharp point and it hangs over my head. I walk towards this volcano with my dead father. I walk towards this volcano with my dead boyfriend John who came to this desert to try to heal himself of AIDS. I walk towards this volcano now with my living boyfriend these ten years, Doug. Even though I'm completely alone. This is the volcano of my life. I crawl up the side of the volcano. Every step I take I sink up to my hips in ash and blasted bits of bone. I feel like each step might be the wrong one. Might shake the earth to its soul. Break its heart. The lip of the crater is high. My breath races. There are cocked Eisenhower era hydrogen bombs and exploded Frigidaires everywhere. Bits of bone blasted from the center of the earth. The smell of rotten grease blasted from a place for burning. I get to the top of the volcano. I didn't go into the volcano when I was here with my dad when I was little. But I will now. I did what you're supposed to do.

I stripped myself naked. *(He takes off all of his clothes and stands in red light)* Bared my heart to the hot sun. Hoping that it might warm the frozen places. Dug my feet into the earth. Ash between each toe. Under each toenail. It felt like an old friend. So familiar. Like the ash we will all become. Bared my dick and butt to the sky. Took a walk around the that crater and far in the distance I could see a billboard for the Bun Boy Restaurant in Baker, California. "We are the Bun Boy Restaurant. We have the best biscuits and gravy in all the Mojave." What is inside my volcano? My fear . . . stronger than life. Sometimes. Who taught me that? My shame . . . deep as the sea. Sometimes. Who gave me that? I'm knocked down. I am grabbed and pushed and shoved along the top of the crater. A hundred hands tear at me. Blood pours from here and here where my first major lover David was stabbed nine times with an icepick in front of a gay bar in Garden Grove. QUEER! QUEER! Blood pours from here and here where my boyfriend Doug was bashed almost killed with the two-by-four and the blood pours over our breakfast linoleum. FAG! FAG! Blood pours from here and here where the catheters pierced my friends' sides so the medicine could go in their bodies. AIDS! AIDS! Broken here where Reagan and Bush smiled their do-nothing holocaust grins while my friends died. Broken here and here where my own embarrassment twisted my spine and threw me off center with the feeling I'm no fucking good. Broken here and here, why is it when I am about to kiss a boy I have been flirting with on Santa Monica Boulevard, do I have to imagine an unkind god above me is going to throw a rock at me and smash my head? Broken here and here, dick and balls smashed off by the hammers of Helms and Buchannan and Sheldon and Wildmon. Broken here and here. Butthole blown open by DIRTY DIRTY DIRTY, they said. DEATH DEATH DEATH, they said. Blow winds. You're cracking my fucking cheeks. I'm dragged down into the crater. Pinned there at the bottom. Naked in the crater. My butt and hole up to the sky. Dick buried in ash. My mouth is full. I whispered secrets into the earth.

I miss my friends and lovers who have died. I am afraid of my mom's body. The tumor on my side kept my shirt on for fourteen years. He was so thin. I was so scared. Don't watch me take a shit. What are my father's secrets? I am embarrassed that I am alive sometimes.

I lay there for nine years. Watching my friends and lovers die before my eyes. Then, a horrible beast came into the crater crawled towards me. It opened my body. Tore at my skin. This beast started pulling corpses out from inside me. Hundreds of them. I recognized every face. It pulled these friends dead from AIDS out of my butthole. Piled them like wood in this giant crater. Filling the hole. The wound. All around me. I was being buried. They were gonna block out the sky. Up here. Up here. I'm gonna stop there. If it's OK with you, I'm gonna stop there. Actually, even if it's not, I'm gonna. Hey, up in the booth! Could I have that bright light we had before? *(The follow spot comes on)*

I made all that up. All that about the volcano and the beast. I lied to you. I'm sorry. Don't hate me. I don't really know what's in my volcano. I don't know much of anything anymore. The only thing I really I know is that I'm here naked in front of all of you right know. *(He walks naked down into the audience)* That's very tangible. I bet it will become even more tangible if I walk around closer to you. Oh yes, much more tangible. I'm here with you and you and you. I *see* you. Even without my glasses. Which are very strong. *(He touches someone's hair)* This person has nice hair. A little too much mousse, maybe. I could learn something from you. You look wise tonight. Many cute boys here. Can I sit down here? *(He sits naked on someone's lap)*

This is the most nervous part of the performance. Here, feel my heart. I see my face reflected in your eyes. I am here with you. I *am* here with you. My body is right here. You are right there. Here, feel my heart. I still feel alone. A little afraid of all of you. And I could tell you another sweet or a scary story like I've tried to do tonight. But whatever I did . . . it would be a lot wetter and messier and human and complicated than when I stand up there naked in the red theatrical light and pretend I'm going into the volcano. I can shove through the bareassed shame . . . I'm pretty good at that. But, I still feel more of my friends slip away so what good is it? After ten years of being scared and angry. No wonder I gotta go into the volcano sometimes. Some nights I feel this strange border between my body and some friends who are really sick right now. It's a coastline I don't like. I want to throw a surfrider to them pull them to shore . . . but I can't do that. Who am I kidding? I wanna tongue kiss them, and I do, even though I'm afraid. I wanna hold our bodies really close together so nobody else slips away and that I can try to do . . . that I can at least try to do. And I'm really glad 'cause I don't think I can manage much fucking else. Please nobody go anywhere. I have one more thing I gotta tell you. It won't take long. I swear. *(He goes back onto the stage)* You want a volcano. I'll give you one. Up here onstage. There are the outlines of hundreds and thousands of people who have died of AIDS. Some of them I know. Some of them you know. You walked across 'em on your way to your seats. Do ya feel them on your shoes? It's a strange crater we're in and there's strange fruit here. This one is Martin and I've told his story before but it hurt much more in real life HA HA and the sex was better than I let on.

This man was Keith and we sniffed around each other and made love a few times in a tiny bed in a room with no windows when we were both intensely young and wanting to be famous artists on the Lower East Side.

This was John. A man I loved but not well enough and left and whose face I see in my mirror and on the faces of my friends if the light is right. And whose body I still feel inside of mine just like it was that one blizzardy Sunday in New York before the snow got real dirty.

Now these three are just my boyfriends who have died of AIDS. The men whose dreams I shared, art we made, lips I kissed, and dicks I sucked. There are dozens of other friends here. People I know or you know. Now, I shout myself hoarse. I've ACTED UP all over. I wash my hands. I put up my stickers. And I'm still here and I'm fucking glad of that, but it means the world makes no fucking sense. I am not USDA choice anything. Why am I breathing *right now, tonight,* and they are not? Now that's a big fucking question. And I'll get an answer if I have to go into twenty volcanoes or pull God down here by his too wide lapels, slap him around until I get some answers.

. . . because I don't understand this pain and this loss anymore than I did ten years ago.

. . . because I try . . . but sometimes I am still the same selfish prick who ran for the hills when love walked in the room.

. . . because I've lost my maps and I don't know where I wanna go on my body.

. . . because we're all gonna die. Right? We all know that. We all bought that ticket. We all signed that lease. We all got our volcano.

. . . but, meanwhile, I am here in my body. I gotta find the chant . . . the rhythm . . . the offering . . . the ritual to be here in my body and remember what is gone. In my breath up here. My spirit all around. To not close my heart. My legs right here . . . through my feet to the center of the earth. My cock in the world. My belly, my friend. My arms up here. My brain on fire. Up here. Up here.

(He stands still. Pause. He looks at his forlorn penis) Uh oh. I've got myself in trouble again. I'm naked in front of all

you people. Painted into a corner without any clothes on.
Plus my dick looks so sad and forlorn. So abandoned. So
soft and so shy. *(He begins to whisper to his penis)* Pssst. Hey
you. You missed your cue. You know you were supposed to
get hard after the psychosexual empowerment litany. Look,
I'm really sorry. This *never* happens to me. It'll just be a
second. Are you trying to make me look bad? Don't talk to
me about performance anxiety. GET HARD! Ooops. We all
know, in this situation, yelling does not help. I'm going to
work with you. Directorally.

OK. I'll suggest some stimulating and arousing imagery
and then you'll get hard and we can leave the volcano. You
can all do this now in your seats or later in the comfort of
your homes. We are in a field. A plain. Warm and sensual
water moves across this field. Reeds and grasses dance in the
wind. Beautiful and muscularly defined black Labrador re-
trievers running through that high grass. Sal Mineo and
James Dean are there naked having hot sex finally rewriting
the last scene from *Rebel Without a Cause.* NOW GET
HARD!!!! Come on. Come on.

You say not until I finish my story? OK. This is a fairy tale.
Maybe I can make up a new ending and maybe we'll find
our way out of the volcano. Now, in that volcano, the corpses
were pulled out of my butthole for a long time. Some
corpses were found that everyone had been looking for.
Jimmy Hoffa. JFK's assassins. All eighty-six of them. An important object, too. The Holy Grail. But, I had always known
it was there.

Then it stopped. I was spent. I bent over and smoked a
cigarette. Then I felt something moving through me. I squat-
ted down over the earth and I gave birth to an egg! Well
not an egg. It's a seedpod, obviously. Wait. I know this seedpod. I know it well. I had left Philadelphia, the City of
Brotherly Love. I walked over the river to New Jersey. I
walked for many miles. I came to a cemetery. I found the
grave I was looking for. At this crypt there were poems,
flowers, offerings of food. They looked like they had all been
put there that day. This is Walt Whitman's grave in Camden,
New Jersey. Queer father, poet guide. The moment I stood

in front of this grave this seedpod fell from a tree far above which had long ago eaten Walt's body and hit me on my head. Inside it was many things. Inside it was a high school ring. The breath of every man I've ever kissed. And a light that could change the end of that old story that tells us our bodies are good only for death. Well, that's my story. It had a magic seedpod ending. That should be enough. So now you'll get hard and we can leave this place and I'll tell you why.

Get hard because it still feels good to be touched . . . get hard because there is so much that is gone . . . get hard because even though it's not the most important thing, it's magic when it happens . . . get hard because it's the least we can do . . . get hard because you can remember you are alive . . . get hard because every time I come, I think of the men I've loved who are dead . . . get hard because once we're gone, we can't . . . I think. Get hard because we can't let the right-wing fuckheads tell us how to fuck . . . get hard because I want these boners before I am just a bag of bones . . . get hard because there's work to be done . . . get hard because I am a queer and it is good and I am good and I don't just mean in bed.

Get hard because it is time to make a move. To transubstantiate. A little alchemy please. Let's turn that rock into gold. The water into wine. The pain into change. The bus is arriving. The alarm is going off. Because I only know one thing. This *is* my body! And these are *all* our times. So . . .

Get hard . . .

Get hard . . .

Get hard . . .

I hardly know what to say . . . except that we're here in the greenish glow again. I'm gonna use this greenish moment to pull up my pants. You'll have to use your imagination for the rest. You might wanna arrange yourselves in case you got a little damp or bulgy. Well, come on, it could happen. Whatever you do, I need you to do it quick. I need your help to help me create a little alternative reality.

We have to project a bit into the future. Not too far into the future . . . otherwise it's just too depressing. OK. Back at the volcano. I said, "Fuck this Jungian mythopoetic stuff. My queer friends are getting beat up back at the museum." I rushed back to the tar pits. Everybody unfroze. As you know, that night we forced the governor out of office. He works in the copy room at the Lesbian and Gay Center in L.A. now. During the '90s and early part of the new century, queers, people of color, women made enormous advances until finally the U.S. elected the first black lesbian president of the U.S. This is where I need your help. We are no longer in this glamorous theatre. We are now at the Kennedy Center in Washington, D.C. It is the inaugural gala for the first black lesbian president of the U.S. She has appointed me performance art laureate of the nation. As you might imagine, I have accepted. But she has given me a very serious challenge. She has commissioned me to create a symphonic homoerotic performance art cantata that will exorcise homophobia and bigotry from our land. Basically she wants me to create a work that will, via a global satellite TV hookup, explain to the planet how fabulous it is when two men have sex together. The lesbian a capella group from Portland, Maine, will be doing the same for dyke/dyke sex during the second half of the program. I have been working with the L.A. Philharmonic for about two months in California and now here in Washington. There is tremendous excitement here tonight. AIDS activists from all over the country are here and both houses of Congress. I'm going to go put on my evening clothes. The lights in the Kennedy Center dim.

There is a buzz of anticipation in the hall. I step out onto the stage. There is immediately thunderous applause . . .

My conductor, Zubin Mehta, steps to the platform. We exchange a meaningful gesture. And I begin.

Good evening. As your performance art laureate, I welcome you to the inauguration of the first black lesbian president of the U.S. I offer this piece in memory of all our friends who have died of AIDS and in honor of the breath and pleasure that exists in everybody here tonight.

Music, Maestro Zubin. (*The music comes up. Yes. It's the*

Bolero. Please, reader, imagine the music brewing towards climax during the rest of the performance)

You look at him . . . sometimes over your shoulder . . . sometimes across the crowded performance art space . . . you make the signals . . . a glance held too long . . . a leg in contact not pulled away . . . the sharing of knowledge . . . the crucial questions . . . "Didn't I meet you once at ACT UP?" "Weren't you in that performance piece at Highways?" "Do you have a boyfriend . . . if so, do you sleep around?" These are the politics of our space and how we bridge it. Close. But not close enough yet. Not for this reporter. I want to *know* this man. What he tastes like. The books he reads. The touch he has. A little neck massage is not out of order here . . .or perhaps a quick game of postmodern mid-plague Twister.

But, finally, the lips touch. I kiss this man. Oh good. Who will stick their tongue in first? Him or me? Who cares! And I claim this wet wet kiss assuming everyone is HIV positive. A little two-day beard on the faces as they rub and EUREKA! we know we're guys.

All right, I admit it. It's that sandpaper cha-cha that gets my fingers snapping and does a soft-shoe on my slutty heart.

The hands grab each other close in a real embrace. So close that no junior high chaperone can shine light between us. You feel each other's backs. His hair. His butt. With pelvoid radar beginning to feel the hard thing . . . Oh that lovely hard thing, in the pants. A coupla bumps in the night start to rub over each other before the embrace pulls away. You look each other in the eye. It's scary, isn't it? Don't pull away.

I SEE YOU NOW

HELLO I'M HERE

Hands move over chests. Get the lay of the land. The cut of the cloth. Pinch the nipples which, yes, we do find get more sensitive with each passing year . . . One of the many benefits of getting older . . . What is inside my heart? What have we here inside this secondhand Walt Whitman breast? There is so much LOVE!

We roll the foreheads together. Pinching each other's tits. A breath or a "yeah" showing what feels good. Beginning the spar. And let me hear a "yeah." Good! This is *not* a joke. Not to be kept at arm's length with a nervous laugh. This is ground zero. A crossroads. The vortex.

THIS IS
THE HIT PARADE

My hands reach down and feel the particular hard dick there in the pants. This is a big moment. Sort of like the lottery. And I don't give a shit whether they're big or small, light or dark, cut or not. Through thick and through thin, I am just glad to be lucky enough to be feeling this particular hard cock at this troubled moment in history, if you know what I mean.

Our hands go under shirts. The tongue tips . . . touch . . . down . . . down . . . the neck . . . The fingers open the shirt, a bite on the nape, a nip on the nipple. The other hand negotiates the buttons or zipper. Struggle with the belt. I hate this part. And finally reach in. Oh it's hot and sweaty here. Where the underwear mashes the curly queer hair. Then you reach down and grab low under the balls. Feeling then heavy like a scoop of ice cream

AND PULL THE DICK
UP AND OUT

The pants may now get cheerfully dropped depending on your fashion. Shirts get pulled over the head and then . . . Oh skin skin skin, thank God for skin. Our pants are open and our hearts uncovered as we get ready to bare our souls and buttholes.

Cocks mushed against bellies. The tongue tip trails down to the tit, up to the pit. Redrawing those maps with our tongues on skin. Down to the place where the pubes and the dick hook up. Where the freeways meet. Where the turf meets the surf. Then the tongue goes up Interstate 35, up up up and around the shaft. Tongue tip dances along that cock. The mouth is open. We pause there now for station identification.

RIGHT THERE
AT THE TOP

Safe sex quandary moment. Is it or isn't it? Only your urologist knows for sure. To suck or not to suck. That is the question. Let's be serious . . . Let's be honest. Of course, we're gonna take a little journey up and over that dick for a while at least. This is a special moment. A sacrament of sorts. Made more sacred for our fears. Speaking of fears, I don't taste any pre-cum. (I once had to explain to a straight women friend what pre-cum is. I told her, "It is the rustle of wings. The rumble afar. It is the taste of things to come.") And when that dick is in my mouth or my dick in someone's, there is a faith in the universe and the rhyme comes out right.

AND IT GOES DOWN

LIKE HOME COOKING

And hands go up and down and around the town to a visit to the balls so pleasant and bouncy. And we're up and there is a kiss. The fingers now do the walking and dance down under beyond the balls to what my friend in Texas calls—he was a cute boy who I had sex with in a hayloft in San Antonio. I lured him back there with my classic pickup line, "Hey, wanna ditch the party and go out back and look at the chickens?" Well, that's another story—Anyway, he told me that where he comes from this area is known as the "t' aint," the area between dick and butthole. The scientific word being perineum. It is called this, and not just in Mississippi and East Texas, because it "t'aint your dick and t'aint your butthole." It doesn't matter to me what words you use or what accent you have.

WHATEVER YOU CALL IT

IT IS GOOD

And then the question, "How much does each of us want our buttholes to be played with and what will we find when we get there?" I know this is a nervous subject so let's assume we have both been swimming in a highly chlorinated pool for seven hours doing the breaststroke. So when we get down there things are extremely tidy and puckered and cool. Our fingers go around and converse, flirt with our buttholes. Getting to know you. Getting to know all about you. And a "yeah" is called for. Which is an affirmation of our place in the universe. Everybody take a breath . . .

LET ME HEAR YA SAY YEAH
PUT IT IN!
And the democracy of fingers. We all got 'em. Lotsa 'em.
Enough to go around. Ten times ourselves. And we got 'em
inside each other now. No one on top. The bottom pulled
out from under us like a sly slapstick rug.

The other hand on each other's dicks. The finger goes in
and the held hand goes up and lips are pressed. And we fall
down over and about. And head to foot. Lip to ball. Finger
in butt.

We're in a universe of our own making. No more waiting.
Our hoped for escape from gravity. Weightless. We're in our
own solar system.

PLANETS IN OUR SEXY ORBIT
Don't you see? This is the promised land where your lips
. . . all of them, and your points . . . all of them, and your
holes . . . all of them, get tended and loved. Get their valves
adjusted and their licenses renewed. It's like this sex will
revive the big identity document that says, "I am! My body
belongs to me!" Flipping the bird to fear. Because even
though there has been so much death, we are still here with
our skin and bones. There is blood and spirit and queer
horndogginess within and about me. Between you and me.
Between your butts and your seats. Between our hearts and
our heads.

I AM IN MY BODY
I AM IN MY LIFE
I've got a hard-on for the universe. Sometimes a yielding
unclenched butthole that might keep the world from blowing itself up . . . And don't tell me this white boy don't have
rhythm because that's all it is now. It's all listening and
sensing . . . and reaching . . . and reaching. And someone
reaches for a condom. They're never where you put them.
There they are. Oh, reminder of plague, we embrace you!
Someone opens it with slippery hands (this has a 9.3 level
of difficulty) and slips it over . . . pinch at the tip . . . roll it
down. Down. Down. Down.

THE AIR IS OUT AND THERE IT IS
And, now, let's flip a coin or consult the oracle. Check

the tea leaves in the tea room and one way or another a dick is going to find its way into a man tonight. And this is no small thing. It makes the world turn upside down. This pleasure that one man can give another. A dick in a butt-hole. A whole lot of peace. A piece of ass.

Now, what's the problem here? Is this love that dare not show up on network TV? Is this the sex that launched a thousand ships and burned the topless towers of Washington? Is this the buttfuck that put the bees in the bonnets and tent poles under the cassocks of cardinals in Columbus?

Are we stuck with their images? Their projections? Their religion?

IS IT ALL OF *THEIR* THINGS?

No. For once, right now. It is just ourselves. Two men inside of each other without a knife, a gun, or a stock portfolio.

And one is close. And then another is closer yet. Full. Fuller. Fullest. There is a nod and a yes and a squeeze and a breath.

I am fucking, I am being fucked. Every single cell. And heads or tails I am glad to be here, my body in the world. The water inside me. The dying that comes to all. And it is faster and closer than we knew. Everything that we hoped for on the jungle gym . . . hanging upside down and twirling around and around on the high bar of our lives. Naked between the sheets after church.

THE CURTAIN RAISES AND THERE WE ARE

Naked in the sight of each other. The only ones that matter. I am fucking, I am being fucked. Touched and touching. Time now to know each other and ourselves. I am fucking, I am being fucked. And so close. The words in my brain fly out the windows like a buncha crazy birds let outta the cage. I am fucking, I am being fucked. Right there. There is wetness and hardness and growing together and quick in my heart and my head.

I am with you now.

And with my friends and lovers who are dead from AIDS.

And with all the queers who got burned up in the con-centration camps. With all the dykes and homos bashed on the streets of our fucked up country. And for the little fag within me who cried so much as a kid and never does now. Not anymore. *(Bolero music reaches its climax)*

But, now, I feel the blessing of being closer than they told us was possible. The fuckers lied to us. I am not ashamed of nakedness and I will not cast out of paradise by right-wing bigots or some fucking hunky archangel with a flaming sword in some garden. *(Music blaring)*

This is one sex between two queer men's bodies in the time of trial on the planet Earth at the very end of the second millenium.

Blackout.

about the authors

ROBERT BERG

Born and raised in Canada, Robert Berg was formerly one half of Bachelor's Anonymous, the infamous electronic pop duo which performed in Los Angeles and San Francisco. Berg cocreated the scores for Judy Perez Performing Ensemble's *Made In L.A.,* Terri Lewis Dance Ensemble's *Bachelors,* and John Fleck's award-winning *I Got the He-Be-She-Be's.* He has also composed for film, children's theatre, and church choirs. For the first production of *AIDS! The Musical!* at Highways in August 1991, he produced and recorded the music and was the musical director. He dedicates this production to the memory of his soul brothers, Thon Kouwenberg, Gary "Guitar" Maynard and George Mocsary, whose love and support he will never forget.

VICTOR BUMBALO

Victor Bumbalo has won an Ingram Merrill Award for playwriting. His award-winning play, *Niagara Falls,* followed its off-Broadway run with subsequent openings in over fifty cities throughout the United States, England, and Australia. His play, *Adam and the Experts,* opened to critical success off-Broadway and has had productions in several cities in the United States and Canada. *What Are Tuesdays Like?* was featured in the 1993 season at Carnegie Mellon's Showcase of New Plays. A number of Bumbalo's plays have been published: *Niagara Falls and Other Plays,* a collection of his comedies, by Calamus Books, and *Adam and the Experts* by Broadway Play Publishing in 1990. *Tell* appears in an anthology, *Gay and Lesbian Plays Today* published in 1993 by Heinemann Educational Books, and *Show* appears in *The Best American Short Plays 1992-1993,* published by Applause Theatre Book Publishers. Bumbalo has also been the recipient of two MacDowell Fellowships and residencies at Yaddo and the Helene Wurlitzer Foundation.

DOUG HOLSCLAW

Doug Holsclaw is a San Francisco-based playwright and solo performer. At Theatre Rhinoceros, he wrote for and appeared in the original production of *The AIDS Show: Artists Involved with Death and Survival* and codirected (with Leland Moss) its sequel, *Unfinished Business*. He also appeared in the subsequent PBS documentary about the project. He is author of the plays, *Life of the Party, In the Summer When It's Hot and Sticky,* and *Get Real* (AIDS education for children produced by San Francisco's New Conservatory Theatre). He has written and performed two solo shows at Josie's Cabaret, *Don't Make Me Say Things That Will Hurt You* and *Tattoo Love.* He is currently associate artistic director of Theatre Rhinoceros.

WENDELL JONES

An activist/performer, Wendell Jones spent five years (1972–1976) writing, directing, and performing with the Bertolt Brecht Memorial Guerilla Theatre Group in Austin, Texas. He wrote and directed *Sugar and Spice and Nothing Nice* for the Austin Women's Workers Theatre. In the last few years, Jones has written and performed several solo pieces including *Hurtling Through the Stars* at venues such as Highways, Different Light Bookstore, LACE, Newport Harbor Art Museum, and the Third Phase Multicultural Gallery. He also performed in a two-man show called *Queers* at 1800 Square Feet in San Francisco. Most of his current work has centered on AIDS issues. Along with cowriting *AIDS! The Musical!,* Jones played the character Christian in the workshop production at Highways in August 1991. He is trained as an attorney and helped organize a six-hour performance demonstration against censorship during the NEA crisis in 1990 along with providing legal support. He has also organized numerous guerilla theatre performances for ACT UP/Los Angeles and helped coproduce the notorious performance club benefits Guy-O-Rama and Naked City, raising more than thirty-seven thousand dollars for ACT UP and other gay organizations. In August/September 1992, Jones presented a full-length solo piece called *Damaged Goods* at Highways.

MICHAEL KEARNS

Michael Kearns is a writer/performer/director who has been concentrating on AIDS art since 1984, establishing himself as one of the country's most consistent and respected theatre artists.

His two theatrepieces, *intimacies* and *more intimacies,* in which he portrays a dozen culturally diverse PWAs, have been produced in Los Angeles, San Francisco, Chicago, Portland, Eugene, San Diego, St. Louis, Tucson, Phoenix, Washington, D.C., New York City, Hartford, New Haven, Northampton, and Sydney (Australia). Heinemann has published *intimacies* and *more intimacies* in *Gay and Lesbian Plays Today.*

Other writing for the theatre includes his autobiographical *The Truth Is Bad Enough* and *ROCK.* His most recent solo work, *ROCK,* premiered in 1992 and continues to tour nationally and abroad. *Myron,* Kearns' first multiple-character play, opened at Highways in January of 1993 and then played at the St. Genesius Theatre in West Hollywood. He also wrote the lyrics for *Homeless, A Street Opera.*

Kearns directed and coproduced the Artists Confronting AIDS' landmark production of *AIDS/US* in 1986 and *AIDS/US II* in 1990. He also directed the Los Angeles premiere of Robert Chesley's *Night Sweat* and *Jerker,* Rebecca Ranson's *Warren,* and Doug Holsclaw's *Life of the Party.*

As an actor, he appeared in *Jerker,* James Carroll Pickett's *Dream Man,* and as an openly gay/openly HIV-impacted actor on a segment of ABC-TV's *Life Goes On.* He also appeared as Cleve Jones in the HBO adaption of Randy Shilts' *And The Band Played On.*

He is a member of the Dramatists Guild and PEN Center USA West.

TIM MILLER

Tim Miller is a performance artist and activist born and raised in Los Angeles. He spent nine years on a life sentence in New York before being let out for bad behavior. He now lives in Venice Beach (L.A.) with his dog, Buddy, and his boyfriend, Doug. He is a loud, obnoxious fag and all his various performance art agitating goes toward articulating a queer cultural identity and trying to find an artistic, spiritual and political response to the AIDS crisis.

His performance works—*Postwar* (1982), *Cost of Living* (1983), *Democracy in America* (1984), *Buddy Systems* (1985), *Some Golden States* (1987), *Stretch Marks* (1989), *Sex/Love/Stories* (1991), and *My Queer Body* (1992)—have been presented all over North America and Europe, including productions at the Brooklyn Academy of Music *Next Wave* Festival, the Copenhagen International Theatre Festival, the London Institute for Contemporary Art, the Walker Art Center, and the New York International Festival. These full evening pieces have been a weird journey through sex and love, the AIDS crisis, confronting the state, and trying to make sense of the world.

Tim Miller was a founder of Performance Space 122 on the Lower East Side and in 1989 cofounded Highways with Linda Burnham, a performance space dedicated to new performance forms and cross-cultural exchange. He has taught performance art at New York University and the University of California, Los Angeles, and has received numerous grants from the National Endowment for the Arts.

A member of ACT UP/LA, he has created performance works for mass protest and civil disobedience actions.

He is currently a California Arts Council artist-in-residence at Highways where he teaches free weekly performance workshops including one for gay men, and is adjunct professor in the graduate theatre program at UCLA.

JAMES CARROLL PICKETT

Playwright and AIDS activist, James Carroll Pickett is the cofounder and executive director of Artists Confronting

AIDS. His plays, *Bathouse Benediction, Dream Man,* and *Queen of Angels* have been produced in Los Angeles, San Francisco, New York, Atlanta, Portland, Des Moines, Minneapolis, Washington, D.C., Dusseldorf, Frankfurt, Edinburgh, and London. He wrote and coproduced the acclaimed docudramas *AIDS/US* and *AIDS/US II,* and received an *L.A. Weekly* Humanitarian Theatre Award for his work with Artists Confronting AIDS. He has also received an *L.A. Weekly* Playwriting Award (*Dream Man*), the *Drama-Logue* Award for Playwriting (*Bathhouse Benediction*), the Alliance for Gay and Lesbian Artists Media Award (*AIDS/US*), an AGLA award for Playwriting (*Dream Man*), and another *L.A. Weekly* Humanitarian Theatre Award for his work as a founder and producer of the STAGE Benefits for AIDS Project Los Angeles. As of this writing (1993), he is living with AIDS.

Currently writer-in-residence at the Beverly Hills Playhouse, Pickett teaches theatre classes and directs the Garden Street Playwrights Lab. He is a member of the Los Angeles Playwrights Group, PEN, the Dramatists Guild, and the direct action AIDS organization, ACT UP. From 1987–1990, he produced the monthly Gay Writers Series for A Different Light Bookstore in Los Angeles, and curated *3 Gay Sons Read On Father's Day* at Highways Performance Space, (*This Is Not*) *An AIDS Reading* for Words Project For AIDS at Barnsdall Gallery Theater, and *3 Gay Writers For Life* for the Otis-Parsons Art and AIDS Exhibition. He recently received a City of Los Angeles Cultural Affairs Department grant, and Brody Arts Fund Fellowship for the development of his play, *Queen of Angels.*

TED SOD

Ted Sod is a playwright/performer/director and arts education advocate who is a refugee to Seattle from New York City. He is presently artist-in-residence in charge of outreach and education at Seattle Repertory Theatre. He has performed in plays produced off-Broadway by the New York Shakespeare Festival, BAM Theatre Company, Second Stage, Playwrights' Horizons, American Place Theatre, Circle Repertory, the Yale and Seattle Repertory Theatres, among others and is the author of *Stealing* (book and lyrics), Seattle Group Theatre, 1989; *Damaged Goods*, Alice B. Theatre, 1990 (also director); *The Kiss* (published and produced as part of *Portrait of Iowa*), Alice B. on tour, 1989–1991; *Three Wishes* (book and lyrics), Seattle Children's/ Madrona Youth Theatres on tour, 1990; *High Risk*, Bainbridge Performing Arts/Straigh-Talk on tour, 1991; and *Make Me Pele for a Day*, Seattle Children's Theatre, 1992. He has received playwriting fellowships from the Seattle Arts Commission (1988, 1990, and 1991) and was awarded residency at the Edward F. Albee Foundation (1992).

DAVID STANLEY

A military brat born in Okinawa, Japan, David Stanley attended UCLA's Film/TV School where he created the film, *Reverb*, and the video, *Torture for Beginners*, along with writing two screenplays. Since graduating, he has written a novel, *Hurt*, created safe sex music videos for Revolver, cowritten and performed in *AIDS Crisis Anthology* at Barnsdall Art Park in May 1990, acted as the editor for ACT UP/Los Angeles newsletter and was coproducer/cowriter of the ACT UP/ LA TV Show for public access. For the first production of *AIDS! The Musical!*, Jones acted as producer, fundraiser, and publicist.